HOPE'S BOY

HOPE'S BOY

ANDREW BRIDGE

NEW YORK

ISBN 978-1-4013-0322-8

Hyperion books are available for special promotions and premiums.
For details contact Michael Rentas, Assistant Director, Inventory Operations,
Hyperion, 77 West 66th Street, 12th floor, New York, New York 10023,
or call 212-456-0133.

Design by Jo Anne Metsch

FIRST EDITION

3   5   7   9   10   8   6   4   2

For Hope and Jim.
I love you both.

Author's Note

IN THIS MEMOIR, I have recounted events and conversations to the best of my memory. A few exceptions, however, are worth noting. My mother and I lived in and were evicted from several apartments, rather than only one. More than a single family took us in. For the purposes of this book, I have included the apartment where we lived and the family with whom we stayed the longest. Where my recollections are incomplete, I have tried to present events and conversations to reflect the thoughts and feelings that remain. Still, memory is far from perfect, exact, or final, and the thoughts and feelings that I express are nothing but my own.

I have changed some names and identifying details of individuals to protect their privacy. My mother's first and middle names are Priscilla and Hope, though her maiden name is not Reese. I have kept the names of David Dolihite and Eddie Weidigger, two children at the Eufaula Adolescent Center. I was able to contact David's family, who had no objection to their son's name being used. Eddie died at Eufaula, and I was unable to locate his parents. The geographic details of my life before foster care, particularly of my life with my grandmother and mother, are as I remember. However, readers familiar with Los Angeles will not recognize the names of my elementary, junior, and senior high schools. I have changed those names, along with a number of other geographic details pertaining to my childhood in foster care—again, to protect the privacy of others. I have not changed the name of MacLaren Hall, however—Los Angeles County's notorious facility for foster children. For myself and the other children who lived there, that name seemed an important one to keep.

HOPE'S BOY

*W*HEN *MY MOTHER* walked down the street, men noticed.

She smoked Parliament cigarettes, which she had me retrieve from the corner drugstore with her handwritten notes. She played cards, mostly solitaire. Despite her modest height, she never wore high heels, preferring boots— especially the kind that zip up the back or the side and wrap around a woman's calf.

She had little patience for childishness. More than once, she snapped at me to stop acting my age.

Her hair was dark and matched her eyes. Her spoken voice was soft, even a little low for a woman. Yet when she wanted, her words could leave a man stammering as though his tongue, or something more, had just been skillfully excised. She was prankish with her girlfriends. Sometimes, a little vain.

She liked rock music, mostly the Doors and the Rolling Stones.

She was smart and said that I was too.

Other than occasional lipstick, she wore little makeup.

She thought that Izod shirts looked best on me, and I liked the alligator.

She enjoyed my company, toted me everywhere with her, and refused to compromise, regardless of what others thought. She sat me on bar stools, took me to Disneyland, and taught me how to bet at racetracks.

She protected me when she knew that I needed it; left me to fend for myself when she knew that I could.

When I was seven years old, they took her from me on a street in North Hollywood and called me a foster child. In all, she was mine for barely two years. But even now, if I were to walk down one of these streets with her, though slightly aged, she would still catch the eyes of a passerby, who would assume that the young man at her side was the son whom she had raised— the same son who was now assuming, for the first time, the role of her protector.

Prologue

No one asks to come back to these places," I whispered.

Next to me, our trial expert glanced up briefly, then returned to her work. My gaze drifted to the clutter of certificates on the reception room's cherry-paneled walls. Escorting us out the night before, Dr. Carlton had paused at the hanging frames. The wall of assurances should have been enough—so the man had claimed—to prove that the children locked inside the old Air Force base were safe. Noticing our expert's empty smile and my skeptical stare, Carlton had cut his argument short, then pointed to the exit and left us to show ourselves out. With his back to us, he had snapped, "Y'all just get back by seven in the morning. I got more to do than usher the two of you around."

"I'm sorry, Andrew. Did you say something?" The trial expert looked up again.

"Oh, no." I turned to her, shook my head. "It's nothing."

Secured with thirteen-foot perimeter fencing, copious spools of barbed wire, and electronic surveillance, the old installation on the outskirts of Eufaula, Alabama, channeled its few visitors—mostly women and children—into a single waiting area. The receptionist, who doubled as Carlton's secretary, had disappeared, and though the expert and I had now been waiting for at least an hour, she had still not returned. Other than the chug of an air conditioner behind the woman's empty chair, the room was quiet. A yellow fluorescent light clung to the ceiling, and opposite the receptionist's desk, a heavy blue sofa—its legs removed for some reason—squatted on the floor. When I relented and finally sat down, the thing had sucked me in like a bucket. Beside me, our trial expert made the most of her wasted time. Resting one foot on the buckled coffee table, she calmly occupied herself with yesterday's notes and a list of chores for us to finish by late afternoon.

Not much was supposed to happen when I left Washington for another round of discovery in Alabama. I was barely out of Harvard Law School, and the lawsuit was already twenty-three years old. Over the decades of courtroom battles, dozens of attorneys and law firms had traipsed through the litigation. By the time my name appeared on the pleadings as the most junior counsel at a public interest law firm, my boss had worked on the lawsuit for thirteen years, longer than any lawyer who remained. He was well known, even famous among civil rights lawyers, and had little patience for a recent graduate who had never filed a brief in court, much less argued a case. The day before I arrived in Alabama, his instructions had been characteristically clear:

"Do what the expert tells you, when she tells you, and keep your mouth shut."

Our trial expert had grown up in the South, and of the two of us, she was clearly in charge—our best chance that the trip would go smoothly. And she knew her way around places like Eufaula. Specializing in children with severe mental illness, she ran North Carolina's largest residential treatment facility for adolescents who were violent and assaultive. Confronted by the most condescending Eufaula employee, she could hold her smile, remember why she was there, and get what she needed. But even she had been shaken by the fear she had caught in a thirteen-year-old boy's vacant stare as she watched Eufaula's staff admit him to the facility.

"Take my advice and behave yourself. There's more going on at that place than you think," she had warned me, driving back into town after our first day touring the Center.

I stared out the waiting room's front window, surveying the gravel parking lot. The Alabama plates on our white rental car stared back at me. I glanced out at the sky, briefly noticing that the morning overhang of clouds had darkened.

Halfway between the state capital in Montgomery and the Gulf of Florida, the converted radar base had been one in a brotherhood of strongholds that guarded the skies of the nation's southern flank. Historians call the region "wiregrass country"—the heartland of the old Confederacy, covered with tall grass and piney woods, remembered for snipe hunts, rattlesnake festivals, and Baptist churches. Nearby settlements, like Opp and Andalusia, had given in to the lure of interstates and the promise of big-box retail and fast-food chains. But not the City of Eufaula. Great planters, merchants, and governors had come from Eufaula, lived and died there. In the center of town, their antebellum mansions survived as private residences, though they reeked of mildew in the summer heat.

The Confederacy may have died, but politics had not. Eufaula's friends in Washington, D.C., and Montgomery had not even completed construction of the town's new forty-five-thousand-acre reservoir—complete with stocks of catfish, bass, and crappie—before granting it a new military outpost in the late 1950s. In a few short years, the base became one of the largest employers for miles, eventually surpassing the reservoir's tourist trade. But the Cold War had not even ended when pork barrel politics failed, and the base was closed barely a decade after it had opened. In the eyes of Eufaula's citizens, what had protected and sustained them had been taken away. They demanded that something replace it.

Eyeing the vacant outpost and ever mindful of jobless constituents, state legislators made good on a promise to do something. A bill slipped through the legislature. Soon after, state crews arrived, the base grounds were swept, the buildings were painted, and the sign out front was changed to read Eufaula Adolescent Center. Meanwhile, bureaucrats in Birmingham, Montgomery, and Mobile, doing as they were told, searched through their lists of lost, abandoned, and unwanted children. Several dozen were surrendered to the care and employment of the local populace. And the largesse of public money and jobs streamed back into the town by the lake.

On October 22, 1970, a group of civil rights lawyers and private law firms sued the State of Alabama over its care and treatment of men, women, and children at its largest state psychiatric hospital. Three years later, Eufaula's new children's institution was added to the litigation. When President Nixon's Department of Justice joined the lawsuit on behalf of the plaintiff class, Alabama's defenses collapsed. Surrendering to squadrons of liberal lawyers and reserves of federal judges, Alabama's governor agreed to a sweeping consent decree. Once again, Washington's tenacity and resources had overpowered the proud but weaker South.

Interviews and records revealed that a few of Eufaula's children were different or, as our trial expert described them, "miswired." But most were simply unwanted, guilty of childhood's host of common crimes: truancy, curfew violations, smoking, breaking family rules, or just not getting along. Diagnosed as "conduct disordered," hundreds of these children had passed through Eufaula's gates. Though officially members of the larger plaintiff class that included thousands of adults confined to Alabama's state psychiatric facilities, Eufaula's children numbered fewer than a hundred, were hardly mentally ill, and were rarely the focus of the litigation that had been fought through the years.

Then, fifteen-year-old David Dolihite hanged himself in one of the base's old dormitories. Eufaula's staff found David in a bedroom closet, dangling by a shoestring that he had taken from his sneakers. David failed to kill himself, though in the minutes that it took his fourteen-year-old roommate, Eddie Weidinger, to chew through the knot, he succeeded in suffocating enough of his brain to suffer what the doctors labeled "severe hypoxic damage." According to his doctor's earliest prognosis, David could be expected to function at the level of an overgrown three-year-old who would require tube-feeding and hospitalization for the rest of his life. The boy's suicide attempt put Eufaula's administration on notice that the hanging bars inside children's closets posed a threat. Still the staff did nothing. Six weeks later, Eddie mimicked what David had done. When Eufaula's staff noticed that Eddie had gone missing and searched the dormitory closets, they found the boy dead.

Both boys had been kept in what staff and children called Building 112. Across the compound from the reception room where we were waiting for Dr. Carlton, Building 112 was an on-site warehouse where children sorted rubber fishing lures for the nearby reservoir's tourists. The building also held three isolation cells. Each cell was nine feet long by six feet wide. Facility staff fastened a steel grate and a single hanging lightbulb above each cell. The doors were painted black and braced shut with U-bolts and wooden two-by-fours. The building and cells were unheated. Children sat on a mud-covered concrete floor. Begging to be released, they banged against the cinderblock walls, leaving behind hand and footprint smears, red from Alabama's clay soil.

The length of time that David Dolihite and Eddie Weidinger had been locked in Building 112's cells was unknown—files and depositions revealed only that it had been more than a week. Yet the time had been long enough for both boys to decide that no more hope was left to borrow from the future. Facility administrators ordered the cells boarded up—hidden behind a wall of freshly cut and painted plywood—the day before our trial expert and I first arrived. Still, children confided in us about yet another place, a dormitory basement where they had been locked away. They called the basement the Behavior Modification Unit, or simply B-Mod. Moments before

Carlton had stopped to show us Eufaula's proud display of framed certificates, the expert and I had informed Carlton that we intended to inspect B-Mod the next morning.

Dr. Melvin Carlton, Eufaula's director of adolescent programs, had earned his degree in psychiatry while he was still in the military. He believed in discipline and guarded his authority scrupulously. He was defensive, usually pompous, and though the lawsuit had been brought against Alabama long before Carlton had arrived at Eufaula or I had finished the first grade, he took personal offense to it, me, and the trial expert whom I had brought.

Weeks earlier, the federal court had ruled that, as a licensed clinician, Carlton could escort us where and when he pleased. According to the court, everything was to be done through him, and he delighted in the small victory that Alabama's attorneys had won on his behalf. The smirk on his face when he finally appeared from his office just beyond the waiting room only confirmed his contempt for the lawsuit and for us.

"Good morning, y'all. I do apologize for the wait." Carlton watched as the expert and I struggled to lift ourselves from the sunken sofa, then glanced at the receptionist, who had finally returned to her post. "Tell anyone who calls that I'm touring a class action lawsuit expert . . . ," he took a long look at me, "and her junior counsel around the facility. I don't think this'll take much time." Then he promptly paced out a side door and led us to the grounds.

"I'm not spending the weekend," our expert reminded me, as Carlton marched ahead of us toward the boys' dormitory. The morning humidity had only thickened. "If it's raining, I want us gone by five. And I'm not sure you should stay here either."

The closest airport was in Columbus, a two-hour drive north, just over the Alabama–Georgia line. In my nascent legal career, I had learned that few commodities carried less value than a young public interest lawyer's time. Our expert would be leaving that evening, before the weekend. I would be staying until Sunday for the cheaper flight home.

"Don't worry," I mumbled, before glancing anxiously at the blackening sky. "We'll make it in time."

The facility's dormitories had been designed for servicemen. But since the conversion from Air Force radar base to adolescent facility, children whom the state deemed in need of intensive mental health treatment now roamed the long hallways, doubled up in rooms, and showered in curtainless stalls. One dormitory was reserved for girls, the other for boys—though keeping the two groups out of each other's sleeping quarters, bathrooms, and stairwells had proved difficult for the Center's frontline staff.

Having already lost so much of the morning, our expert decided that we would work through lunch, but by midafternoon, the children's interviews were taking longer than we had expected, and we had still not toured all of the grounds. With the two-hour drive to the airport still ahead, and with the weather getting worse, she ordered me to the basement with Carlton, while she finished with the boys upstairs. She told me to hurry, to meet her out front by the facility's gates, then reminded me again not to be late.

Left alone with me, Carlton knew he could take as much time as he pleased. First, he claimed that he needed to make a call and meandered across the wide lawn to his office. Forty minutes later, he sauntered halfway back, yelled that he had forgotten his keys, then took another thirty minutes to retrieve them. By the time he returned to the stairwell that sunk down to the basement door, the black clouds overhead were already bursting. His shirt was splattered with rain, soaked at his shoulders and down his sleeves. My jacket and tie were faring no better.

At the top of the stairwell, Carlton insisted on leading the way down. His form carried the bulk of middle age descended from high school football. Thrust out at me, his backside left little room to move. The afternoon heat radiated from the walls, and the concrete enclosure filled with the tang of his day-old aftershave and sweat. I waited as he flipped through a ring of keys, successively stabbing each into the bolted door.

"Dr. Carlton," I finally demanded, "if you don't know which key, then who would?"

The man stiffened his face but kept his eyes on the door. "Would you like me to sit down and memorize keys? Because, if that's the case, I'd be happy to get back to my office and do it."

"That's fine, you just take your time. You know, we'd love to come back." Of course, nothing could have been further from the truth. Immediately, I regretted the stupid taunt that now hung in the soggy heat. *Dumb bluffs are for dumb lawyers,* I remembered a law school professor chiding me. *A good lawyer never asks for something he doesn't want.* Carlton knew he would always have more time than our expert or I ever would. I had been dumb to remind him of it.

As expected, Carlton seized the moment and turned to face me. "We've got all the time down here that you and all your experts do, Mr. Bridge. Probably more." He glanced at the wall, sucked at his teeth, then stared back at me. "Or, Counselor Bridge, allow me to put it another way. Making sure we're both comfortable." He smiled, leaned nearer, then drawled sarcastically, "Now, I myself is ignorant. But, even I knows that we godst rights." He inched closer to me. "Jew git dat, boss?"

I flinched. My eyes darted down at the concrete drain between our feet. *OK, Doctor Frankenstein,* I thought, with the same smart-alecky voice that had always threatened to get me into trouble as a boy. *You win. Now just get the key and open the door.*

As if he had heard me, Carlton lifted the ring to his stomach, then isolated one key from the dozens of others. "There, I think this one could be it." He dangled the key in front of me like a satisfied jailer.

"Thank you, doctor. Should we give it the old college try?"

"Why, I'd be happy to, Mr. Bridge." He turned to the door and plunged the key into the lock. "Like I said when you got here, we all want to be as cooperative as possible."

Peering over his shoulder, I watched his wrist turn and anxiously pressed forward. "I can handle it from here, thank you."

He shoved against the door with his forearm, jolting the barrier open. "I'm sure you can 'handle it,' Mr. Bridge. But I know you won't mind if I come along." He stepped aside, holding the door open for me. "After you, counselor."

Squeezing between him and the door frame, I stepped inside. The underground passage was a brightly lit pocket of silence that smelled of the mildew growing in the earth around us. I hugged myself, chilled after the humid heat outside. "The air conditioner keeps it cold down here, doesn't it?"

Carlton ignored the question, slamming the door shut behind us.

Stepping forward, I passed a windowless alcove, then stopped between the first set of large, dark doors. Carlton remained at the threshold, the key ring at his side. I turned to the corridor ahead and noticed the sound of my own breathing. "Stick to the law," I whispered to myself. "Act like a lawyer. They all know you're here. Just stick to the law."

A few yards down, I looked over my shoulder and tossed out a lawyerlike question. "Dr. Carlton, I want to be clear. Are you telling me that this is the only basement on the institution's grounds?" The corridor strengthened my voice, but the inquiry was weak, almost desperate.

"Mr. Bridge," he began, his tone drawn and bored, "I have already told you that I will answer your questions only in the presence of my counsel, Mr. Henson. He has advised me, and I know that he has informed you . . ."

In a rush of confidence, I cut him off. "Mr. Henson is not your counsel in this matter, Dr. Carlton. Mr. Henson is counsel for the State of Alabama. You have no counsel here, as far as I know, unless you've hired your own."

But my words tumbled to the floor. Guarding the corridor's only exit, he smiled in triumphant silence.

I started down the hallway, my dress shoes clicking on the gleaming tiles. Slowly, I opened each door, reached into the dark, flipped the switch, and peered inside.

"The rooms, are they all empty?"

"Isn't that what you're here to find out, Mr. Bridge? You have your job. I have mine. Isn't that so?"

Nervous and hanging through a door frame halfway down the corridor, I persisted with Carlton. "Is this what the kids call B-Mod?"

His gaze lifted from the floor and he shrugged his shoulders.

"It's just a bunch of empty rooms," I muttered to myself. Anxious to get back outside, I spun toward Carlton, ready to leave.

But he confused the quick move for something more. He mistook it for discovery.

"We take the doors off, where we keep the children," he suddenly shouted down the hallway.

Startled, I looked again. There, at the end of the hall, I saw what Carlton had assumed I could not have missed: a splash of light across the floor.

"We keep it all in accord with clinical practice, and of course, that consent decree that you and that *expert* are here for," he yelled, watching as I approached the vacant threshold.

The quiet box of light revealed the back of a sleeping boy, fully dressed, huddled into a ball on a bare mattress. He wore an oversize T-shirt, jeans, and white gym socks. His dark hair was unkempt and greasy. His arms were thin and white—two nearly blue sticks. The odor of unwashed sleep filled the air around him.

He stirred, then quickly sat up. For a moment, he observed the intruder at the door before scooting on his heels to the mattress's far corner.

"That's all right. That's all right," I whispered, crossing through the doorway, moving toward him. "It's all right. I promise. It's all right."

A few feet from him, I picked up the single blanket from the floor and extended it to him. He refused it, pulled his knees to his chest, hugged his legs, and locked his hands in front of him. The sharp bones of his elbows poked at his skin. Scars of countless widths, lengths, and shapes were scattered across his arms and up under his shirtsleeves. Some wounds were clean, stretched, and white, while others lay thick and purplish. Still fresher lacerations broke his skin— bloody, brown, and scabbed. Dozens of the children upstairs had the same. He caught my stare and cast his eyes down to his white socks.

He looked to be thirteen or fourteen years old. The earliest swath of adolescent acne covered his forehead; wisps of sideburns crept down his cheeks. Still, guessing ages of institutionalized children— especially the boys—was difficult. Their time was spent mostly indoors, making them unusually pale. They were often smaller, thinner than other boys their age. Their familiarity with life's reservoir of cruelties was undeniable; yet the facilities that housed them isolated them from their peers and from the outside world, giving a startling innocence to children who had otherwise lost all claim to it.

I glanced around the room. After the staff had removed the door, they had stripped the room like practiced thieves. The closet doors were lifted from their guides. Inside, the drawers for the built-in dresser were gone; the hanging bar was taken. Above him, stringed blinds had been unscrewed from a narrow strip of gray window that ran along the ceiling and sliced the basement's skin at ground level. I looked back to the boy, who had not moved.

I placed the blanket on the mattress. Then, carefully leaving sufficient space between him and me, I sat on the floor across from him.

Where to start? What to say?

The day before, our expert had provided me an introduction and a list of questions. I began as she had instructed. "My name is Andrew Bridge. I'm a lawyer—your lawyer." The boy shifted his gaze to the side. "I won't repeat anything that you tell me." The boy said nothing. "As a matter of fact," I wandered off script, "I think they'd take my license from me if I did." The room remained quiet. I glanced to the side, trying to find the spot of wall where the boy was staring.

Suddenly, the boy turned back, looked me in the face. His eyes were dull and hard. I thought of myself as a boy, meeting a new lawyer or social worker, another stranger who had come calling, claiming to care, promising to get to know me and to want to stay. *So, tell me about yourself. . . . I hear you're good at school. . . . Your foster parents and I are very proud of you. . . . Maybe we can go to the movies next time. . . . I have to go, but would you like me to call you in a couple weeks?*

I smiled at the boy in front of me. "So now that you know my name, what's yours?"

"Jeff," he mumbled.

I nodded, thinking for a second. "You know, my best friend's name is Jeff. We've been friends for ages." I had tried the same line on at least a half dozen other boys upstairs. Several had rolled their eyes, demanding that I come up with something better. But this one, hidden in the basement, broke into a sheepish, twisted-tooth grin.

A second passed before he fumbled out a question. "How long did you have to go to school to be a lawyer?"

"Four years of college. Three years of law school. Do you want to be a lawyer?"

"No," he answered. He looked beyond my shoulder to the empty door frame. "Is Dr. Carlton with you?"

"Yes, he's here. He's at the end of the hall." I thought of what the boy might want. "I don't think he can hear us, but I can tell him to leave if you want," I added, making a promise that I probably could not keep.

The boy briefly considered the offer, then ignored it. "He came down earlier and brought that." He nodded at the blanket on the mattress.

"That was nice of him," I muttered, eager to move on. "How long have you been here?"

"Eufaula or here?" he asked, glancing around the room.

"Let's start with here, in the basement." I smiled.

"Five or six days, maybe more. I'm not sure."

In a later review of therapy and progress notes, our expert concluded that nearly thirty percent of all the children were secluded in the basement at some point during their stay at the facility. However, as Dr. Carlton had already informed me, he did not consider confining a child to the Behavior Modification Unit to meet the legal definition of seclusion. Therefore, why a child was put in the basement and how long the child remained went undocumented.

"Do you leave to eat or sleep?"

"No," the boy answered. "Mr. Ginder from upstairs leaves a tray for breakfast and dinner." The boy pointed toward the floor at the room's entrance. "Then he turns out the lights at night."

I had met Mr. Ginder the day before. He was a large, powerful man who carried the title Mental Health Worker, Level I. As he put it, he believed in "tough love." Ginder was responsible for frontline supervision on the boys' unit. He had also been the subject of dozens of incident reports, in which boys claimed that he had done everything from referring to their mothers as "bitches" and instigating fistfights between children to slamming their heads against walls and punching them in the back. Nearly every incident took place at night, usually on weekends, when he and the complaining child were alone. Investigating the charges, the facility's administration concluded that, with only Ginder and the boy present at the time, nothing could be substantiated. Few matters were investigated further.

"Why did the staff put you here?" I asked the boy.

"I wouldn't get out of bed for school."

Seclusion in a basement was a tough but effective remedy for a boy refusing to follow staff instructions. I had once unintentionally provoked the staff at MacLaren Hall, the sprawling children's facility where Los Angeles County housed me as a boy. The response was equally potent, and as a seven-year-old, I quickly learned the importance of complying with the smallest request from any of MacLaren's staff.

"You're not from here, are you?" he asked. "I mean you're not from the South. I can tell by your accent. Besides, anyone from Alabama would know to get outta the rain." He grinned. "Your shirt and tie are soaked."

"Yeah, I guess I'm not from here. I grew up in Los Angeles." Jeff's face brightened at the mention of the land of surf and sun, then dimmed when I added that I had left it and moved to Washington, D.C. I noticed the cold again and looked above us. The strip of window was darkening. It was getting late. Our expert would be finishing soon, waiting for me outside the gates. "How long have you been at Eufaula?"

"Since March." He quietly popped out the months on his fingers. "Five months."

"Do you see your parents? Do they come to visit?"

"My daddy called in Birmingham to tell me someone would be picking me up from the group home to drive me down here."

"Where are you from?"

"Athens." The boy noticed the questioning look on my face. "Up north, 'round Huntsville."

"And, your mom? What about her?"

"Daddy says she loves me. She just got mad. She won't tell me, but I know she wants me back."

We sat quietly for a moment. He looked away, back at the mysterious spot on the empty wall.

"My Uncle Stevie, he's Mamma's brother," he began with a flat, almost rehearsed tone. "He don't work, so he used to watch me and my baby brother afternoons after school. I told Mamma I could do it, that my brother and me didn't need no babysitter." The boy turned to me. Unsure what kind of encouragement he wanted, I nodded quietly. Apparently what I gave was enough, and he moved quickly to his point. "Uncle Stevie never did anything to me."

Outside, the rain strengthened, sinking into the ground around us. As the basement darkened, Jeff kept his voice steady, defending his uncle, his mother, and his father, calling himself a liar and a fraud.

After months of afternoons with his uncle, Jeff went to his parents. But his mother refused to believe him, choosing her brother over her eldest son. Jeff hung tough for several weeks, but eventually he decided that he needed his parents more than the truth. He went back to his father to undo what he had said, to set everything right again. He told his father that he had lied, as his mother had accused, but that he had never meant to hurt anyone. His father was grateful, quickly giving in to the new claim; but his mother resisted, insisting that there was evil in Jeff and vowing never to forgive him. The boy refused to surrender and fought to win his mother back. He tried to do everything right, remembering every chore, carefully selecting every word and phrase, even returning to Uncle Stevie in the afternoons. But nothing worked. The truth still hung in the house.

Finally, late one night, Jeff took the family car without permission or a license. Outraged, his parents called the state troopers. When the squad cars tracked Jeff down, his mother insisted on pressing charges. Vindicated, she claimed to have been right all along—Jeff was a liar who had grown into a thief. Father and mother discussed the matter and decided that the boy had to be held accountable. He had to learn, and the best way to teach him was to give him up to the state.

The boy grew quiet.

"Is there anything you want?" I naively asked. "Anything you need me to do?"

Jeff mulled over my offer. "If you see my mamma, would you tell her I'm sorry, that she can come see me now."

To the end, he proved himself a loyal son. He gave his mother everything that she could have wanted. Months later and miles away, concealed in a basement, he stuck by her, still hoping somehow to win her back. Whatever his mother had done, he forgave her. Uncle Stevie stayed free, and the truth left the house—at the price of only one childhood.

I glanced at my watch. We had been together for nearly an hour, and it was ten past five. Our expert, now waiting by the car, would be angry.

"You're going, aren't you?"

I winced, knowing that I was no different than the countless others who had asked Jeff for his story, listened as he surrendered it, then packed it up and left.

"I have to take someone to the airport. It'll take about two hours." I thought of the rain and the two-lane roads, then finally made an offer that I could keep. "I'll make it back, Jeff."

In front of me, the boy was already withdrawing.

I stood. "I promise, Jeff. I'll be back. Tonight. No matter what time. I promise."

From the empty door frame, I looked back into the room.

"Good-bye, Jeff."

He was already as I had found him, flat on the mattress, his back to me, his face to the wall.

I walked past the open, darkened rooms. At the end of the hall, I was polite to Dr. Carlton. "I have to go now. Our expert needs to get to the airport."

He threw open the basement door. At the top of the stairwell, the wind snapped at my hair as I looked back down.

"I think he's cold, Dr. Carlton," I said quietly, then repeated it louder. "I think the boy's cold. Can you get him another blanket?"

He turned, stepped inside, and slammed the door.

I rushed to the front gate and found our expert cramped under the building's awning, trying to protect herself from the rain. The parking lot was nearly empty, and the swath of forest across the road loomed over us as if it had surrendered enough of itself and would give no more.

"I'm sorry I'm late."

She glanced at her watch, well within her right to be annoyed.

Crossing to the passenger side, I nervously dug in my pockets for the keys, then opened the door for her. I unlocked the driver's side, climbed in. Her arms folded, she looked ahead at the tall chain-link fence. I pulled out of the gravel driveway, at last leaving the facility behind us.

The roads were narrow, and the rain poured over the dark silence between the woman and me. Through the windshield, the dim headlights of passing cars washed across our faces. The glow of small towns fractured and cleared over the glass, and as we approached, their radiance strengthened, shoved aside the darkness, then just as suddenly vanished somewhere in the black behind us.

Nearly a generation separated me from the boy in Eufaula's basement. We spoke differently, looked nothing alike. Our lives had begun half a continent apart. Yet little of that seemed to matter. The heavy cotton in the stuffed mattress where he slept smelled the same, and the cloth that cased it remained as rough. When Mr. Ginder came down to turn off the lights in Eufaula's basement, the darkness surely felt as it had in MacLaren Hall's basement. And Jeff, too, fought the great wars of loneliness on his skin.

I was seven years old the last day that I lived with my mother and the first night that I slept in foster care. By the time I was a teenager, I had spent half my life in county custody and still had the remainder of my childhood to go. I had no idea who Jeff's mother was, the woman he wanted me to find, to tell that he was sorry, to explain that he needed her. She may have been good or bad, kind or cruel, or more likely, a mix of it all. Yet, what I did know was that Jeff would never forget her, though everything and everyone around him told him that he should. Stubbornly, he would hold out, become the sole believer that, despite his mother's failings, her memory was worth keeping. Quietly, he would wait and hope for her return, as I had done for my own mother and thousands of other children have done for theirs—all of us assigned to new families or facilities, then expected to ignore that they were not the people or the places from which we had come. And the few of us who survived—the ones who learned early the swift consequence of failing to please—never revealed that we had long forgiven the mother whom so many had condemned, that we had refused to forget her, that we missed her and still loved her.

My mother was a beautiful woman, with short black hair, pale skin, and a slender figure. Her left eye was flawed by a black pupil that had bled into its green iris, as if, when making her, God had forgotten to stay within the lines. She was selfish, impulsive, and irresponsible. She forgot birthdays, ignored Christmas, and might tend to the cat's needs before mine. She cashed welfare checks to buy clothes and a pair of boots, then waited outside a McDonald's while I begged inside for hamburgers to feed us both. Like her eye, her mind had burst its boundaries, failing her and me. Yet, as a boy, I forgave her. Even as a man, though the reasons have changed, I forgive her. Because I will always be her son.

CHAPTER ONE

My earliest memory of my mother was her absence.

The white clapboard house stood quiet. The sun hung in a barren blue sky. Beyond a patch of yellowing grass was a road, beyond that a great plowed field of stubble. Not a curb nor fence nor even a ditch separated them. Later, the swath of loneliness would remind me of the San Joaquin Valley, the great sink of farmland that descends across California's backside like the dent down a lying man's spine.

I was not a baby, though I had only begun to grow into a boy. Someone must have been left to watch me. Yet, the emptiness lay uninterrupted. If I had been told why I was there, I had forgotten. I remembered only that I was supposed to wait.

"I'll come back for you," my mother had said, kneeling to give me a kiss. "I'll come back for you, Andy. I promise. I'll come back."

IF I HAD answered the questions at school, if I had told the truth and been as honest as my heart had wanted, what words would have come from me? Where would I have started? Everything would have begun with Mom.

She grew up on the eastern plains of Colorado, where the final stretch of the Midwest meets the Rocky Mountains. From a dusty bungalow outside Colorado Springs, she knew Pikes Peak, the summit named for Zebulon Pike—the white man who, after seeing it, tried to climb it and failed, then tried again and got lost. Nearly a century later, Katherine Lee Bates, an English teacher from Wellesley College, took a carriage to the top, announced that she had found the Gate of Heaven, and wrote "America the Beautiful" on her way back into town.

My mother's family came from the "dry land" farms in the shadow of the peak, where survival depended on grudging rain and stubborn wits. The high point of my family's wealth came when my mother's grandfather acquired a withered plot, which he passed down to her mother, Katherine Reese. The first woman in family memory to have something more than herself to bring to a marriage, Katherine chose a man who was a generation older than she and who had been gassed as a young soldier in the First World War. He widowed her with their two children: my mother, who had just reached her sixth birthday, and her brother, who was still working toward his third. The local child welfare agency suggested a children's home. In desperation, Katherine married a second man, who shortly thereafter sold Katherine's patch of dirt for promised oil royalties. When the payments never arrived, Katherine's second husband abandoned the family. Katherine had chosen poorly—twice—in a life that offered few accommodations for mistakes. Her daughter and son went in and out of children's homes while she did her best to keep them for as much of their childhoods as she could.

When my mother, Hope, was sixteen years old, she met Wade—a twenty-one-year-old outsider stationed at one of the several military bases nearby. In Katherine's words, Wade was an angry man who loved my mother selfishly. Against Katherine's wishes, my mother dated Wade for nearly a year. She left school in the middle of tenth grade. Then, in a final act of defiance, she married Wade in the town clerk's office a week after her seventeenth birthday.

Following his discharge, Wade convinced my mother to see what they could of the world in a Chevrolet station wagon. They left Colorado, traveling for months on a grand tour of America's dust bowl. When they were in Missouri, they called Katherine to announce my arrival, describing me as a blond baby boy who looked more like him than her. They did what they pleased and stayed where they wanted, paying first with the savings that Katherine gave them, then with bad checks. Outside Bakersfield, California, they were arrested for bank fraud. Barely in their twenties, they were sentenced to state prison. I was not quite four years old when I was sent to live with my grandmother, who had moved to Chicago.

Like Katherine before her, Hope had chosen badly. After her release from prison, with me safe in Chicago, my mother settled in Los Angeles, refused to return to my father, and demanded a divorce. On a bench in a public park, Wade agreed to the breakup, but on his terms. If my mother insisted on retrieving me from Katherine, Wade promised a meager monthly stipend for child support. He refused to pay alimony of any kind. There were no assets to divide. Wade declared that their agreement would remain a private one, without the intervention or enforcement authority of a court. If his young wife refused his offer, if she asked for more, if she went to a judge, Wade reminded her that, with or without legal permission, a little boy would never be hard to steal.

From her own mother, my mother knew how easily a woman could lose a child. She accepted Wade's deal, and in return, he abandoned any claim to me. She kept the boy she loved from the man she despised. Yet even with Wade gone, my mother's fear of losing me always lingered. "You have to be ready," she warned. "Someday, someone may come to take you."

"IT'S TIME TO put that away," Mrs. Gordie yelled over the television's racket from the other side of the living room. I looked up from the floor next to the sofa, noticing the darkened room for the first time. "She said she'd be here at a quarter to six. You don't want to make her wait, do you?" At my knees, an embankment of LEGOs that Mrs. Gordie and her husband had given me as an early Christmas present barely restrained a band of identical plastic dinosaurs—all branded SINCLAIR OIL across their bellies—that my Grandma Kate regularly stuffed in her purse for me as she left work for home.

Mrs. Gordie's form lingered in the kitchen doorway. "Come on. Let's hurry up, sweetheart." She nodded at the clock on top of the television. "Your grandmother will be here soon. Get your things in your backpack. Kindergarten means homework, doesn't it?" She pointed toward the small pile of chewed pencils and mimeographed alphabet sheets that I had pulled out, then promptly abandoned beside the front door. I shrugged at the clutter and watched Mrs. Gordie disappear back into the kitchen, leaving her husband to watch me. "You've got a birthday coming in February. Six years old means you'll be a big boy. One of the older ones in your class!" she yelled through the door as I began reluctantly dismantling the LEGO barrier. Knowing me well, she cried out again to hurry me along, "But before your birthday, you know, there could still be another present coming for Christmas!"

The Gordies had lived across the street from my grandmother and me for as long as I could remember. Every afternoon, when the school bus dropped me off at the end of the block, Mrs. or Mr. Gordie—occasionally both—was always there, patiently waiting.

Mr. Gordie leaned over the sofa to see if I was doing what his wife had told me. Beneath me, the LEGO wall lay demolished, its bricks broken and scattered into chunks just small enough to be crammed back into the shoebox that he and his wife kept in the coat closet beside the front door. The pocket-size dinosaurs remained tame. From the corner of my eye, I watched Mr. Gordie linger to catch my attention. A smile dashed across his face. He lay back into the sofa and returned to the television's late-afternoon rerun.

"You want the rest of your soda?" he called from the sofa, his face out of view from the floor. His hand appeared over the armrest, dangling a half-empty glass bottle of RC Cola by its lip with his fingertips. I reached, but he plucked it from my grasp. I scrambled for the drink again and he laughed. With my third effort, he surrendered the bottle. "Don't spill that thing or we'll both have hell to pay. I can promise you that," he cautioned, leaning over the edge and shaking his head. After securing the bottle with both hands, I pressed its base into the dusty carpet between the sofa and me.

Our apartment in Lincoln Park was just north of downtown Chicago, a few train stops from the Loop, where my grandmother worked as a secretary at Sinclair Oil. She did her best to get off work no later than five in the evening, sometimes skipping lunch to beat the clock. During the summer, she might do a little shopping on the way home, taking advantage of the late sunlight. But the winter sun rested early, and she disliked being out alone at night. With the evening and the chill, she rushed home. Mrs. Gordie teased her regularly about it. "My goodness, Katherine, try living a little, for God's sake. Who stuffed you with such an old, anxious soul? What are you, thirty-seven, maybe thirty-eight?"

My grandmother nodded back, inevitably declining to answer Mrs. Gordie's bigger question and sticking to the smaller. "I'm forty-three."

By the late sixties, when my grandmother arrived with me in tow, the grandeur of the Lincoln Park neighborhood was in steep decline. The redbrick row houses where we and the Gordies lived had been divided and redivided, stretching into rows of tenements where a half dozen families might squeeze into the space that only one family had occupied in better years. The kindergarten and elementary school where my grandmother enrolled me eventually fed their charges to Waller High, which Chicago's Board of Education later renamed Lincoln Park High in a vain effort to shake loose the school's reputation for violence.

Mr. Gordie's afternoon Western was exploding into a final round of gunfire, and my grandmother's faint knock was nearly lost in the volley. But expecting it, I dashed to the front door and found my grand-mother on the porch, a small bag of groceries under one arm and her bulky purse hanging at her side. Bundled for the cold, she wore a heavy overcoat that she had bought from a woman at church, dark gloves, and a small yellow knit hat over a head of thick gray and black hair. She was a young-looking woman with strong, dark eyes, though lines creased her forehead, especially when she scowled. She wore lipstick, but reserved it exclusively for work. With me at her side, she was of-ten confused for my mother. But each time—regardless of the place, person, or circumstance—I jumped to correct the error. "She's not my mom," I lectured ignorant strangers. "She's my grandmother." Then I pointed at her to confirm what seemed to me an apparent fact. "She's old."

Still waiting on the porch in the cold night air, my grandmother peered into the Gordies' apartment, then adjusted her grocery bag. "Grandma's sorry she's late."

Lying on the sofa, Mr. Gordie lifted his hand in recognition. "Hello, Miss Katherine," he yelled across the room before slumping back to the television.

"Did you get enough TV?" she asked me.

I smiled and without a word retrieved my coat and backpack from the living-room floor. Mrs. Gordie reappeared from the kitchen, and my grandmother apologized again.

"Don't you want to come in, Katherine?" Mrs. Gordie asked, fold-ing her arms from the open door's chill.

"Oh, he won't take long with his coat." My grandmother threw me a glance to hurry up. "We really have to get home. Maybe to-morrow night."

Outside, the lingering clouds of an evening flurry warmed the air a little. Locked in ice and buried up to their bumpers, neighbors' cars rested like great metal fossils, waiting for discovery with the first slush of spring. Clutching my hand, my grandmother steadied her footing down the stairs of the Gordies' frozen porch, onto the softly packed sidewalk. We reached the first of two ridges of crusted snow mounded over the curbs of the neighborhood's streets. She lifted my arm to help me scale it. Over the ice crest, I twisted my hand from her grasp, darted into the middle of the street, looked back, and teased her with a smile.

She glanced to the left, then to the right, down the long, white canal. Without a moving car or person in sight, she raised her eyebrows and grinned, nodding her head to accept the challenge. She dropped her purse in the grocery bag, then with her free arm, slowly reached to her side for a fistful of snow. I hastily fell to my knees, began packing together my own ball. She lobbed one, deliberately missing me by inches. Still at the curb, she waited, unarmed and laughing. I fired back, but the toss was weak, dropping closer to me than to her. She bent to gather a second round. My fate sealed, I scrambled across the second embankment of ice, onto the sidewalk, to the row house where we lived. Crouched behind the stairs, my hands stinging from the cold, I listened for the coming onslaught. I peeked over the railing. My exhausted grandmother appeared in front of me, one hand clutching her grocery bag and the other holding the backpack that I had left in the street. Not a snowball was in sight.

"Come on, sweetheart," she sighed. "It's time to get inside."

Our boots crusted with snow, we trudged up the four flights of stairs, passed our neighbors' well-secured doors, and finally reached our own. Balancing the groceries on a lifted knee, she fumbled inside the grocery sack for her purse and keys, unlocked the first and second dead bolts, then the doorknob that she complained was useless anyway. We stomped our feet just outside the opened door, leaving a jumble of snow prints on the hallway's threadbare carpet.

My grandmother grinned down at me. "Good enough to scare away the prowlers?" I nodded in agreement. She reached inside, flipped the wall switch, and led the way.

The two of us crowded into the apartment's small foyer. My grandmother quickly shut the door, flipped the dead bolts back into place, then twisted the button on the knob sideways and softly ran her fingertips across it, making certain that she had gotten it right. She latched the chain, took a final look at the secured barrier, and when assured that everything was as it needed to be, turned toward the apartment's cold, unlit rooms. She stepped forward and I scooted behind. She slipped off my backpack, which I grabbed with both hands. I waited at the threshold of my darkened room and watched as she passed through the apartment leaving a chain of light behind her. Then, with every other room ablaze, I turned to mine.

I plunked my backpack onto my bedroom dresser, disturbing the clutter of books that my grandmother bought from catalogs and that arrived at the beginning of every month addressed to me. As always, she had made the twin bed that morning, and now in the evening shadow, the tucked bedcover rested smooth as ink. I flopped down, my legs hanging at the side, my ears and nose still cold from the trek across the street. Tired, my mind emptied slowly into the raven night of the room's deepening corners.

Down the hallway, my grandmother dropped the grocery bag on the kitchen table, walked back across the wooden floor to the living room, and was now struggling with the radiator knob.

"Andy, after supper, do you want me to read some of your Bible to you for Sunday school?" she hollered through the wall. "We can practice learning that story your teacher assigned you in class." The radiator sputtered with steam. She turned back for the kitchen. "Is that all right with you, Andy?" Her footsteps halted in the hallway as she strained to tug off her wet boots. "Did you hear me? I asked if—"

"Yeah," I hollered just to give her something. Her lightened steps drifted back toward the kitchen. I slid off my bed, wandered to the cold of the bay window that, even with my eyes adjusted to the dark, barely lit the room. I gazed down at the clean view of the street where, across and several houses down, a gray rectangle of light marked the apartment where Mrs. Gordie, finished with the cooking, must have sat down for dinner with her husband in front of the television.

"Andy, could you come in here and give Grandma a hand?" My grandmother's voice echoed from the kitchen into my room. I glanced at the door, then up at the old walls that framed it. Long, bent cracks spread down the chipping plaster. I thought of the legs of a stalking arachnid dangling around the sides of the room, its hairy abdomen having descended from a silky wisp overhead.

"Andy!" she cried again.

I sprang to the hallway and the kitchen. The table was set for two.

"Are you hungry, honey? Grandma got spaghetti for dinner." She stirred a battered aluminum pot on the stove. "Why don't you put the empty cans in that grocery sack and throw 'em away for me?" She lifted the sauce-covered spoon to point at the containers on the counter next to her, then to the paper bag upright in the middle of the room. I looked at the kitchen door leading to the balcony, then back at her. She rolled her eyes, exhaling loudly. "Sweetheart, it's just outside. I'm really too tired for this tonight." She returned to her stirring. "Come on, let's be a good boy, and help Grandma out."

I dropped the cans loudly into the bag and dragged it across the floor. Reaching the door, I pushed it open, inviting in the cold and stepping into the night. Across the wooden balcony, the kitchen light beamed across several patches of rough ice that had frozen from the winter's melted snow.

"Don't forget to close the door, sweetheart," my grandmother yelled from the stove. "Remember how I told you heat's expensive?"

With my free hand, I gingerly pulled the frigid knob toward me, leaving a careful gap.

Dozens of nailed scaffolds wrapped the back sides of the neighborhood's nearly identical row houses. Reaching chest-high to me, a wooden railing bound our hanging framework. I glanced down the long alley that split the neighborhood block in two. The muffled cry of a woman—undoubtedly closer than she sounded—echoed against the walls of the gleaming corridor, broke the quiet, and halted with the sudden slam of a door.

Mounted at eye level, the incinerator hatch was wider than the width of my shoulders and big enough to swallow me whole. Rust had crept across the shield's face and eaten into the two heavy hinges that held the little door in place. In the humid heat of Chicago's summers, the pong of rancid food swelled up the long chute from the basement and out the catch's flaking edges. The winter cold suppressed the rot, but even then, the sweet smell of smoldering garbage clung to anything—or anyone—that neared it. I placed the grocery bag at my feet, reached for the handle and tugged. The hatch swung at my face.

"Andy, sweetheart," my grandmother's voice called through the door, "is everything OK?"

"Yes," I yelled back, grasping for the bag in the dark, then flinging it down the shaft. The cans tumbled between the brick walls, clattering toward the basement and the waiting inferno. Hoping to glimpse the flames, I leapt but saw nothing. The lattice wobbled beneath me, and I grabbed for the wooden guardrail.

"Andy!" my grandmother cried.

"Coming." I struggled to shove the metal casing shut, then scrambled across the icy balcony to get back inside.

Next to the kitchen table, she held a chair for me. Two bowls were brimming with spaghetti, my place marked with a glass of milk, hers with water.

"Your feet, young man." She pointed at the set of tracks that marked my path from the doorway to the table. I kicked off my slushy sneakers and carefully placed them beside the oven to dry.

She pushed me into the table before sitting down herself. She folded her hands at the table's edge and nodded at me to do the same. Then, speaking for both of us, she thanked God for her day and for her job, invited him to bless the spaghetti that cooled in front of us, and asked Him to keep her children safe—Terry, a son in the army whom I had never met, and Hope, a daughter in California whom I had convinced myself that I remembered. She then appealed to God to protect me in the days and nights to come.

Bored, I looked up early, scrutinizing her closed eyes.

By her thirtieth birthday, she had been widowed by one husband and abandoned by another. Hope and Terry had long left too. As dinner waited, God and a grandson were all that remained. Watching in silence, if I had understood that she was lonely, even frightened by what life had done, I would still have had it no other way. I was five and a half years old. She was mine. I was hers. And that was all that I required.

She mouthed a last, private plea, then, looking to the side, caught my stare, and asked if I had something to add.

"No," I quickly whispered, alarmed at interrupting her conversation.

She shut her eyes again, announcing to the room, "Amen." She lifted up her head, then her fork, and began to eat.

I never heard the light knock on the front door. The faint disturbance might have gone unnoticed had my grandmother not suddenly glanced up and listened to the evening air. At the second tap, she took a quick swig of water from her glass and scraped her chair away from the table. I turned to follow her.

"That's all right, sweetheart." She put her hand on my shoulder, signaling me to stay put. "Grandma will only take a minute." I watched her walk toward the front hallway.

A moment passed as she peered through the peephole. Two sharp flips from each dead bolt ricocheted through the apartment, the entrance cracked open, and the door chain snapped across the breach.

"I'm sorry to bother you, Katherine"—I recognized the landlord's voice—"but there's someone on the phone for you upstairs. She said she was calling from Los Angeles." Immediately, I abandoned my spaghetti, slid from my chair, and scampered toward the front door.

"Did you want to take it?" the man asked through the rift between the door and the wall.

"Oh, of course. Thank you." She shut the door, fumbled with the chain, and re-opened it. He thumped up the stairs and back to his apartment to retrieve the telephone. She looked at me expectantly.

Evening calls were a rare event. Most of the buildings on the block had not been wired for telephones, though a few of our neighbors had spent the extra money to have their apartments hooked up, agreeing to pay the monthly service charges that—as my grandmother pointed out—came whether or not a single call was made. My grandmother decided to do without. The Gordies had a phone, and mornings when I was sick or she was running late for work, my grandmother walked across the street to make a quick local call to my school or to her boss at Sinclair. If the Gordies were not home or it was too early, she ran to the pay phone around the corner—a handful of nickels and dimes bouncing around her dress pocket. The landlord and his wife volunteered their telephone number to take calls for us and even bought a cord long enough to trail from their apartment down the flight of stairs to our front door.

Telephone and receiver in hand, the landlord reappeared in the hallway. "My wife thinks it's your daughter. Should I just put it here?" He bent down and rested the apparatus on the floor at the base of the stairs.

"That's fine. Be sure to thank your wife for me." My grandmother stepped forward, aware that minutes on the line were being wasted.

"It's no problem, Katherine. Just do me a favor and bring it up when you're done." The man lingered, then spotted me just inside the door frame. "You likin' school, Andy? That new school bus working out all right?"

I grinned eagerly.

"Well, that's good." He looked at my grandmother, whose face had frozen into an impatient smile. "He's a good boy, Katherine. Isn't he?"

She nodded.

"Well, don't worry about the time. We're not headed for bed anytime soon."

"Thank you." She sat on the staircase, then waited for the landlord to pull himself up the railing. She lifted the receiver from her feet, covering the mouthpiece with her hand. Overhead, the man's apartment door closed. She allowed another moment to lapse, assuring herself that the hallway was as private as it could be.

"Hello, Hope?" she asked. "He's fine." She glanced up from the staircase. I smiled widely. "No, the weather hasn't been too cold." She paused. "What? I didn't hear you." She stared at the telephone box between her feet. "I'm not sure. . . ." She shot me a scowl, mutely waving me back into the apartment.

I retreated to the door frame. "Well, it's barely halfway through the school year. I feel like I just got him enrolled. The school's holiday break hasn't even—" A longer pause followed. "Can't you wait until the end of—" Her voice rose. "I know he's your son. Of course, I know you have every right. . . ." She halted, then tried again. "I'm just saying he's a little young."

I crept out of the door, back into full view. Her tone softened. "Hope, honey, I'm not sure that you're ready to—" The caller's faint voice cut her off. My grandmother listened impatiently, then suddenly accused, "Wade's there, isn't he? He's there, putting you up to this." The caller's voice grew louder until my grandmother interrupted. "I'm sorry . . . I know you don't need him, Hope . . . I never thought you did . . . Yes, I think it's good that he's gone."

She looked up again. I expected her to be angry and order me inside for the last time. Instead, she stared blankly, as though she had stopped listening to the call.

I looked back. "Do you want me to talk to her, Grandma?"

She ignored me, went back to the phone. "I can't. He's already in bed." I stared at her, stunned that she was lying. She hung on the phone a while longer, saying less and less, agreeing to more and more. Finally, she stopped entirely and limply extended the receiver to me. "It's your mother," she announced flatly. "She needs you to say good night and that you love her."

I put the phone to my ear but said nothing.

A woman's throaty voice broke the silence. "Andy? Is that you?"

"Yes, I'm here."

"Remember that I promised to come back?"

"Yes."

"Have you been a brave boy without me?"

"Yes."

"Do you promise not to forget me?"

"Yes."

She went quiet.

I looked up, unsure what more to say. "I think she wants to talk to you, Grandma." I handed back the receiver. She sat on the staircase, did her best to smile. "What's wrong, Grandma?"

"Why don't you go back inside now?" she said gently. Suddenly, the voice on the line called out my name. She clamped her hand over the mouthpiece and whispered, "Go get ready for bed, sweetheart." I looked into her resigned eyes, and though she could not say it, I understood that already she had begun to give me up. Of the little that Grandma Kate had, more was about to leave.

I walked to my room, just a few feet beyond the open door. As the conversation carried on, my grandmother's voice remained calm, though she sounded tired when she finally said good-bye and hung up. Sometime while she was climbing the stairs to return the telephone to the landlord and his wife, I fell asleep, and, after locking the front door again, she forgot to wake me to change my clothes.

Halfway through kindergarten, on New Year's Eve morning, Grandma Kate took me to O'Hare Airport. She insisted on boarding me herself, and even after the flight attendant had buckled me in and assured her that everything would be all right, she lingered in the aisle. The last of the passengers was seated, yet she crouched beside me, stroking my knee and staring out the oval window.

"Grandma, you have to go," I whispered. "The plane can't take you, too," I added, unsure where the plane was taking me. "There isn't a seat for you."

"Will you remember me?" she whispered. She turned to me, her eyes red with loss. Then, taking a moment to steady herself, she instructed me firmly, "You mind your mother and you be a good boy for both of us."

I nodded, then watched as she disappeared down the aisle.

WITH THE TAP of the flight attendant's hand, I knew to get up. I looked around and saw that the plane had emptied. Emerging from the boarding tunnel with my escort at my side, I saw two young women waiting among the thinning holiday crowd. The taller woman looked a bit like me. She was blonde and tanned, dressed in red and yellow striped pants, a low-cut white blouse with great puffy sleeves, suede moccasins, and a wide-brimmed orange felt hat. The other woman was dressed as confidently, though more conservatively. Her hair was black, short, and closely tapered. A sleeveless turtleneck—ribbed and dark blue—exposed her pale, slender arms and left her torso a silhouette beneath the terminal's bright lights. Her jeans clung to her hips and legs. A pair of smooth black boots wrapped her calves, then ended in two small feet.

There was no one who told me that she was mine. Still, before she knelt or opened her arms, I ran to the darker of the two women. Quietly, she wrapped herself around me, her small frame eclipsing mine. Her turtleneck scratched against my face and her arms were cool against mine. She pulled me closer, pressing one hand against the back of my head, the other against the back of my thighs. A mingle of cigarette smoke and light perspiration, her scent was warm. In the quiet of her body, I could hear her breathe.

"Andy," the throaty voice sighed, almost sadly. I looked up at her. Seeing the worry in my eyes, she loosened her grip, held me in front of her, then laughed at the sight of me. "Mom waited for you for a long time." She gave me a little shake, then furrowed her brow, mimicking my consternation with a grin. I smiled back, surrendering myself to her. Then I said what I knew to say, what I had learned from Grandma Kate and surely before that from this young woman as well. "I love you, too."

"This is Carol." My mother glanced to the side.

The blonde woman smiled. "We've heard a lot about you, Andy." She bent to extend her hand.

My mother picked up the bag that Grandma Kate had packed, then waited beside her friend. "Go ahead, shake Carol's hand, sweetheart."

I reached for the woman's hand.

"It's nice to meet you, Andy," the woman said formally.

"Is that a cowboy hat?" I asked.

"No, it's a cowgirl's hat." She tapped the orange felt crown, then lifted it and threatened to drop it on my head.

I ducked, darted to my mother's side.

"Andy," my mother scolded, pushing me back in front of the two of them.

Carol shrugged, returning her hat to her head. She reached for the bag from my mother's hand. Then the three of us proceeded down the long, bright corridor. While Carol retrieved her car, my mother and I waited quietly beside the curb. The temperature was cool, though the jacket from Grandma Kate kept me warm. Carol pulled up, at the wheel of a red Rambler. Battered and faded, the car idled and choked as Carol fumbled to clear some trash from the front seat. Finished, Carol nodded. My mother grabbed my hand and ran around to the passenger side.

Wedged between the two women in the front seat, I looked at the overcast sky. Palm trees lined the streets, their bare trunks reaching through the air before ending in hanging feathers of green. "Is it going to rain?" I turned to my mother. She glanced out the passenger window.

"If it does, I hope it clears up. We're supposed to go to the Rose Bowl tomorrow. Well, not the football game. Those tickets are expensive. But the parade. . . ." She leaned in to me, whispering jokingly above my head. "The parade is free."

Unsure what parade or football game she was talking about, I nodded and returned to the passing line of palms outside. A moment later, I blurted, "Are we in Hawaii?"

My mother looked at me, smiling but confused.

"The palm trees." I pointed over her lap toward the sidewalk. "Palm trees grow in Hawaii."

Carol laughed, shook her head. "No, this is definitely not Hawaii." She let out a snort. "Welcome to Los Angeles."

THAT NIGHT, I woke to a sharp laugh in the back of a van. In front of me, I saw a man driving and my mother sitting beside him in the passenger seat. Ahead of them, the windshield wipers cleared glaze after glaze of water. Under me, the metal floor was cold. My sneakers and socks were soaked to my feet and clammy. My shirt collar clung around my neck.

"Who's the kid?" a man sitting on the floor across from me remarked to no one in particular. The light bounced off his face, and his body shook with the road. In the shadows, he seemed gaunt, and his thin beard gave him the look of an overgrown adolescent. I had never seen a man with hair to his shoulders, and I watched him intently. A cigarette danced between his lips as he spoke in a louder, irritated tone. "I said, who's the kid?"

Crouched next to him with her eyes closed, Carol mumbled to the empty space in front of her, "God, would you shut up? Some of us are trying to sleep." She slid her backside across the van's floor to slouch farther against the side. Then she grumbled louder, "What the fuck are we doing, anyway? It's raining *and* freezing."

The driver glanced back toward the three of us on the floor. "Come on, Carol, it's the Rose Parade. I've never seen the floats, except on television. And Hope wanted to do it." He looked back to the road. "She thought the kid would like it. You might even like it too."

The longhaired man yelled again. "Is anyone going to answer my fucking . . ." Wondering why my mother had not said anything, I tried not to move.

"For Christ's sake," the driver finally answered, "he's Hope's kid. I thought I told you."

"Hope's got a kid?" the longhaired man asked, leaning closer in the dark to get a better look. I turned to my mother, whose head rested on the back of the front passenger seat, bobbing with the road.

The driver answered, "Yeah, he was with Hope's mother in Chicago. Before Christmas, she called and said she wanted him. Old lady put up a stink, threatened not to send him. Then Hope threatened to take her to court if she had to." The driver chuckled and lowered his voice. "You know, the bitch woulda done it, too." The longhaired man grinned and shook his head in the shadows.

"Anyway, the threat was enough. She put the kid on a plane this morning. I told Hope to leave him in Chicago." The driver's voice deepened. "What's she gonna do with a five-year-old? For weeks, he's all she talked about." He changed his voice to a mocking mimic, waddling his head with every sentence. "He'll need this. He'll need that. What should I get him? What should I do?"

I slid deeper into my jacket, pulling it farther over my legs and gloving the sleeve cuffs over my knuckles. My toes had begun to get numb, and my hands hurt.

"What's his name?" the longhaired man yelled over the rumble of the road, inspecting me from a few feet away.

"She calls him Andy," the driver answered. "After they got him home this afternoon," he sniggered, "I tried getting him to call me Dad. Christ, when Hope found out, she came after me." His words trailed into a whistle. "Shit, I was just fuckin' around. You think I want him?" He raised his head to look back through the rearview mirror, and I caught a glimpse of his eyes.

Finally, my mother stirred. I watched as her dark form leaned across her seat toward the driver. Her words were low and deliberate.

"What was that, Louis?" The question hung in the silence. My mother waited until the driver glanced at her.

"It's nothing, baby. I think your kid's awake."

My mother turned and looked in my direction. She motioned me to her. I pushed my hands out through the jacket sleeves and began making my way toward her; but I slipped on the wet floor, nearly falling. The longhaired man sprang forward and clasped his hands around my ankles to steady me.

"I got you." He smiled, lifting me by the waist and swinging me forward between the driver and my mother. "There you go, buddy," he whispered.

My mother's hands replaced his grip as she pulled me into her lap. She tugged her coat from under her and wrapped me inside against her warm body. She pushed her face into my jacket collar and I felt her warm breath against my neck. I looked out at the dark strip of glassy highway that lay ahead and watched the rain as it lingered on the windshield, only to be quickly slapped to the side like thousands of unwanted tears. I glanced at the driver, the one my mother had called Louis. He shook his head. Then, in the silence of my mother's arms, I fell asleep.

THE CROWD OF spectators was still thickening along the parade route when Carol announced that she was going for coffee. Shoving her way back to us, she returned with a steaming paper cup and a box of malt balls. She tossed back a fistful, then spotted me covetously staring up. She threw me a scowl, but I refused to relent. Handing me her coffee, she rolled a few more chocolates into her palm and was about to surrender the remainder, when an onlooker's leg knocked my hand.

The paper cup flew to the sidewalk, splashing coffee over Louis's pants. He began to yell; yet my mother quickly intervened, screaming back. Grabbing my hand, she abandoned her friends on the curb. In the morning drizzle, she and I walked for several blocks before she stopped at a pay phone and rang for a cab. By the time the first float tottered past, my mother and I would be gone.

As the driver pulled up, she ran to the street, then held the door open for me to climb inside. Pushing me deeper into the wide back-seat, she sat down and reached for my hand. The driver twisted toward us and waited.

She glanced at him, then turned to me. "What do you think we oughtta do?"

"I don't know," I whispered, anxious that the man was still staring through the plastic divide.

She waited for a better answer.

I slipped my hand from hers, pushed my back against the seat. Then, avoiding both adults' eyes, I focused on my sneakers dangling over the muddy, black floor well. "I've never been in one of these cars before."

"Well, I hear they've got them in Chicago." She tapped her finger against my hand.

The joke fell flat, and the driver grunted. "Lady, where are you and the kid headed?"

"I don't know yet," she answered tersely, keeping her eyes on me. She sighed, then wagged her hand toward the empty holiday street. "Just get us out of here."

Heading nowhere in particular, the driver turned, flipped the meter, and drove.

My mother cocked her head in a funny sort of way as she peered briefly out the window to think. "I got an idea." She turned back to me. "You want to see the city? Why don't we try Hollywood? There's always something open there."

I smiled at the vaguely familiar name.

"All right." Giving me a nod, she looked relieved. "It's a deal." Then, before I said anything, she rapped at the plastic barrier and declared our decision.

The driver quickly swerved, turning back toward the block we had come from and driving down several more. As his two passengers jostled behind him, the man sped up a ramp, rolled through a red light, then descended into the low green hills that cradle Los Angeles.

Across the seat, my mother grinned, then surveyed the length of me. "Hey, didn't Katherine ever give you any of the clothes that I sent?" She looped her finger into my shirt collar and gave the damp ring a tug.

I looked back, confused.

She leaned closer, widened her eyes, and shook her head with a grin. "Katherine? You know, Kate? What do you call her? Grandma? Granny? That old lady who put you on the plane in Chicago?" The cab hit a bump, and she and I jolted against the seat. Still holding her smile, she furrowed her brow and scrutinized my feet. "And don't you know how to tie those things?"

I glanced down at the loosened knot.

"Hmm?" She waited.

Overwhelmed by the plane ride, exhausted by the long night in her arms, I mistook her tease for irritation. I tucked my hands under my thighs, retreated across the seat, and felt my eyes redden.

Her expression changed to concern. "Sweetheart, it's nothing to be upset about." She pulled me back to her. "We can get you some new clothes. And shoelaces. . . ." She bent to knot them for me. "Shoelaces are easy."

Pressed against her, even I knew that she was not used to children. She had gotten it wrong, assuming that a five-year-old boy cared that much about the clothes he was wearing or that he had not yet learned to tie his shoes. In the cab, I knew that Grandma Kate would have never made those mistakes. She would have known that I was tired and would have announced that it was time for a nap. Still, in the flood of questions that this twenty-three-year-old woman asked, in her anxious look after I pulled away, even I could see that she wanted desperately to get it right.

As she watched the window, the driver took us into the city streets. When the HOLLYWOOD sign came into view, she motioned to the glass, making sure that she was the first to show me the jumbled line of white block letters wedged into a hillside, just below the crest. About ten minutes later, she leaned toward the man, pointed to a large intersection, and told him to let us off.

"Looks like we got some time to kill before things start hopping. " She peered down the quiet row of caged businesses. "You got any ideas now?"

I looked up. "I'm hungry."

We stopped at a corner coffee shop with a sign shaped like a rocket ship. The waitress handed my mother one menu, which she turned over to me. Across the banquette, I clutched the oversize, brightly colored folder, watching as she ordered a cup of black coffee. When the waitress returned, my mother nodded, signaling me to order. I looked across the table and pointed to a picture. Then as her cup was refilled for a second and a third time, my mother watched as I wolfed down a BLT and fries for breakfast.

By the time we left, a few stores were open, and though they were mostly for tourists, my mother insisted on shopping. As I stood in the middle of the aisle, she pressed shirts against my shoulders and pants against my hips, checking for the proper size and arguing with herself about which ones she liked most. Then, doing what I had never seen Grandma Kate do, she picked out an armful of blouses and tiny skirts, disappeared into a dressing room with one set and left me with the rest. As she called for more items, I retrieved them from the pile, reaching blindly through the drawn curtain and handing them to her. Every few minutes, she emerged barefoot, wearing something new, modeling it a bit for me but mostly for the mirrors.

The morning drizzle slowly strengthened, leaving the two of us and our handful of bags soaked by midafternoon. She halted outside a random hotel, threw me a quick grin, then tugged me inside. She glanced around the dull walls, pausing briefly to admire the colossal ceiling. Wrinkling her nose at the mixed perfume of the dust from the lobby and the damp from outside, she shrugged at me, then glanced toward the sound of a television spilling in from a small bar off to the side. She took several minutes to convince the bored desk clerk to let us check in early without charging extra. "My kid and I'll catch pneumonia before we get home." She ignored him as he reached for the paperwork, muttering something about what she and I were doing out anyway.

"Just me and you is good enough for me." She bent to meet my face, as the desk clerk finished up. Passing her fingers through my wet hair, she spiked it in every direction and stuck out her tongue. Looking back at her, I smiled then quickly pressed my bangs back into place. She shook her head. "Grandma Kate has made you a very good boy."

We went up to the room, which reeked more than the lobby. Lying side by side on the bed, we watched television, then dozed to the sound of the rain outside. Around dinnertime, she ordered a pizza. As night fell, she told me to get ready for bed and wash my face. Emerging from the bathroom in my T-shirt and underpants, I watched as, wearing a bra, she dug through a shopping bag, hunting for something to wear from our afternoon purchases. A few feet from the bed, she had opened the window to the fire escape, which hung above an alley. The rain had nearly stopped, leaving the wet sweep of a few passing cars and a cool breeze to meander through the room.

Tearing the tag from a new blouse, she absently remarked, "Sweetheart, it's time to go to sleep." Obediently, I climbed into the sagging bed, shivering between the cold sheets.

After buttoning herself up and slipping into her shoes, she strode across the small space, then stopped at the mirror to adjust her hair. As she leaned closer to put on lipstick, I felt ignored, insignificant. She stepped back to give herself a final once-over before turning toward the dresser at the foot of the bed. She took a few bills from her purse, walked to the bed, sat down, and finally looked at me.

"Are you going someplace?" I asked, holding on to her gaze. "Please don't leave me alone."

"Aren't you a bigger boy than that?" she asked, her fingers tucking my hair behind an ear. "I'm just going downstairs for a drink. One drink, that's all. I'll be back soon."

"Are you mad about your friend? I didn't mean to spill the coffee on him."

"You mean Louis? Of course, you didn't. Don't worry about him."

"Can't you stay? We could watch more TV."

"It's getting late for you. And I won't be long." She answered firmly, then gave in a bit. "Come on, sleepy boy. Be good for Mom. Close your eyes, and I'll wait until you fall asleep. I'll be back before you wake up." She plumped the pillow around my head. "You won't even know I've left. I promise. Now, be a good boy for me." She leaned over me, her head hovering above mine.

"What's that?" I asked, hoping to delay her.

"What's what?" She grinned curiously.

I tugged my hand from under her weight and pointed my finger in the space between us. "There." She pulled away, but I saw that she knew what I meant. "What's that in your eye?" I stared at the black pupil that had burst through its line, crossing into its circle of deep green, nearly reaching the surrounding white. "Were you born that way? Did God do it?"

She laughed, squeezed my sides. "God? No, God didn't do it." She looked ready to leave, then added, "A man I knew did."

"Who?" I persisted.

Her smile tightened. "Wade. Your father."

With her body sheltering mine, she explained that she had known Wade for only a few months when he took her to a bar. After bullying the bartender into giving his underage girlfriend a drink, he began bullying her. "He called me an ugly name," she explained. "One that you should never call a woman." She slapped him, then got up to leave. Drunk and humiliated, he yelled her name, and when she turned, he threw his glass at her face. The cuts across the side of her face were light and had healed without a scar. But the shard that reached her eye went deeper, left its mark.

That night in the hotel was the only time that she gave Wade the title of father. Thereafter, when the subject of him arose, I would follow her lead. I would use the man's first name too. Had I insisted on calling him Father or even Dad, she might have tolerated it. Yet I understood that calling him Wade pleased her more, and that was what mattered most. When I considered his absence, her presence quickly overcame it. Her smile was the one that I pursued.

She leaned over the bed once more, kissed me on the forehead. "When I come back, I'll hold you," she promised, glancing at the empty pillow beside me. I gazed at her with sleepy eyes, then felt the covers around me loosen as she rose, leaving only the warmth of her body behind.

She could not have been gone long, before I woke in the room's shadowed light. Something had fallen in the dark. I rolled over, looked down the length of the bed. My eyes focused slowly on a black shape beyond my feet. The wide slope of a man's shoulders and back grew clearer. His head turned to the side, and he glanced across the bed from the corner of his eye. His body and mine waited in the darkness. When the shadow of my mother's purse caught his attention, he returned to the dresser in front of him. He extended his arm, gently grasped the strap. He lifted the purse slightly, then, with more confidence, a bit higher. A tube of lipstick rolled across the dresser's glass top and tumbled to the floor.

I screamed.

He turned in anger.

I screamed again.

He rushed toward me.

His knee hit my ribs, just as my mother's hands began slapping against the outside door. "Andy!" she screamed, fumbling with the lock. "Andy! Andy! Andy!"

The light from the hallway spread into the room. My mother ran toward the bed. As she and I watched, the man's backside vanished through the empty window frame. He banged his way down the fire escape and into the alley below.

Whatever the prowler managed to steal has fallen away, lost in a fault of memory. Yet later that night, as my mother held me in the bed, she told me never to scream again if I woke in the dark to the sound of a stranger in the room. "Be still, sweetheart," she whispered in my ear, slowly rocking me in her arms, watching the desk clerk and two policemen inspect the room. She turned, stared at the open window just beyond the bed, then pressed closer. "Be still." She wiped a tear from my cheek. "No matter what's there. Hold it in. Be still."

Chapter Two

∽

M y mother and I lived in the other Hollywood, the one behind the Hollywood sign. Over the hill, in the San Fernando Valley, North Hollywood had none of the pretenses of its southern cousin. Stars had never lined its sidewalks; no one drove there looking for a good time. Cut into a grid of hot, flat avenues, the neighborhood's most abundant resource was stucco. Gallons of it draped the walls of the gas stations and car dealerships that lined its central artery, and still more remained to swath the modest, single-family homes and squat apartment complexes that spread through its smaller streets. Like most Los Angeles neighborhoods, no one really knew anyone else, everyone existing anonymously. Though not poor, most lived only a paycheck or two from poverty's bite.

"Do you like it?" my mother asked, holding my hand at the bedroom's threshold.

Before her first call demanding me from Chicago, she had anticipated my arrival. She had rented a small two-bedroom apartment that she could barely afford, then decorated the spare room for the boy that she wanted back but barely knew.

"Do you like racing cars?" She pointed at the bed's brightly printed sheets. "Aren't boys supposed to like cars?" Before I could answer, she shifted her attention to the window. "I gave you the room overlooking the front." I glanced at the view of the building's front lawn. "Hey, you like Tweety Bird, don't you?" She took a step inside, turned toward the wall beside the door. I followed her. The yellow hatchling's immense head and eyes glowered at me, his tiny arms folded in consternation. "You know, he's always looking for that stupid cat." She sat on the bed, stared at me. "If you want, we can paint."

I glanced at the room's spartan furnishings: the twin bed covered with racing cars, the battered dresser waiting with empty drawers, and Tweety Bird taped to the wall. "That's all right, Mom." I moved toward her, felt her arm reach for me and pull me backward onto the bed. Lying beside her, thinking that she wanted more, I whispered, "I like it this way."

A few days later, she enrolled me in kindergarten at a nearby elementary school, only a few blocks away. Each morning, she sat on my bed, quietly waking me. Then she walked me to school. A month and a half after arriving, I had my sixth birthday. The most that I recall of the celebration is that she and Carol took me to McDonald's, near the Page Beauty School and Salon, where my mother had enrolled herself. If there were gifts, they were small ones, as they had been with Grandma Kate. In those early weeks, I remember little of Louis, only that if I woke too early, before my mother came to my room, I sometimes found him in the kitchen or bathroom getting ready to leave.

After school, when my mother picked me up, I spent the afternoons at the beauty school, watching as she cut and sprayed hair, plucked and waxed eyebrows, and soaked and painted fingers and toes. In a pink trainee uniform, she could last for hours, smiling at the endless vanities and complaints of unknown women enveloped in the reflections of hundreds of mirrors and the comfort of freshly laundered robes.

For me, the salon was a great chemistry set. Everywhere was a clutter of contraptions that I borrowed as I chose: squeeze bottles with pointed tips that shot streams of water at targets yards away, eyelash clamps that pressed paper into the shape of half moons, tweezers that grabbed at the smallest hangnail, and tinfoil squares that folded into airplanes or simply crumpled into hard, wrinkled balls. Meandering through the back room, I swiped nail polish from trays of rainbows, stuffed the heavy, tear-shaped glass bottles into my pants, then snuck outside to an abandoned shed. The space smelled of rotting wood and moist dirt. With beetles and spiders as my only audience, I pulled what I had taken from my pockets and admired my loot. I painted twigs into striped snakes, dribbled the gloppy gloss onto the sides of discarded boxes, and swirled new colors that inevitably turned into the same chocolate brown. Bravely, I tried the paint on my own small nails, then panicked and rushed to wipe it off.

Emerging from my silent mysteries and experiments, I returned to my mother and the welcoming tribe of women who doted on me. My mother's working companions liked me, and as I listened to their warm gossip and endless chatter, weeks at the salon stretched into re-assuring eternities.

"Well, hello, Mister Andy. What have you been up to, you little blond beast? We heard you had your sixth birthday." Wearing frilled pink like my mother, a young woman called to me as she hunched over a customer and yanked at a tangled clump of gray hair. I shrugged, stepped closer to her workstation. "Could you hold this for me for a second, sweetheart?" She handed me an extra comb as if she were awarding me a diploma. "Thank you, sir."

I scrutinized the woman in the chair, her head cut from her body by an enormous black plastic bib. Her forehead tightened with each tug at her scalp. She endured the pain and ignored the boy standing next to her gawking at her torture.

On the other side of me, dressed in more professional white, an older stylist tended to another seated woman. Leaning toward me, she pressed against her customer, who grimaced at the intrusion. "Did you have a good day at school? Did you do what your teacher told you?"

"Yeah."

Down the aisle of chairs, another hairdresser interrupted. "Baby, would you get me a coffee from next door? You can pick up a candy bar for yourself. Just don't tell your mom. And don't forget, cream with lots of sugar." I put down the brush and walked over to her. She reached into her side pocket and handed me a five-dollar bill.

As I made my way through the rows of women, I heard a familiar voice casually remark, loud enough for me to make out. "Did you know he's Hope's boy? She brings him in every day after school and he waits for her." More than anything, I loved to hear the women mention my mother, connecting me to her, making me belong. As I reached the door to retrieve the coffee from the neighboring family deli, I turned, and the same woman smiled and waved a brush in my direction. "And he's always a big help around here."

"GO ON, HOPE. Wake him up," Carol whispered in a girlish giggle, just outside my bedroom. Flat on my stomach, I looked to the half-closed door and the strip of light that connected my room to the hallway.

"Carol," my mother hissed back, "it's nearly two in the morning. And he needs to go to school tomorrow. His kindergarten teacher already sent home a note."

"God, Hope, it's not that late. What's it, the last week of kindergarten? You think he's reading *War and Peace?* Who cares?"

"I do, Carol."

"Damn it, Hope. We'll never find a sitter now," Carol whined. "Come on, the kid'll love it. Give him a cup of coffee, or something else." She giggled again.

"That's not funny," my mother snapped. "I get enough of that crap from Louis. I don't need it from you."

The conversation halted.

"This is ridiculous," my mother sighed. "What if we get caught?"

"Oh, Hope, we're not gonna get caught. And with a six-year-old, who's gonna do anything to us? Come on. Where's his coat? I'll get the pillowcases."

The voices paused again, before my mother gave in.

"He left his jacket on the couch. You go get it. I'll wake him up. It scares him when someone wakes him up in the dark."

"OK, OK. You get the kid. I'll get the jacket."

Carol's footsteps moved down the hall. A moment passed. From the corner of my eye, I watched the door slowly open. The light from the hallway flooded around my mother's figure and spilled like a puddle onto the floor in front of her. Still on my stomach, I shut my eyes and lay perfectly still.

"Andy?" she whispered, creeping toward me and trying not to scare me. "Andy, sweetheart, are you awake?"

She waited a moment, leaning over the bed before sitting down. I felt her light touch through my T-shirt as she rested her hand on my back between my shoulders.

My mother insisted that pajamas were for little boys. Since I arrived, she had always dressed me for bed in my underclothes. "Everything's about getting ready to be a big boy," she said.

She leaned over and kissed the nape of my neck. "Sweetheart, do you want to come with Carol and me?" Her cheek felt cold. Her leather jacket smelled of the outside and a recent cigarette.

Playfully, she whispered in my ear: "I know you can hear me, mister." I warmed at the touch of her breath, and recognizing the sound of her smile, I struggled not to grin. She moved her hand to the other side of me. With her body canopied over mine, I rolled over, doing my best to look groggy, still knowing I could never fool her.

"What's wrong?" I asked. "Is Carol still here?"

Smiling, she waited for me to finish my ruse. Then, aware that I had been awake all along, she pierced the darkness with a normal tone: "Let's go, sweetheart. I'll get your clothes. Carol's looking for your jacket."

She got up, walked to the door, flipped the switch on the wall. My eyes burned from the light.

"Where'd you put your shoes?" She moved closer to the bed and tugged at my feet through the blanket. "This'll beat anything you ever did with Grandma. Are they under here?" She leaned to her side and looked under the bed. With an exaggerated gesture, she stood straight and spoke like some kind of investigator. "Hmm, Mr. Panda, no shoes and no monsters." She smiled at me as I sat, consuming her attention. "Maybe they took them and wore them. I hear they have tender feet."

I shook my head and pointed across the bed. "I put them in the closet. Where you tell me."

She walked across the room.

"Well, here they are, all right. One empty pair of little boy's shoes." She turned back to me, dangling my shoes between her fingers.

I jumped from the bed to the middle of the room, eager for her to continue the game. Yet she ended the moment, abruptly tossing the shoes on the bed, walking past me to the bedroom door, and announcing, "Come on. It's time to get dressed. Carol and I have to go."

Several minutes later, I walked into the living room, fully clothed. Carol and my mother were leaning against each another, whispering and laughing, at the front door. Each held a pillowcase, and each was clad from head to toe in black, except for Carol's orange hat, which she took everywhere. They continued talking as my mother gently pushed me ahead of them onto the balcony. As she shut the door, I reached for her hand. Absently, she accepted.

Outside, the night was late. The air felt moist and cool, and the moon was small. The streets were long and empty. The three of us walked several blocks, advancing into increasingly unfamiliar territory.

"Where are we going?" I whispered to the two of them.

Neither woman answered. I was quiet.

Finally, we stopped at the entrance to an alley. Carol spoke up first: "This one looks as good as any, doesn't it?" My mother looked straight ahead. "I mean it's light enough," Carol continued, "but not too light. You don't think we know anyone who lives here, do you?" She laughed, as my mother continued ignoring her, examining the corridor of back-yards. Carol grabbed her shoulder and gave her a light shake. "Come on, Hope. Relax. This'll be fun if you let it." My mother looked at her blankly.

Then Carol bent down to me and began speaking in that childish voice that adults had used with me before. My mother let it go, though she hated the slow, overstated tone and, whenever she heard it, corrected people and asked them to stop using it. When they per-sisted, she snapped at them, "He's a little boy, not a moron."

"Andy, your mom and I thought we could play. . . ." Carol stopped and looked up with an expression that asked for help, but my mother ignored her and made her carry on alone. "Your mom and I thought we would play cat burglar." Trying to reassure me, she held her hands overhead and clawed at the empty air. "But first, we have to remem-ber to be very quiet, because cat burglars never want to get caught."

I stared at Carol, then felt my mother's hand tug at mine.

"For God's sake, you're scaring him to death. I'll do it."

Carol grimaced and my mother bent down to take her place. Crouching in front of me, she reached for my hands.

"I need you to listen to me, sweetheart. Your fath—" She inter-rupted herself, looked away for an instant, then back to me. "Wade stopped sending money weeks ago, and now we've run out."

"Can't you ask your boss for some money?" I asked, offering the only suggestion that I could think of.

"No, the salon won't pay me until next Friday. And he said we'd have to wait." She looked to Carol, then returned to me. "It's very late, and everyone's sleeping. So, like Carol said, we have to be quiet." She squeezed her hands around mine. "I've always told you, I need you to be brave for me. Can you be a brave boy for me?" I nodded mutely. "You can't ever tell anyone what we're doing. Do you under-stand me? Can you promise me that, sweetheart?" I nodded again.

She kept her eyes locked onto mine. "There, that's my big boy." She caressed my face, gave me a quick hug, stood up, and announced to her friend: "OK, we're ready."

Standing between the two women, I gazed down the alley. It ran the length of a block and was dimly lit by streetlights that broke the dark corridor at either end. Other than the rush of an occasional passing car, everything was silent.

As the three of us walked deeper into the darkness, backyards alternated on each side, guarded by fences of cinderblock, brick, redwood, and chain-link. Porch lights spread across the stucco walls and over the dark windows of several homes. At our feet, a thin trickle of water split the middle of the concrete passage. The sour smell of rotting food drifted from trashcans and hung in a filthy fog around us.

Carol stopped at a fence. "Shit, it stinks."

My mother ignored the complaint.

Carol looked at the house closest to us and whispered, "What about this one?" My mother shrugged her shoulders. Carol walked to the chain-link fence, peered into the backyard, then swaggered back. "The windows are dark. They've gotta be sleeping. Maybe they're not even home." She stuck her hands in her back pockets and nudged my mother in the side. "So, whadda ya think, Hope?"

My mother considered the flat swath of dirt behind the fence. She looked at me for a long moment before answering. "We shouldn't have brought him with us. I told you it was crazy. What'll happen if I get caught with him? His teacher already wants to talk to me." She lowered her voice and stared straight into Carol's face. "I told you what they could do."

"And if you can't feed him? If you can't pay the rent? Christ, Hope. He's six years old. What's gonna happen then? You think he'll be quiet all day at school? You think he won't say anything to his teacher? You were the one who wanted him, now he's yours."

I listened to the two women argue above me. Then, increasingly aware of the dark around us, I pushed into my mother, hoping that she would tell Carol that it was time to go back home. My mother draped her arms over my shoulders, pulling my head squarely below hers. Carol glanced at the two of us, then took a breath and lowered her voice.

"All right, I'm sorry, Hope. But you have to lighten up a little. You talk about it day and night, and I've told you a dozen times. Nothing's going to happen, not to you and not to Andy. No one's going to take him away from you." She moved closer. "You're all the kid has, and he loves you." She glanced down at me. "Look at him, clinging to you. God, he's like a puppy or something."

I felt a sting of anger, shot Carol a look. *I'm not puppy,* I thought to myself. *Just leave us alone.*

Carol smiled at my mother. "He can't get enough of you. All right?" She glanced at the fence next to us and joked again. "Besides, who else is going to fit through a window?"

"All right. All right," my mother answered, pulling herself from my grasp.

The three of us walked to the fence and stared at the darkened house that lay beyond it. Then my mother looked at me.

"We're going to climb over the fence and run to that tree next to the barbecue. Remember, don't say a word." She looked into the backyard, then back at me. "If you hear anything, I want you to run. Get back over the fence, and wait for me at the end of the block. Run as fast as you can, all right. Carol and I'll find an open window. While we're in the house, I want you to take whatever you can from the yard."

She shot a command at Carol. "He's not going in the house. He wouldn't know what to do anyway. It's this house, and that's it. Understand?"

"For Christ's sake, whatever." Carol smirked. "You think we could get going before someone sees us?"

My mother walked away to get a better look at the side of the house, leaving Carol and me alone. Carol turned to me. This time, she spoke like an adult. "Andy, can you see the garden over there?" She pointed to a patch of dark growth at the other end of the yard, away from where my mother was standing. "Grab everything that you can, and put it in this." She pulled the wadded pillowcase from under her arm, then shoved half of it down the front of my pants. "Remember what your mom said. Be quiet. And if you hear something, run as fast as you can. Your mom and I'll find you."

I had no idea where we were or how to get back to the apartment on my own. "What if you can't find me?" Carol glanced down at me, annoyed.

My mother returned and explained the plan. "He goes over first, then me, then you. We hear anything, we run. If the cops find one of us, we say nothing about the other. If one of us gets caught, we're on our own." She stopped for a moment. "Except for Andy. Whoever's left finds him." She pointed at Carol. "If I'm gone, then you take him until I'm back. No matter what."

"All right. Jesus, all right." Carol shrugged.

My mother could have ended everything there, and her friend would certainly have relented. What drew her to the back of a stranger's house in the middle of the night? Was it the lack of money? Was it just about stealing, getting something for nothing? Was it because she was twenty-four, still driven by impulses, willing to go too far, simply too reckless to know right from wrong, good from bad, for herself, for her son? Or was it about taunting the dark, daring the dangers it held, proving that she was stronger than all of it? Whatever her reasons, she decided to go ahead.

My mother looked at me. "Sweetheart, you know how to climb a fence. Can you show me?" Frightened, sensing only that I should do as she told me, I leaped at the chain-link. It rattled wildly. My mother ran and grabbed my waist from behind. Beside me, Carol threw her body against the links, hoping to silence the sound. When the shaking stopped, my mother whispered in my ear, "You need to do it slowly. Be careful when you get to the top."

I wrapped my small fingers through the damp metal diamonds, inserting my toes below me for support. I reached the top but froze, frightened by the height, unsure what to do next. Only a few feet below me, my mother hissed from the alley. "Pull yourself over, one leg at a time." I tried, but my legs were too short, and the fence swerved with my every move. I clung to the wire and looked to my mother in panic. "Stay there," she whispered, "I'll help you."

She gripped the fence and climbed up to rescue me. For an instant, she and I clutched at the top, as the wobbling wire lattice bowed under our collective weight. She motioned me to stay quiet as she reached for my foot, slowly prying it from its metal stirrup. I stared at the backyard ahead and felt my mother's fingers dig into my ankle as she pushed my unwilling leg over the entanglement. Struggling, I managed to swing the other half of my body over the edge. Trying to avoid the top's metal spears, I snagged the pillowcase that Carol had tucked into my waist. As I struggled to save the cloth bag, the rubber soles of my sneakers slipped on the wet wire. I plunged down the fence, my face slamming into the links, until I tumbled to the ground inside the yard.

I watched my mother as she made her way over and down the buckling mesh. She reached the ground, then threw me an angry look. Jabbing at the night air in the direction of the house behind us, she mutely mouthed, "Tree, tree." I turned, recognized the blackened form of a trunk and barren branches, then ran and stood beneath it. My mother waited for Carol to make her way over. Alone, I eyed the two women as they crept across the yard to the side of the house and disappeared.

Beyond the protection of the yard's single tree, the flat ground lay completely exposed to the moonlight. With the pillowcase in hand, I moved into the empty space toward the small garden. The owner had seeded the plot with tomatoes, but the plants were now exhausted, their souring fruit abandoned for next season's mulch. The rows of staked plants barely reached my waist, leaving me in clear view of the alley and the house. Frantically, I began grabbing at the spindly vines and dropping the soggy tomatoes in the cloth sack. With every step, something on the darkened ground snapped or rustled. I was no more than a few feet into the tended earth when a dog's bark ripped through the silence. I looked up just as a light shot across the yard from the far corner of the house.

Suddenly, a man's voice cried out from the side of the house where Carol and my mother had disappeared. "Who the hell is that? Call the police!"

A moment later, the two of them fled across the yard and threw themselves at the fence. The dark figure of an immense dog tore after them. Alone, I watched as the women pulled themselves over the wire, out of the reach of the animal, and into the alley.

Behind me, room after room inside the house began to brighten, igniting the darkness. Soon, a woman's voice spilled into the yard. "Are they gone? Did the dog scare them?"

The dog kept barking, hurtling itself against the fence and blocking my way as I looked desperately at the two dark figures peering into the yard from the safety of the alley. One of the shadows ran to the far corner of the yard, banging at the chain link and drawing the animal's attention. Closer to me, I heard my mother yell.

"I'm here! I'm over here. Andy, run! Now!"

Blindly, I followed her order, dropped the pillowcase, and ran to the fence.

"Climb over it! Come on! Jump!" she screamed through the wire, her face filled with terror.

The light from the house behind me had already spread into the neighboring homes, while the canine snarled at Carol from the far corner of the yard.

I lunged at the fence and heard the man's voice from the house. "Is one of them still back there?" I was only a few feet from the ground when Carol saw me and ran to help, drawing the dog with her.

The porch door slammed. The man's voice was closer now,

encouraging the dog, "Get him, boy. Go on, boy. Get him!" Following his master's commands, the animal threw himself at me.

My mother began climbing the fence on the other side. I was a few
feet below her when she reached the top and lurched toward me. The
wire buckled, pushing me back toward the dog that was snapping at
my dangling legs and feet. I kicked and scrambled nearer to her as she
grabbed for my jacket. Clutching me by the back of the neck like the
puppy Carol had called me, she yanked me toward her and over the
fence. My weight fell against her slender arms, and she and I tumbled
to the pavement and safety.

Scrambling out from under me, my mother seized my hand and
rushed us down the alley to the sidewalk and street. We were nearly
two blocks away before she finally stopped, spotting Carol's shadowed
figure loitering ahead at the corner. Panting, we looked behind us but
saw no one in pursuit. She bent in front of me, pressed her hands
against the sides of my face, then patted my body down to my ankles.
Over her shoulder, I watched Carol saunter toward us. Ignoring her
friend, my mother stared at me.

"Are you all right, sweetheart?" she asked, still holding me.

"I'm all right," I answered. My heart was pounding, but I did my
best to be still.

"Is your leg all right?" My mother reached around me, then tugged
up both of my pant legs.

"He didn't get me." I glanced at my ankles to make sure. The headlights of a passing car suddenly approached. The three of us froze,
watched it slowly drive by.

My mother looked into my face a moment longer before standing
up. She glanced at Carol, shook her head, and muttered something
like, "I told you." We walked another block in silence until finally she
gave Carol a sidelong glance, and the two of them burst into giggles.
Unsure what to do, I listened to their giddy laughter, then mimicked
them and began laughing too.

Safe in the apartment, with me half asleep on the living room couch, my mother and her friend recounted our foiled heist. Leaning to light each other's cigarettes, the two of them teased and argued, acted out moments, each rushing to interrupt when she felt the other was about to leave something out. When the joking grew too rowdy, my mother glanced at my open eyes and quickly shushed Carol. They lapsed into whispers, then as my sleep approached, another round of girlish cackles broke the night. In every bit of chatter, neither said much about having decided to bring me along.

Lying on the couch, I knew what we had done was wrong, and when I thought about it too closely, I frightened myself, remembering how near we had come to getting caught. Yet when my mother walked over to me and passed her hand over my dozing head, the fear disappeared. Even the wrong diminished. Listening that night, I never wanted to judge her, to cast a vote of right or wrong. Had there been a crowd of arms reaching to catch me from that fence in the back of a stranger's home, I would have still chosen to fall into hers.

THOUGH HE ALWAYS left in the mornings, Louis began spending more nights with Hope. He held only the slightest physical advantage over her but he was rough. His hair was dark and thin, though not yet balding, and the skin on his neck was badly pocked. Removing his shirt exposed a blanket of acne across his shoulders and down his back. He rarely smiled, though when he did, his face appeared weak and guarded. He was by nature lazy; the smallest request provoked him.

I once heard my mother describe him as "swarthy" to Carol, who looked at her disbelievingly before they both burst into laughter. Carol eventually dubbed him Monkey, referring both to his appearance and to the difficulty he had reading, though I never heard her call him that name to his face. Whatever his vulnerabilities, Louis more than compensated for them with explosive rage. He was quick with a slap and wildly possessive of my mother. He enjoyed the feel of a good, solid hit, and on more than one occasion, she had warned him never to try it with me.

My mother never mentioned how she met Louis or why she refused to make him leave. That summer, he and I had been scarcely introduced when he suddenly moved in. Kindergarten had just ended. My mother and I were supposed to spend the summer alone, together. Instead of school in the morning, I could go with her to the salon, spend the day with her and the evenings, too. So she had promised. I was angry when she broke her word.

On the condition that I would behave myself, the beauty school manager agreed to let my mother bring me in from the morning to the early afternoon. Sometimes I stayed until three, maybe even four o'clock. But the manager soon tired of my roaming through the back room and dallying beside workstations. When the shop filled with customers in the late afternoon, I was to be gone. "Your apartment's not that far," he lectured my mother. "He's six. Send him home on his own." Trying to learn a trade and afraid of offending him, she reluctantly agreed.

Louis's life had fewer complications. Lacking a job, his days and nights were free. Late afternoons, when I came home from the beauty school, I inevitably found him in the apartment. His daily activity encompassed little more than eating, watching television, and going to the bathroom. For weeks, I tried my best to behave, spending most of my time beside him on the couch.

"You here already?" Louis grumbled, as I walked into the apartment late one afternoon. Lying across the couch, he kept his gaze on the television. He was unshaven, still dressed in his underwear and a T-shirt. I said nothing and walked into the kitchen to find something to eat. He yelled over the television's blare: "Your mom left you a sandwich in the fridge. You better eat it. I'm sick of you wasting good food."

In the nearly bare refrigerator, I found a thin sandwich, tightly wrapped in plastic, resting on a plate. I walked into the living room

and sat cross-legged on the floor, a few feet from Louis but in view of
the television. He lay on his back, ignoring me and laughing stupidly
at the afternoon program while I unwrapped my snack. I have forgotten why all of it began that afternoon, but I looked at Louis and
hatred swelled inside me. I despised him for the food that he ate, the
space that he took, and the bed where he slept. Why had my mother
let him in, and why had she let him stay?

I got up, walked to the television, turned the channel, and sat back
down. Louis turned his head to me and yelled, "What the fuck you
doin', you little son of a bitch? Turn the fuckin' channel back, now!"
Ignoring him, I sank into myself until nothing more than the shell of
a little boy sat alone with the man.

He sat up, leaned toward me from the couch, and bellowed in a
heavy, deep voice, "Get your fuckin' ass up and turn the channel!"

The assault shook me, but I withstood it and did nothing.

He jumped up. For a moment, he recovered a sense of his own authority and spoke almost calmly. "This is the last time I'm saying it.
Get your little fuckin' ass up and turn the channel."

Knowing what I had started, I gave the precise response required to
complete our exchange: "No."

His hand clamped on the back of my neck. He picked me up and
threw me to the floor, over and over, my knees crumpling under me
and elbows burning against the carpet. Looking me in the face each
time, he screamed, "Turn the channel. Turn the fuckin' channel." To
his every command, I answered: "No."

He gave up on whatever he was watching, dropped me one last
time, and stalked across the room. He picked up a glass table lamp,
smashed it on the floor, and ripped the electrical cord from its metal
stem. Returning to me, he grabbed a fistful of hair and dragged me to
the bathroom door. If I said anything, it was nothing more than "No."

Inside the bathroom, he hulked over me, wrapped the cord around
his fist for a better grip, tore off what remained of my shirt, ripped
down my pants and underwear. The cord was of a sufficient length to

snap across my spine, around my back, over my sides. Careful to avoid my chest and face, he finished what he had to do with about a half dozen swipes.

When my mother got home from work later that evening, Louis had returned to the couch and television. I was sleeping in my bedroom, fully dressed.

"In bed already?" she asked softly, as she sat down next to me. "You're still dressed. Come on. Let's get you ready for bed. Time to brush your teeth and wash your face."

From her voice, I knew she was tired, but running her forefinger across my cheek, she joked, "Is that a beard I feel or just more peach fuzz, mister?" I was quiet. "OK, here we go," she sighed, slipping her arms around my stomach and pulling me up from the bed. "Haven't you grown into a little sack of potatoes?"

We walked to the bathroom, where she flipped on the light, found my toothbrush inside the cabinet, turned on the tap, and squeezed out a dollop of toothpaste. Finishing in a couple of strokes, I spat into the sink. She grimaced.

"Is that all we can manage tonight?" she asked, crouching on her knees in front of me, brushing my hair from my forehead. "Well, we'll do a better job washing your face. This isn't the shirt you wore this morning. Beginning to think about appearances, huh?" She grinned. "OK, big boy, up with your arms." I lifted my hands over my head. "Come on, you gotta help me out here, honey. Higher." I stretched farther; and she dragged out her voice in a tired, playful tone: "Higher."

With my arms in the air, she reached around my stomach and pulled the shirt above my chest, tugging the collar over my chin and head. Then she was silent.

"Turn around," she ordered as she grabbed me by the waist. I hesitated, but her grip strengthened. "I said turn around and let me see." I did as she ordered. From behind my back, I heard her suck in a deep breath. Then her fingers touched the crisscross of thin welts in the bright bathroom light.

"Who did this?"

I was silent.

She spun me around to face her, shook me angrily, and repeated, "I want to know who did this."

Still I said nothing.

She cast her head to the side and thought for a moment. Then she pulled me closer and whispered, "Louis did this, didn't he?"

I nodded.

"Is that all he did?"

"Yes," I whispered.

She waited for me to wash my face. Then she put me to bed, where I fell asleep immediately.

My mother never told me what she did to Louis. She was a slight woman, with little physical strength, and I wonder what it took to get him out. Maybe her rage was enough. All I know is, by morning, Louis was gone.

CHAPTER THREE

◇◇

I NEEDED A BUNNY suit. My first-grade teacher was Mrs. Nagami, a well mannered, middle-aged, Japanese-American woman who spoke with a gentle accent. She brought us homemade food to sample, talked about the hard lives of coal miners in Japan, and taught us to fold tiny paper cranes. By early October, she had already proven that her patience with even the slowest and most restless among us was inexhaustible. Every day, as we piled in from lunch and settled in our chairs, she walked to the front of the class, pulled her chair from her desk, and lifted a book from her drawer. With our heads on our tables, our hands and arms nearly still, we waited and listened. Then in the warmth of the fall afternoon, her voice rose and plummeted through the adventures and misdeeds of Peter Rabbit, his three brothers, and their beleaguered mother. Finished with her third and on to her fourth storybook, Mrs. Nagami announced that our first-grade class would be performing a Peter Rabbit Pageant.

"Now, all of you have to get ready," she announced, walking through the rows of small desks and placing a large envelope in front of each of us. "And I don't want you opening this until you get home and give it to your mother. I'm sure she'll be able to manage these. They're very simple patterns and all the same."

I stared at the wrapped assignment, my apprehension rising. I was six and a half years old, had lived with my mother for only nine months, but had already discerned that she was different from other mothers. Barely twenty-four, she was likely the youngest of any parent and certainly the least cooperative when it came to domestic chores. I had never seen her with a thimble and thread. I never questioned her devotion but simply understood that she was a woman who sat more comfortably on a bar stool than behind a sewing machine.

Walking into the beauty shop that afternoon, I clutched the envelope at my side.

"What's that?" one of my mother's friends asked me.

"Nothing," I yelled back and smiled, putting the pattern under my papers from school and running to the supply room for my afternoon research.

Walking home with my mother, I considered mentioning Mrs. Nagami's homework assignment, then thought better of it. Sitting in my room, I did my best to peel the tape from the paper flap without ripping it and carefully pulled the envelope's contents onto the floor. In addition to the paper designs, Mrs. Nagami had included two colored felt swatches—one in light pink and the other in baby blue. Apparently, my mother was expected to search out and match the prescribed fabric and, using the pattern, precisely tailor a bunny suit for my upcoming performance. The chances of my mother sitting in the evening and stitching together a four-foot-three-inch, blue felt bunny were about as flimsy as the tracing paper on which the patterns were drawn.

My mind began hopping through solutions. I could make the outfit myself, though buying the cloth and piecing it together would be difficult. Maybe I could glue it. I could ask Carol for help, which would be ridiculous. Or, just maybe, my mother had hidden her ability to do what came so easily to other mothers. I chose this last and most impractical of solutions, decided to turn the project over to her and hope for the best.

I emerged from my room with the restuffed, now lumpy envelope in hand. Still in her uniform, my mother was sitting behind the coffee table, her legs up, watching television, smoking a cigarette, absently slicing the air in front of her with jets of smoke. "Wash up for dinner, sweetheart. I thought we could go out tonight. My feet are killing me." She kept her eyes on the television set.

"OK. I'll get ready." I paused, thinking how to begin. "My teacher told me to give this to you," I muttered. I lifted up the large envelope and waited in the middle of the living room.

She glanced up, took a drag on her cigarette, and returned to the television. "What is it?"

"It's something for school. We're supposed to dress up like bunnies or something," I answered, mildly embarrassed at the thought.

She nodded, still looking away.

Watching her, I steadied my words. "My teacher said you're supposed to make it, but it's not hard. There's a pattern inside." Afraid that she would know I had looked at it without permission, I volunteered, "I already opened it."

"That's great, sweetheart," she answered, completely distracted and waving her cigarette in the direction of the kitchen. "Put it on the counter, and let's get ready for dinner. I'm starving." Relieved and disappointed, I left the envelope in the kitchen and went to the bathroom to get ready.

At school, weeks passed and the litter of bunny suits steadily grew. Each comprised of a felt headpiece with one ear hanging at each side, plus a matching body suit with foot pouches. The first two or three outfits, prepared by the most zealous mothers, arrived in a few days. As the Peter Rabbit Pageant neared, the pace quickened. Not a single suit was out of hue, as though all of the mothers had gotten together, purchased two massive bolts of cloth, and cut each outfit to identical perfection, allowing for only minute differences in size. My spirits sank.

"They're just a bunch of pajamas," I grumbled, staring at the array of bunny suits from my desk.

Eventually, every bunny had arrived, and they all hung on a rack in a corner of the classroom—every one except mine. Mrs. Nagami must have hesitated to ask where mine was, much less send a reminder note home with me.

By the end of the second week of first grade, my mother had begun showing up occasionally outside my classroom uninvited. As she peered through the window from the hall and my classmates stirred around me, my face flushed with embarrassment. When she smiled and waved through the glass, I looked away, hoping she would leave before Mrs. Nagami noticed. But she always noticed. She would ask the class to quiet down, then step into the hall and carefully close the door. Several moments would pass as the two women moved out of view. Then Mrs. Nagami would return, glance in my direction, and the window would be empty.

After school, I complained to my mother, telling her that other mothers never arrived at school in the middle of the day.

"I was on a break. I just wanted to see if everything was OK." She shrugged. Noticing my unabated irritation, she grabbed me, then tickled and teased, "You know, make sure no one takes you."

"Who's going to take me?" I tried asking, before surrendering to cackles of laughter.

"Oh, I don't know," she answered, a little defensively.

Less than a week before the pageant, Mrs. Nagami pulled me into the hallway. "Andy, where is your outfit?" I stared at her blankly, trying to think of an excuse. "You didn't lose the pattern, did you? Did you bring it home like I told you?"

I thought for a moment. "I gave it to my mother," I spat out. "She has it, and it's almost done."

"Oh, that's a good boy," Mrs. Nagami said with relief. "But you have to tell your mother to hurry. Remember, we're having the Peter Rabbit Pageant next week. Can you bring it before Friday?"

"Yeah, she'll have it done. I promise."

Arriving at the beauty shop that afternoon, I told my mother that I needed my suit by the end of the week.

"What are you talking about?" she asked, staring at a customer's head and violently teasing a patch of hair.

"My suit. My bunny suit. My teacher said I have to have it by Friday," I answered in a panic that bordered on a whine. "I gave you the pattern. Remember? It's in the kitchen!"

Later that evening, my mother grabbed the envelope from the counter where it had waited for weeks. Sitting at the coffee table, she tugged out the thin paper and cloth swatches. Perplexed, she stared at the instructions, then muttered, "Shit." She looked up at me and saw that my eyes had already begun to redden. "Oh, sweetheart, don't worry. Mom will take care of it, I promise. You need it by Friday?"

I nodded.

"Come here." She motioned me toward the couch. Pulling me into her, she whispered, "Mom will take care of everything. I promise. It'll be fine."

The next day, I arrived at the beauty shop and found every woman smiling. "He'll look adorable," a customer remarked, turning in her chair toward me. As I walked by, she repeated herself: "He'll just look adorable!" My heart jumped, unsure what the gaggle of hairdressers and customers had concocted for me. My mother called me from the back of the salon.

"Andy, come over here." A large box sat on the floor beside her. "Carol drove, and I found it!" my mother exclaimed, proudly sharing in the credit. She was beaming. "Remember when I said I'd take care of everything? Well, it's only Thursday, and I've got it for you!"

The box was large enough to hold bunny suits for my entire class. Walking a gauntlet of smiles from a dozen or more women, I approached her. She untucked the box lid and reached inside. "We got the smallest to make sure it fit you." She struggled with her arms until the box finally gave way.

"There!" she cried, to the crowd's fawning approval.

Between her hands, she clasped an enormous costume rabbit's head, bigger than a basketball. Two large, black, shiny eyes stared blankly at me, each under a nest of sharply curled, plastic eyelashes. The body was covered with reddish purple velour. The creature's ears stood erect, joined together by a faded garland of artificial flowers. A straw hat, clearly too small for a head of such proportions, was laced with orange and white ribbons and lovingly perched between its ears. Above its grinning mouth, several thick, black whiskers extended from its nose like evidence of budding puberty.

"Well? Can you believe we found this? I mean, it's perfect!" she exclaimed, smiling at me from the side of the thing's head. "Not to mention adorable."

I stared, dumbfounded.

Eager to win me over, she returned to the box, pulling out the rest of the costume. There were the shoes shaped like rabbit feet, crafted from the same red purple fuzz. Then came the body suit. Several small carrots had been sewn onto one of its sleeves, as if to reassure observers that, despite its menacing appearance, the thing remained herbivorous.

"The flowers," I whispered.

"What flowers?" my mother asked, confused.

"On its ears." I pointed to the head that sat smiling next to her on the floor. "The flowers. None of the bunny suits at school have flowers. Boys don't wear flowers." The horde of watching women giggled at my struggle for masculinity.

My mother picked up the head and stared it in the face. "Oh."

She paused and looked at me. "Carol and I liked them. You don't think they're pretty?" I grimaced and said nothing. "Well, I can fix that." She looked around and reached for a pair of heavy shears. Smiling at her solution, she held the scissors up in front of her and began stabbing between the thing's upright ears. After several thrusts, she held out the handful of plastic posies like a bride's bouquet, then promptly threw them back in the box.

"Ta-da!" she announced, extending the reformed head toward me.

Apparently, the flowers had provided support as well as adornment. Now, the animal's ears split apart, like two spikes jutting horizontally to each side. *Oh, there's an improvement, Mom,* I thought.

"Oh, honey, it'll be great," she said to reassure me.

I forced a smile as she stuffed the costume back in its cardboard home.

At school the next day, I told Mrs. Nagami the truth. "My mom is done with my suit."

"Well, why didn't you bring it in? She's coming to the pageant next week, isn't she?"

"Yeah, she's coming. Her friend helped her and it's at our house. But I'll have it. She promised."

For the next week, I stared at the cardboard box by the living room sofa, desperately hoping that something might yet transform the creature that lay lurking inside. But nothing did.

The morning of the pageant, even my mother understood that stumbling my way to school in my rented, overgrown hare suit would be impossible. "Honey, I called Carol. She said she'd pick us up," she yelled from the bathroom as she finished her makeup. "Carol told me she wouldn't miss this for the world."

Carol arrived late, and the three of us rushed to load the creature's lifeless shell into the trunk of her car. By the time we got to the school's auditorium, the pageant had nearly started. Most of the parents had already assembled, and Mrs. Nagami was onstage with the rest of my class. While Carol took a seat in the audience, my mother hurried my bunny box and me backstage.

She knelt in front of me, holding open the oversize velour suit while I stepped inside. Zipped from the back, the costume hung between my knees at the crotch, leaving yards of legging at my toes and its white, grapefruit-size tail dragging behind me. The rabbit's feet were several times bigger than mine. As the music began, my mother struggled desperately to secure the feet, finally resorting to anchoring their laces around my ankles. Then came the matter of the gargantuan mask. I slipped my head through the neck. As the creator had intended, I could see through the rodent's grinning mouth. Yet, with every step, the head toggled back and forth, first blocking, then allowing my vision. I complained, but my mother snapped at me. "Don't be such a baby, honey." She blew me a quick kiss and vanished down the hallway to take her seat with Carol.

The curtain was drawn. My classmates were waiting. The audience quieted. Then suddenly, I lurched onstage like some immense and drunken pubescent gargoyle piling into a hutch of innocent bunnies. Parents watched in amazement as I searched for my assigned position—ears flapping, mask stupidly grinning. Desperately, I held the head in place with my hands, which only made me appear terribly confused. When I finally found the spot where I belonged, I turned to a girl classmate, who looked at me and screamed.

But the final blow was yet to come. A simple song would never have satisfied Mrs. Nagami's enthusiasm. A master of many trades, she had also choreographed a dance.

"Remember, children, one step to the side, one step back, turn in a circle, and double hop," Mrs. Nagami had told us in countless rehearsals.

Inside the hollow, echoing head, I heard the needle drop heavily on the record. I straightened my back. A second later, the song began.

I started moving. However, my feet slipped inside the creature's huge, three-toed shoes. Instinctively, I confined my dance to the most secure areas of my body—my knees and waist. As my classmates stepped, turned, and jumped, I remained in place, squatting up and down, over and over, my crotch drooping to the floor as if I desperately needed to urinate, or worse. After several repetitions of our song and dance, Mrs. Nagami stopped clapping, the music abruptly halted, and the performers froze.

Silence persisted, hanging heavy among the parents. Then came the hoots and hollers of two audience members, girls more than women, who loved me. Shamelessly shattering the room's silent pall, their cries and applause sailed over all the other parental adoration combined, marking the beginning and end of every sound of praise.

Behind my enormous mask, I smiled wildly.

Lingering as my classmates shuffled offstage and out of view, I stared at my mother, who was still clapping even as the others had begun to stand. There she remained, refusing to notice as more than one parent aimed a quick look of disapproval at her and her equally boisterous companion before moving on between the rows of folding chairs. Instead, she elbowed Carol to keep applauding, then quickly returned her full attention to me. In a pink-patterned dress cut well above her knees and a matching pair of calf-high vinyl boots, she fit in the crowd no better than I fit on the stage. Yet, from inside my costume's warming bobble head, I claimed her and every one of her differences. She could not have seen my eyes, but I recognized in hers the uncompromised delight of claiming me as well.

IT MAY NOT be right or fair, but I have always thought that when Louis came back, he intended to take everything. He arrived in the middle of the night and must have been in the apartment for some time before I woke to my mother's screams. I jumped from my bed and ran down the hallway into the empty living room. Every room in the apartment but mine was brightly lit. The front door stood open. I ran to the kitchen, where I found my mother with her back pinned against the far wall. Her blouse was torn and her bra was ripped from her shoulder. Her skirt lay on the floor. Louis was in front of her.

When she saw me, she screamed. In response, Louis clamped his hand at the top of her throat just under her jaw. In his other hand, he held a steak knife, pointing it at the base of her neck above the spot where two slender collarbones nearly met. His pants circled his knees, exposing his flexing backside and thin legs. As he pressed himself against her, her head lightly tapped the wall.

Unsure what to do, I watched as she gasped for a breath and choked out a single word: "No." Louis's hand moved up from her neck and spread over her mouth, pressing hard against her face, as if to sink inside her. His other hand, now dangling the knife, crept down and clasped her breast.

I screamed at her, "Make him stop. Make him stop." Louis turned his head. From across the white linoleum floor, he glanced contemptuously at me before returning to his half-finished chore.

I ran to the front door, down the stairs, and to the first apartment, which belonged to the landlord. The windows were dark, but I began pounding at the door with my fist. Nothing happened. Frightened that no one was home or that I had not knocked hard enough, I pressed the bell, refusing to release it, then began kicking at the door.

Still more time passed.

Finally, the door swung open.

The landlord was a middle-aged, potbellied man, and my mother had gotten the better of him in more than one tangle. She had taken to calling him Pinhead. But that night, to me, he seemed gigantically strong and the only authority available to stop what was happening upstairs.

I waited as he leaned against the darkened door frame, clad in nothing but his underwear and socks, resting his hand on one hip. He knew who I was, and his tone was immediately hostile.

"What do you want?"

As quickly as I could, I began sputtering out what was going on, telling him about Louis, how he had come back, how he had a knife to my mother's throat. I begged the man for what seemed a simple deed: to step from his doorway, walk up the stairs, and remove Louis from my mother. I finished my plea, but the man stared at me blankly. Certain I had not been clear, I began again, repeating what was happening to my mother and what I needed from him.

He waited while I jumbled through the story a second time. For another long moment, we stood together silently, listening to my mother's screams stumble down the stairs then gradually diminish to whimpers. Finally, he moved. He bent down, with both hands on his knees, to get a good look at me.

"Tell your mother to pay the rent on time." He stood, slammed the door, and yelled from inside, "And to shut up. Some of us are trying to sleep!"

I walked back up to the apartment, where every light still blazed. I waited in the living room until I heard the back door slam. Louis had finished. I went to my room and left her alone.

After that night, what I remember most is the quiet. My mother spent hours in her bedroom, leaving me to meander the apartment on my own. I crept about, doing my best not to disturb her. I noticed that she went to work less in the morning. Instead of sitting on my bedside and waking me for school, she would yell down the hall that it was time for me to get up and go. In the kitchen eating dinner or in the living room watching television, she might ask a question or two, but her eyes inevitably faded halfway through my answers. Mostly, we sat in silence, ashamed of what Louis had done and more ashamed that I had seen it.

My mother never talked to me about what had happened the night of Louis's final visit. Her only reference to the event was a vague warning over breakfast: "People can be dangerous."

Already I felt what it meant to be without her.

CHAPTER FOUR

∽

THE FIRST OF my mother's collapses happened on a street corner.

November had just arrived. I was close to the halfway point of first grade, and though it was still weeks away, I was already thinking about Christmas. My mother had asked Carol to watch me for the evening, and giving in to my pleas, Carol agreed to McDonald's for dinner.

In a skirt short even by California standards, that orange, floppy hat over her long, blond hair, and a blouse that only a young woman could hope to pull off with any self-respect, she was dressed more for the benefit of the pimple-faced, gangly boys, sweating in the maze of grills and bubbling fryers, than for her best friend's six-year-old son. With a lingering interest in the menu above, Carol shoved herself into the counter, her breasts nearly slamming into the young cashier's forehead. Regardless of his burgundy outfit with gold trim and matching paper hat, the boy shot out a lascivious, gummy, braces-bedazzled smile.

"He'll have a plain hamburger and small chocolate shake," Carol ordered, ignoring me. The boy glanced down at me for the first time. Noticing the brief shift in attention, Carol piped up, "Oh, he's not mine. I'm just babysitting." The boy's face froze into another grin as

Carol cast her stare on him, before looking down at herself admiringly. "I'll just take a Coke. Gotta keep up with my diet."

Finally, I interrupted. Objecting to having been ignored, I spoke to the boy taking our order. "My mom gave us this money for dinner."

"No, she didn't," Carol answered flatly, then handed the young cashier several bills.

Our order in hand, Carol chose a table in the middle of the room. After a few predictable questions about school, my teachers, and if I was excited about Christmas, she ended all efforts to engage me. I watched as she daintily sipped her straw, scanned the room, and exchanged glances, brief smiles, and an occasional smirk with our fellow diners.

Outside, the day had begun to darken, but it was still too early for bedtime. The streets were crowded with holiday shoppers. Capitalizing on the attention that the company of a little boy inevitably brought, Carol decided on a walk.

We had only made it down a block or so when she stopped and pointed toward the large intersection ahead. A crowd had massed at the corner and was spilling over the curb into the crosswalk, their backs to us.

"God, what's that all about?" she asked.

But I ignored her, staring at the pavement as I leapt from square to square along the sidewalk behind her.

She looked back and held out her hand. "Would you knock it off and get over here, young man."

Reluctantly, I marched toward her and accepted her hand. I was trying my best to keep up with her quickening pace, when just shy of the corner, she let go and left me watching as she sifted through the crowd that was now well into the street, blocking any clear view of the intersection. A police car was parked across the street, its red and blue lights twirling in the evening dark. Soon another pulled up alongside me, halting traffic. Carol's head popped over the throng, as she jumped to get a better view.

I could have walked beyond the curb to try to catch a glimpse of whatever was taking place, but the mob frightened me, so I kept my distance and wandered toward the light of a drugstore window. I peered through the sheet of glass into a treasure house of neatly stacked Christmas tree ornaments, jumbled tubes of wrapping paper, pyramids of detergent, cleanser, and soft drinks. Inside the store, shoppers stood sandwiched, patiently waiting at checkout stands. Still gazing into the store, I ignored Carol when she emerged from the crowd and called to me from the curb.

"Andy, come on. Let's go." She was anxious, which was unlike her, and I hesitated. "Now!" She marched up to me with a glare and grabbed my hand with a jolt. "I told you, we need to go."

I followed her lead as she tugged me down the sidewalk and around the edges of the crowd, which had expanded and backed its way into the drugstore's corner entrance. Carol said something, but tempted by the excitement, I looked away and into the street. She yanked at my arm again and scowled. "I said not to look."

Seeing that her scolding was no match for the attraction of the boisterous crowd, she paused and, reconsidering her approach, bent down to me. "Sweetheart, you need to listen to me. When we get to the corner, I want you to close your eyes until we're across the street. Don't look behind us, OK? Do you understand?"

Unsure what else to do, I nodded.

She took my hand and moved forward, but she had trouble maneuvering for both of us. The confluence of exiting customers and street-corner spectators blocked us at the drugstore's entrance. Their voices cascaded through a forest of legs and shopping bags down to my ears.

One asked, "Who is it?"

Another answered, "Some freak show. I've seen her before." Carol strengthened her grip on my hand and shouldered our way through the strangers.

We had advanced a few more steps when I heard it, a casual

observance from a woman standing over me that struck like an unexpected slap across the back of my head. "You know, she works at the beauty school down the street."

Carol shoved herself against the woman and, as we passed, spat out at her, "Excuse me, ma'am."

Finally, we reached the curb. But the middle of the crossing held too much temptation, and I could not resist glancing over my shoulder. Carol must have felt me turn. In fact, with the clean view afforded by our new position, not even she could ignore the spectacle.

A few yards away, my mother stood trapped in the empty street. Three policemen stalked her at a distance, batons drawn. Despite the evening cool, her hair stuck to her face with sweat. Wild with fear, her eyes darted from side to side. Barefoot, she had already fallen several times. The rear and sides of her tight slacks were smeared with grime. She let out an exhausted grunt, then lunged toward one of the men in an apparent effort to escape. In a quick response, he swung, catching her forearm. She grabbed her arm and cried out in pain, retreating a few steps, surrendering ever more ground to her pursuers.

The officers were closing in around her, when Carol reached for my hand. "Let's go," she said softly.

"Doesn't she need our help?" I asked.

"No. She'll be fine. We need to get home." She pulled me to the other side of her. "She wouldn't want you to look."

I did as Carol told me. We walked away, without anyone knowing that the woman's best friend and son had, for a moment, been a part of the crowd and left early. Down the block and away from the noise, Carol looked straight ahead and attempted the only explanation for my mother that I remember. "It's not her fault." Carol's voice faltered before she continued. "Just remember that she loved you. And that it wasn't her fault."

.   .   .

IN THE DAYS that followed, my mother's mind consumed her with increasing ferocity. Her fears rose and broke like fevers; her weaknesses became familiar. Half-believing the dangers that she described, half-knowing that they could not be real, I feared with her. The more I saw, the more vigilant I became.

At some point, she told me to stop going to the beauty school to wait for her, and though she claimed to have quit, I knew that she had been fired. With the rent unpaid for weeks, the landlord cut off the electricity first, then several days later, he stopped the water. Still, we clung to that stucco apartment in North Hollywood.

Alone in the living room, my mother sat for hours in the dark, smoking and playing solitaire. Flipping cards in a careful monotony that I never fully understood, she played against an invisible foe that shifted with each new hand. On the few occasions when she left the table, she alternated between talking incessantly about strangers trying to steal me and an eerily withdrawn silence. Yet, in the cards, she found a pervasive calm, as though she were resting, preparing herself for some great, unknown challenge soon to come.

At night, when she thought I was sleeping, I listened to her whispering in tears, as she sparred with the darkness.

"You can't have him."

Darkness.

"I know who you are."

Darkness.

"Shut up!"

Darkness.

"I said, no!"

Darkness.

I never got up to help her fight with the nothingness or to tell her that no one but she and I were in the room. I never fought for her, as I should have. Those nights were my great lessons in doing nothing— when I understood the quiet shame we feel in spotting a man or woman crying on the street. *What happened? Should I do something? Would I be told to go away, left embarrassed? Better just leave it alone.* Eventually, her illness grew so immense that not even a six-year-old could imagine how to tame it. And, other than me, she trusted no one.

One evening, when my mother tried to slide the key into our front door, we discovered that the landlord had changed the lock. She began screaming at the barrier, pounding it with the palms of her hands, kicking the sliding window next to me. Then, in an instant, she was calm. She told me to wait, walked down the long balcony, and descended the stairs.

The sound of scraping metal came first. Then she reappeared, dragging a large trash can up the concrete steps. She lugged it the length of the balcony, ordered me to move, and with a wide swing to the side, heaved it through the sliding window next to the locked door. The wall of glass shattered with an enormous, thundering crash. Daggers of it flew across the balcony and into the apartment. I watched quietly as she walked over the shards, pushed the curtains aside, and made her way through the front room. She ripped a sliding door from the closet next to the bathroom and dragged it to the broken window, covering what she could. Finished with her task, she unlocked the door and let me inside, ignoring everything that had just occurred.

We began living on food stamps and government checks, and she spent less time with me. The apartment was empty when I returned from school in the early afternoons. Most days, she came home before dark, but sometimes she stayed out late. Without her, the landlord frightened me, and I avoided staying in the apartment alone. Maybe no one noticed the six-year-old sitting on the curb or aimlessly wandering the neighborhood at night, or maybe I was good at avoiding notice. Whatever the reason, no one stopped to ask who I was, what I was doing, or where my mother could be found. And no one invited me in.

A week or two before Christmas, my mother and I found a gift at our door. The woman living next to us had filled a coffee can with hard candies, covered it with red and green felt, and tied a note with a ribbon. "For Hope and Andy, Merry Christmas!" Cautiously, my mother peeled off the lid and flicked at the candy with her fingers.

After a brief examination, she looked me in the eye. "I told you. I knew it. They said they were going to poison you." She picked out a candy and held it a few inches from my face. "See? Can't you see how they wrapped it?"

Unsure what she meant, I moved to touch the candy, but she snatched it away. "No!" she yelled, flinging it back in the can. As if I had mistakenly reached for a hot stove, she lowered her voice to a gentle reprimand: "Don't touch." Turning her back to me, she walked a few feet, halted at the woman's apartment next to ours, and smashed the can against the front door. Pieces of candy flooded down and over the balcony, then rained onto the sidewalk and driveway below. My mother ushered me inside and quickly shut the door.

By the time my school's holiday break began, she had begun refusing to let me out of her sight. I slept alone some evenings, but mostly I slept at her side in her bed or mine. I thought of the holiday now only days away. In the morning light of the living room, sitting next to her on the sofa, I summoned the courage to ask, "What about Christmas?"

She tapped her cigarette into her coffee cup. "We don't need Christmas, do we?" she said into the empty space.

I said nothing, waited.

Then she turned to me with a smile. "What about if you stayed home from school? You know, just for a few days after the start of the New Year. We could make it a birthday and a Christmas gift."

"But I'm supposed to go to school. . . ." I objected.

She pulled me to her side, then whispered, "You're supposed to be with me."

We sat quietly, staring into the shadowed room. The problem was, both of us were right.

On Christmas Eve morning, I woke with her sitting beside me. Her hair crimped from sleep, she was naked beneath a knee-length coat. "It's time to get up, sleepyhead," she said softly, then pulled me from bed and told me to get dressed.

We walked to the drugstore at the same corner where Carol and I had seen her in the street. After loitering in the aisles together, she bent to me. "Sweetheart, let me shop around a little bit. You can meet me up front." Doing as I was told, I meandered my way ahead of her, but eyeing a cluster of hanging toys, I took a detour of a few yards. Admiring the collection in front of me, I glanced to the side and was surprised to spot her again halfway down the aisle. Half-hidden, I spied with a grin. She nearly caught me with a sidelong glance, but I ducked. Then just as I returned, she reached for a small plastic bag and shoved it down the top of her coat.

I waited at the front beyond the registers, but after several minutes, I went outside, not wanting to see my mother argue with the guard. On the sidewalk, I was watching the empty street when, from behind me, she wrapped her arms around my chest. "Weren't you supposed to wait inside?" she teased.

I nodded, noticing the small bag clutched at her side. Ignoring it, I reached for her free hand. Several feet down, and safely out of view of the store's immense window, I glanced at her. "Did you get what you needed?"

She stepped ahead, dangled the bag in my face.

"What is it?" I asked.

"It's Christmas!" she joked, then waited. "Don't you want it?"

I reached for the bag. For a moment, I examined the green rubber soldier that she had stolen from inside. I had asked for Christmas, and now she had done what she could to give it to me.

I looked at her tired eyes. "I didn't see you get it." Her face broke with joy. I took her hand again, and on the way back to our darkened apartment, I said nothing about what she had done. At her side as her bare legs turned blue from the cold, I let her be the mother that she wanted to be.

A few days after Christmas, she decided that the woman next door who had left the tin of candy was no longer dangerous and asked her to watch me for the night. Leaving me there, my mother told me to be a good boy, as if I had ever done any less or could do any more. She was going out for the evening but promised to return in a few hours. In the gentle quiet of the woman's apartment, I fell asleep, exhausted and fully dressed, on the living-room sofa.

The night air from the open door must have wakened me. In the dim room, red lights flashed on the walls. *Where is she? Why is she late? Why has she forgotten me?* Slowly I got up and walked through the doorway onto the balcony. Feet away, I saw a crowd gaping into the apartment where my mother and I lived. Wholly absorbed in the theater of it all, no one noticed the mad woman's son as he pushed his way inside. Strangers huddled in clusters as policemen took notes and names. Whispers filled the air as witnesses competed to give the best facts, opinions, and events. Then for a moment, my mother silenced them all. From somewhere, her cry sliced through the room.

At the first scream, I froze. With the second, I ran to her in the bathroom. She had convinced herself, or her voices had convinced her, that a group of men had taken me, punishing her for having left me alone. They had found me sleeping on the sofa next door, stuffed me into a burlap bag, kidnapped me. Miles away, they had then packed me in a barrel and were threatening to roll me down an unknown hill and into a river to drown me, unless she complied with their demands. The voices had told her that she had one way to prove that she was worthy—only one way to save me. With no other choice, my mother had readily agreed.

She had walked into the kitchen and taken a plastic bowl from the cupboard. She had found a razor in the bathroom and sat down on the toilet. Carefully, she had pressed the blade into her arms and watched the blood drip from her veins. Having collected as much as she needed, she had dipped her hands into the bowl and smeared my name across the bathroom walls.

ANDY. ANDY. ANDY.

The white plaster had absorbed so much of her. In the small bright room, my name was everywhere. Standing next to a man in a uniform, I gazed at my mother, lying in the bathtub, her soaked clothes stuck to her small frame. Paper-thin cuts stretched across her wrists and arms. The blade had produced clean, surgical slices, though she had fumbled and cut her hands. Her black hair was matted to her face and only revealed blood when her head slipped against the porcelain.

In the crush of her mind, she still loved me, and she had done what she could to keep me. For now, her ransom had won me back. She kept her eyes fixed on the empty space in front of her, whispering my name.

"Andy. Andy. Andy."

After that, my memory is blank.

I DO NOT remember if she was taken to a hospital. I do not remember how long the cuts took to heal. In February, my seventh birthday came and went. If I said something to remind her or we did something to celebrate, I have forgotten that, too. What I do remember is that the nights were still. Whether my mother had punished or merely tamed them, her voices relented. Slowly she gathered the pieces of life, trying to put them together again. She kept her promise, gave me an extra week of vacation after the New Year, but then agreed that I should return to school. After I overslept several mornings, she came home with an alarm clock. She remembered to pick up the bundles of food stamps, to get groceries for the kitchen shelves. She cashed the government check, then counted the bills in front of me, reassuring me that we had enough money to get by. She asked for her

job back, and when her old boss refused, she went to other salons to
start again.

Though her voices could be restrained, our landlord could not. On
a cold spring morning, he finally won the long war with my mother;
and I awoke to the sound of her name being shouted from the balcony outside.

"Mrs. Bridge. Priscilla . . . Hope . . . Bridge."

Still in bed, I crept into the living room. From the sofa where she
had slept that night, my mother shot a look at me and sharply motioned me to stay still. A moment passed. Relieved, I stepped closer to
her until the voice spoke directly into the door. "Hope. We're here."

Another pause, then a knock rapped through the apartment, demanding to be let inside. My mother stared across the room at the
door, thinking how to fool the intruder. The voice persisted and only
grew louder. "We know you're in there." Footsteps moved down the
balcony, past where my mother had leaned the closet door across the
shattered space. Finally, two figures waited where only the curtain
hung between them and us. This time, the voice was clear, as if it was
already in the apartment. "Open up, Hope. Or we're coming in."

At the last threat, my mother stumbled off the sofa. With a blanket
wrapped around her and blocking the entrance, she opened the door.
Shyly and still dressed only in my underpants, I moved to her side. We
stood exposed in the bright morning light. In front of us, two policemen waited impatiently, their hands resting on their weighted belts.

"We need to come inside," one of them ordered. He stepped toward
the door and handed her a piece of paper. She backed away, tightened
her hold on me, and immediately dropped the paper to her side.

"I'd look at that if I were you. It's a court order, Hope." He spoke
as if he knew her. "You need to get out."

The other officer slid his flashlight from his belt and aimed it at me.
"Is that your boy?" he asked, holding his look on me. "How old is he?"

My mother narrowed her eyes and said nothing.

Angered, the first officer interrupted. "When was the last time he went to school?" He glanced at the apartment behind us. "Or for that matter, when you went to work." Hate streamed from her, as she braced herself, frozen and staring. He ignored her and bent toward me. "What's your name, son?"

My mother recoiled, whipping her arm around my chest and pulling me behind her. The man looked back to her. "We'll be back this afternoon, Hope. We need you out or we'll take you in." She masked her face with boredom, and the man raised his voice. "Hope, do you understand me?" She looked away to the side. He shook his head with a grunt. Then he and his partner turned to the balcony. I listened for them to walk away, relieved she had not argued with them.

The men had barely begun descending the stairs when she kneeled to me. "Sweetheart, we have to leave now, and you have to help. I need you to be a big boy." I nodded. "Remember, they can hear us when we talk, and they always come back." She paused. "I need to get dressed, and I need you to pack. Don't be frightened. I'm here."

She walked to the bathroom and shut the door, while I sat on the floor waiting for her, unsure how to begin. As if she could see me, she yelled from the bathroom, "Andy, I promise to be back before they come! But you have to hurry! You have to get your clothes on."

She emerged to find me half dressed and waiting on the couch. "You need to get started," she said, grabbing a bag from under the kitchen sink and dropping a pair of shoes in it. "See?" I nodded. "Go around and pick up as much as you can." She bent down and held my chin to kiss me. Her lips moved against my forehead, as she whispered to reassure me. "If you see them, hide. Don't forget that I can always find you . . . that I'll always know where you are." She made her way around the apartment, filling several grocery bags, making several trips downstairs and back. Then, finished with the heaviest of our things, she walked out, leaving me alone, with the door open.

Nervously, I collected her clothes. I fumbled with a pair of her panties, then awkwardly folded a bra. I stuffed the remaining bags, then
carried them downstairs to the street. The lamps, tables, and dresser had
come with the apartment. If we owned her bed or mine, they were too
big for me. I left them for my mother to help.

Finished packing what I could, I meandered the living room, unsure what to do next. Suddenly the curtain over the shattered glass
swung open, and the landlord walked inside. He paused to get a clean
look at the disheveled room, crouched down to me, then whispered,
"Your mother's a cunt."

Outside, I sat on the curb, guarding the grocery bags, dodging
glances as people walked by staring at the little boy among the sidewalk clutter. I folded the tops of the bags, trying to hide that we had
been thrown out. The day warmed as my mother wandered through
blocks of houses and apartment buildings, knocking on doors, begging for a place to stay, explaining over and over that her boy was
waiting for her. I watched the street, hoping she would return before
the police.

It was nearly dark when I spotted her in the passenger seat of an
approaching station wagon. I stared nervously at the unfamiliar driver
as he neared the curb. A tall, proper-looking man, he emerged from
the car and approached me.

"You must be Andy."

My eyes darted to the side.

He smiled gently and looked around at our belongings. The passenger door slammed, and my mother moved toward the two of us.
He glanced at her and sighed.

"Well, you can't take everything. Pick out what you need, but you'll
have to leave most of it."

My mother moved quickly to the sidewalk and motioned me to
help. She began emptying bag after bag in a trail of small piles on the
pavement. Everything that had carried us through life became garbage.

From the bathroom: nail clippers, a brush and comb, a can of hair-spray, a nearly empty bottle of orange cough syrup for my unending colds, tampons, a curled and gummy tube of toothpaste, her tooth-brush and mine. From the kitchen: a box of cereal, some plastic bowls, a cigarette lighter, mismatched forks, knives, and spoons. From the bedroom: my sneakers, jeans, brightly colored T-shirts, her boots, pants, skirts, blouses, my socks and underwear, her nylons and panties. On the sidewalk and out of place, every belonging, every bit of meaning-lessness, acquired enormous importance. While the man waited and passing neighbors gawked, I learned the intimacy of the things we throw away.

"You heard him," my mother barked. "Get your stuff."

Her instruction was vague and left me unsure what to do. I watched and tried to mimic her, picking up a pair of her shoes, but she yelled, "Not them." She pointed in the direction of another pile. "Them!" The man watched as papers and several empty sacks flew into the street. I ran to retrieve them, but my mother snapped at me. "Forget it, Andy."

Bent over, nearly on her hands and knees, she trawled through our things, picking out what she wanted, ignoring the remainder that spread down the pavement, over the curb, and across the wet grass of the landlord's lawn. When she finished, she had reduced every-thing the world had given us to three grocery bags, which she handed to the man, who deposited them in the backseat of his car.

As she walked to the car, I clung close to her. Exhausted, she shoved me away with her arm and got into the front seat. I stared awkwardly from the street, caught between her in the car and every-thing she had abandoned on the pavement.

"Andy, get in. Now!" She jabbed a look at me. "What's wrong with you?"

I edged toward the open car door. Impatiently, she dragged me over her lap and slammed the door shut.

"Can we come back later and get the rest? What if someone steals it?"

The car pulled from the curb. Ignoring my questions, she turned her head to the window and smiled into the emptiness.

"You'll like where we're going, sweetheart. I promise."

CHAPTER FIVE

∽

M Y MOTHER NEVER went through all the details. After nearly a day of going door to door, halting whoever passed by, she found a neighbor who relented enough to listen. As my mother peered into the woman's apartment, the neighbor slowly closed her door, explaining that she felt sorry for what had happened but drew the line at taking in strangers. Yet when my mother lingered on her front porch, the woman yelled from inside that she would try to think of something she could do. Finally, the neighbor cracked her door open again, said that she had called a church, and if my mother would wait a bit closer to the street, a minister would be driving by to talk with her. Twenty minutes later, the man drove up. After pacing up and down the sidewalk several times, listening to the young mother's desperate chatter, he interrupted and volunteered an extra bedroom in his own house on the strict condition that there would not be any trouble from her or her seven-year-old son. My mother gratefully accepted, then ran back to the neighbor's door to thank her. The woman refused to answer.

The minister's family was out when we pulled into his garage. Glancing at me in the front seat, he said he had two sons, one my age and the other about three years older. His wife's mother also lived with the family.

"They'll like you. I know it," he reassured me.

My mother took two of the bags and left me to struggle with the third.

Other than two twin beds, a dresser, and a ceiling light, the extra bedroom was bare. When I woke in the morning, the sun streamed through the room, turning its four white walls into a single blinding box. Looking out the window, I saw a large courtyard with patches of dirt and crabgrass, bordered by a two-story building identical to the one where we were staying. I smiled at my first backyard.

Our time with the minister and his family was an odd reprieve. His sons were wild, poorly behaved. A nearly matching set of deceitful little thugs, they roved through the neighborhood, goading other children to commit offenses, then claiming innocence. The man's wife was quiet and rarely spoke to me. She disapproved of my mother, and that meant she also disapproved of me. The grandmother was clever and capable of kindness but enjoyed casual cruelties more. Still, with the family, my mother remained calm. The voices that had hunted us seemed to have lost their way.

The family woke promptly at half past six every school morning. My mother made certain that I was up, dressed, and ready when the family gathered for breakfast at a punctual seven fifteen. That first morning, having already wet and combed my hair, she knelt and hugged me in the middle of our new room.

"We can't mess this up, sweetheart," she whispered in my ear. "I know it's hard, but do what they say."

"I will," I promised.

"It won't be that long," she reassured me, locking her thin arms around my sides. "Just wait it out, sweetheart. We'll be back on our feet soon. I promise."

For that first breakfast and for every meal that followed, I watched the minister raise his head and quickly survey the freshly laid meal. Then I bowed my head with my mother, closed my eyes in silence, and waited for the man's voice to fill the room. I obeyed my mother's

command, and for the first time, I did what I could to settle into a
home that could never be mine.

For the remaining school year, I rode with the boys in the back of
their father's station wagon. The family's two boys attended school at
their father's church. The route to my school required a small detour.
As the older boy elbowed and pinched me and his younger brother
yammered away, I stayed quiet, looking out the window and waiting
for the old familiar blocks to come into view.

At the end of the first week, the minister intervened at the salon,
asking my mother's old boss to give her another chance. When I
walked into the house from school, she rushed me upstairs, ecstatic to
tell me the news. She described the minister, attired in his preaching
garb, asking for the salon's owner, then cornering him as the crowd of
women watched. The man agreed, or more accurately, succumbed.
"There's nothing like having a minister tell your boss he better give
you your job back," my mother advised me from the edge of the bed.
Then she grinned. "Well, I guess you could get a nun to do it."

With the end of school and the arrival of summer, I met a friend.
She lived in the apartment opposite where we stayed. Even in North
Hollywood's flattening heat, she dressed warmly, usually in sweaters
that hugged her aging body from her chest to her hips. She tended to
her hair, and I wondered if she knew that the way it had receded above
her forehead made her look like an old man. Meandering through the
courtyard that we shared or walking the sidewalk that circled the
block, she went nowhere in particular. From the bedroom window, I
watched as she climbed the stairs to her apartment across the yard—
resting after each step to recover from the last, as if all that mattered
was to keep moving forward. There at the glass, I gazed at her, one
outsider spying on another, waiting for the old woman to reach her
threshold, not turning from the window until she had safely shut her
door. The minister's sons were responsible for our introduction.

"Grandma said she's crazy, the way she walks around dressed up,
doing nothing," the older boy informed me. Down the sidewalk, the

woman continued her humped and halting gait, oblivious to the cruelty that lashed at her from a few houses down. "She's stupid, too," he continued. "Senile, Grandma says." The three of us mulled over an insult that none of us really understood, until finally, the younger boy took advantage of the silence.

"Why can't she just stay up in her apartment?" he asked his brother.

"What's wrong with her?" I asked, trying to please them.

"The idiot can't even count," the older boy groaned. "Watch this." He cupped his hands around his mouth, taking aim at the old woman.

"Hey, lady! Hey, laaydee!" He shouted several times, dragging out his words. The old woman turned and I glanced around nervously. The older boy held his ground, then yelled and motioned her to come closer. "Hey, you!" In the distance, she appeared to think for a moment, then began hobbling closer.

"She knows who I am," he bragged, holding a frozen smile. "Come on, hurry up!" he rasped under his breath. His younger brother and I fidgeted, waiting for the old woman to amble the half block that separated us. Frustrated, the boy finally approached her less than a single house away. With exaggerated politeness and for the benefit of his little brother and me, he spoke loudly. "Excuse me, ma'am. May I please have change for a quarter?"

He dug a coin from his pants pocket. The old woman waited a moment, perspiring under the sun. Then she slipped her purse from her elbow, unclasped the top, and dipped her hand inside.

"Thank you, ma'am," the boy remarked, as the old woman peered into her purse, collecting stray change. The boy surrendered his quarter, then held out his palm, which she filled with nickels and dimes. With the woman's purse still hanging open, he gave us a sidelong grin. "Thanks, lady!" he yelled.

He ran back, extending his small, sweaty hand. "See!" A pile of change, clearly worth more than twenty-five cents, glistened in the sunlight. "Told you she's too stupid to count."

From nearly the same spot, several days later, the two brothers and I watched the old woman again as she made her way through the sunlight. Only this time, it was my turn to ask.

"Go on, Andy! Do it," the older boy bullied, shoving me forward. "Do it! Unless you're scared." I hesitated. "Don't you have a quarter?" he sneered, then pushed me harder. I stumbled, barely catching myself.

"Or didn't your mom have one?" his younger brother piped up.

I answered defensively. "She gave me two quarters. See." I held out my hand, then looked down the street. The old woman had nearly reached the corner. The younger boy screamed in alarm, "She's getting away! Do it!"

I began to run. Suddenly, I found myself confronted by the old woman's back. "Excuse me, ma'am," I panted, then froze over what next to say.

Her large head turned, and her watery blue eyes settled on me. Her face was lined from cheekbone to jaw, and below the base of her neck, her skin crinkled as she moved. As the air drifted through her hair, I noticed the faint pink of her scalp. Bashfully, I turned from her eyes, glanced downward. Supporting her purse, her arm bent at her waist. Hanging between us, her hand was little more than a clutter of little bones and knotted joints, wrapped in spotted skin and strung together with large, purple veins. A thin gold band, battered and dulled by countless casual assaults, hung on one finger.

"Yes?" She gave me a hard look. "Your name is Andy, isn't it?"

I stared mutely.

"Don't you live across the yard with Hope? Such a very pretty girl and lucky to have such a handsome little boy." The sound of my mother's name fell like a clap of thunder. "Did you want some change?"

She knew exactly what I wanted, and immediately I knew that she had always understood the plottings of the neighborhood's three little boys. Unmasked, my face flushed as the old woman opened her purse.

"My mother gave me a quarter," I answered, stumbling to catch up with her.

She glanced at the coin between my forefinger and thumb. "That's all right, Andy. You keep it."

As I watched in silence, she unsnapped her change purse. Then one by one, as if her fingers were tweezers, she plucked out three dimes and handed them to me. "Thirty cents, by my count," she concluded.

I continued staring.

"I think your friends are waiting," she reminded me, then looked at the two brothers lingering in the distance. "You better hurry or they'll run away and leave you with me." Her eyes turned back to mine. "Good-bye, Andy."

Taking her cue, I answered softly, "Good-bye, ma'am."

I walked back, and I still remember that I forgot to thank her. As for the brothers, I never confessed that the old woman had offered me the change before I had the chance to ask for it, that she refused to take my quarter in return, or that she was perfectly capable of counting.

THOUGH MY MOTHER offered, the family refused to accept her money for rent or groceries. "You need to keep your cash," the minister told her, then suggested that she and I might begin attending his sermons. She immediately agreed.

Every Wednesday evening, she and I faithfully arrived for Bible study classes. Then, on Sunday mornings, we returned for worship. If she disagreed with the schedule, she said nothing to me. When I argued that I had seen her mouthing rather than singing hymns, she snapped that I should pay attention to the services and not to her.

I spent the summer learning about Satan and the importance of being a good and respectful boy. The church gave me a Bible, and the Sunday school teachers read passages that were intended to save a child's soul. Perhaps it was all the talk of the devil or the work of my imagination, and though the safety of a minister's house was an odd

place for them to arrive, the best that I can recall is that my nightmares began there.

Every night, it was the same. The prowler who had broken into
our hotel room, after my mother had turned out the lights and promised to be back soon, returned to find me in the dark. Alone in the
bedroom in the minister's house, I did what I could to keep the Night
Man away, lifting the Bible from the dresser, squeezing the book as
hard as I could, as if my hands might force out its words. I thought of
Grandma Kate, prayed as she had taught me, and whispered lightly for
protection. Finished, I held out the book with both hands, then waved
it in the dark in front of me, convinced that it might save me from the
demon that waited for my eyes to close.

Still, the Night Man came, and as she had done before, my mother
rushed to quiet me. "Be still, sweetheart. Be still," she whispered, night
after night, cradling me in her arms. Yet no matter how quiet she and
I tried to be, our time with that family never felt entirely safe.

By midsummer, I had abandoned the greater neighborhood to the
minister's boys. I preferred the solitude of the courtyard, occupied by
the dirt and weeds. Rarely interrupted, I jumped when I heard the
soft voice behind me.

"Where did your friends go?"

I swung around, then saw the old woman. With a pink china bowl
in one hand and a silver spoon in the other, she stepped closer and
waited.

I shrugged. "They're not my friends."

"Well . . ." She thought for a moment, then pointed conspiratori-
ally to a corner of the courtyard. "Do you know what's over there?"

I shook my head, then glanced at the bowl and spoon.

"I have enough for both of us." She extended her hand. "See?"

I peered into the bowl, recognized a clean slope of sugar. The old
woman shot me a glance, then abruptly turned and left me to follow.

She halted at a dead sapling, staring at the packed ground. "Can
you see them, Andy?"

I looked down and saw an outpost of red ants just beyond my shoes.

She sank the spoon into her bowl, then began dusting the soil with sugar. Confusion immediately broke out among the creatures. Hundreds streamed from the colony's central entrance, while others rushed from smaller holes excavated in later expansions. The ants spread across the ground, hoarding their glorious windfall.

"Aren't they the kind that bite?" I asked, watching the insects swarm at our feet.

"Not if you let them be," she admonished, then grinned and held out the bowl. "Would you like to try?"

I eagerly tossed out three heaping spoonfuls, instantly burying dozens of the industrious creatures in white granules. The pandemonium intensified.

"That's enough for now." She took back the bowl and spoon.

Like two smiling gods, we bent to admire our work and the commotion we had stirred.

"Just think of it, Andy," she mused, "the secret tunnels and rooms, the hiding places only they can find—the deepest one guarded for their single, loved queen. Everything done for her."

Suddenly, another old voice interrupted from across the yard and inside the house. "Is that old idiot out there feeding ants?" I looked up, alarmed.

"Dang it, how am I going to get rid of those things?" the same voice yelled again. "I don't believe it! What the heck is she doing with that kid?" The screen door creaked open and violently slammed. With a broom in one hand and a large spray can in the other, the boys' grandmother began marching toward us like a soldier armed for battle. "Stupid fool!"

Beside me, the old woman kept herself steady over the mound. The ants feverishly seized what they could before descending back into the safety of the ground as the grandmother shoved her way between us.

"What are you doing here?" she demanded of me. Then she bent and yelled into the old woman's ear. "If these things get in the house, you're paying for it, you old nut. I've had it! Move!"

The old woman remained kneeling in the dirt.

The grandmother snapped at me, "You know, young man, your mother will be hearing about this."

Immediately, I countered with my own threat: "My mother gets mad at people who yell at me."

The grandmother stared in shock, then glowered. "Just who do you think you're talking to? What do you and your mother think this is? The welfare office?" She glanced at the old woman beneath us. "Both of you, living off people like bums." She brushed her broom over the old woman's shoes. "I told you to move! Get out of here!"

The old woman looked up with an empty expression, then gradually rose to her feet. Silently, she shuffled across the courtyard, up the stairs, along the balcony, and into her apartment. While I watched my friend retreat, the grandmother stood beside me, stomping at the ground and spraying out pesticide in misty swaths.

LIKE ANY GOOD fight with a bully, this one lacked a reason. Coming back from an afternoon errand for my mother, I made out the minister's older son sitting on the curb in front of the house. His feet in the gutter and his eyes cast dumbly into the street, he was eating a hot dog. A crumpled bag from 7-Eleven lay next to him. Sighting me, he stuffed the remainder in his mouth and, holding his stare on me, brushed off his hands.

"Hey, Daisy-Boy!" Humiliation shot through me as his voice flooded the street. With one hand hanging at his side, cradling something, he stepped to the middle of the sidewalk and blocked my path to safety.

"Where you been, Daisy?" he asked, making his way to my side. Terror swelled down my throat as I looked at the stretch of gray pavement left between the house and us. He waited for me to respond to the name, delighting in my hesitation. Then prompting me, he flicked his finger against the side of my head.

I grabbed at my stinging ear.

"Didn't you hear?" he yelled. "I asked, how's it goin', Daisy?"

"OK," I answered, giving in to the name.

He snorted. "I'm still hungry. Wanna go get another hot dog with me, Daisy?" He pressed his body against mine. The two of us hobbled like a pair of mismatched, conjoined twins, one ridiculing and terrifying the other. I glanced at his hand, still dangling suspiciously at his side.

He swung his foot under my heel, forcing my own leg up into a great goose step. I tripped but caught myself as he ratcheted up the momentum. Dropping his arm from my back, he transferred whatever he was holding from one hand to the other.

"So, why can't you and your mother pay for your own house to live in?"

I looked at the distance to the apartment, a little over two buildings away.

"Mom and Grandma say if your mother and you don't leave soon, you'll stay forever."

"No, we won't," I answered softly.

The boy ignored me. "Aren't you hungry, Daisy? You like ketchup, don't you?"

My mother appeared on the front porch, watching the boy and me like an indifferent bird staring at her abandoned gosling.

My collar yanked against my neck as the boy grabbed my shirt, held me briefly from behind, then slapped me on the back. I heard a snap, like a tiny balloon popping, then felt something warm shoot up my hairline. My hand jumped to my neck. I looked down and saw ketchup on my fingertips. Having burst his little condiment bomb, the boy grinned with satisfaction.

I broke for the safety of the house, then ran into the living room. Trembling, with humiliated tears welling in my eyes, I looked at my mother, who had seen everything but done nothing to intervene.

"What?" she asked blankly from the base of the stairs.

Panting with fear and shame, I stood mute.

"I can't be here forever," she chided, then pointed limply at my shoulder and arm. "Did you see what he did to you?"

I tugged at my shirt to get a better look. The boy's tiny armament had exploded ketchup across the back of my white shirt and into my ear. "Tell him to leave me alone," I begged her. "He's bigger than me. He's ten!"

Relief washed over me when she glanced to the side, reassessing the match and my last appeal. Then, an instant later, she looked me in the face.

"He's not *that* much bigger than you are. Is he?"

I stared disbelievingly.

"Boys have to live through their own battles." She reached for what I had retrieved from the store, then locked her eyes back on mine. "You better get yourself out there, before that little son of a bitch runs away."

By the time I returned outside, the minister's son had fled. Alone on the sidewalk, I looked around, confused about what to do. The red sugary gunk across my neck and sleeve was now thick and tacky. I pulled off my shirt, turned it inside out, then headed to the courtyard.

A pang of humiliation struck me when I glanced up and saw the old woman on her balcony, waiting. I looked at her glumly and was about to retreat to the house when she motioned to me from the railing. I meandered across the yard and up the single flight of stairs, halting short of her apartment.

"Alone again?" she mused.

I stood silently, hoping to avoid recounting the day's events and their evidence under my shirt.

"Do boys still like cookies . . . do you like cookies, Andy?" She glanced at her apartment's open door. "Maybe you'd like to come in for one?"

I nodded with a close-lipped smile before glancing at the graying sky.

She grinned. "I haven't had a guest in a long time." She bent, then for the first time, touched my face. Her wrinkled fingertips trembled against my cheek. "You are a good boy, Andy." She peered into my eyes, then to the sky above. "Well, I think we should hurry before it gets dark, or your mother Hope will start to worry."

She straightened herself as much as her body allowed and turned to begin the few remaining steps to her apartment. From behind, I stared at the form of her back, which her mind, legs, and heart were gradually abandoning, leaving it alone to carry her in these last few years, rounded, hunched, and sore. She reached the threshold with me still behind. Then she stopped, lifting her arm enough from her side to tell me it was safe to take her hand. She walked through the doorway, gently pulling me along, unaware that this was my first invitation into a friend's home.

"Andy, you can sit down there." She pointed toward a boxy tweed sofa.

"Thank you, ma'am," I answered. Awkwardly, I remained standing, looking at the old woman's home. The apartment's entrance opened into a living room. Beyond it was a small kitchen. The rooms felt quiet.

"Sweetheart, sit down," she instructed, motioning with her hand. "I'm just going to the pantry."

I perched myself on the sofa's edge, gazed down at my feet. After several moments, I glanced up and noticed the old woman waiting at the kitchen doorway.

"I said, would you like some milk?" she asked.

"Yes, please, ma'am." I move to stand again. "Thank you."

"No, I can do it." She disappeared back into the kitchen. "Such a polite little boy," she complimented me through the open door. "Your mother must love you to bother teaching you such manners."

Her tribute felt enormous. At some point, adults had stopped talking about, much less complimenting, my mother to me. When I entered rooms, conversations halted abruptly, and when I left, they resumed in whispers.

The old woman emerged with a dinner plate stacked with cookies and a plastic glass filled halfway with milk. She placed both on the coffee table, then sat on a chair that she had borrowed from the kitchen. She took a quick look around the living room, then returned to me.

"What should we talk about?" she inquired.

Eyeing the plate in front of me, I seized the initiative. "May I have a cookie, please?"

"Of course."

The cookies were store-bought, pressed into shapes of windmills blowing scattered slivers of almonds. Crumbs tumbled over my chin and into my lap as I forced one into the corners of my mouth.

"Aren't they delicious?" she asked.

In truth, the almonds were nearly tasteless, but the hard cookie quickly dissolved into a wonderful mix of saliva, nutmeg, and sugar.

"Yes, ma'am," I spluttered, exposing the mashed brown paste that had spread across the roof of my mouth and tongue.

The old woman took more time, carefully selecting a cookie that suited her, nibbling on a corner, then gently raising her hand to her chin to catch the crumbs. "These have always been my favorites," she said, grinning as she chewed.

With the old woman still on her first, I swallowed my second in two bites. Then, feeling proud of my accomplishment, I reached for a third.

But she interrupted me. "Aren't you thirsty, sweetheart?" My arm halted. Hardened bits were glued to my lips, and inside my mouth, pieces were stuck between my cheeks and gums. I took her suggestion, reached for the milk, then sat quietly, absorbed in my drinking.

As silence drifted into unease, I anxiously scanned the wall across the room. Above the television, a clutter of frames filled the space with a gallery of faces, bodies, landscapes, rooms, and flowers. Among them, a fat woman sitting naked beside a bathtub caught my eye. Her breasts were exposed. Her head bent backward as a pair of heavy hands tugged a brush through her hair. I promptly shifted my gaze to the farthest end of the wall.

"Andy, do you like art?" she innocently asked. "My husband and I loved art. Of course, these aren't real. They're just prints." She glanced at my confused face and clarified. "They're posters, sweetheart."

Disappointed, I nodded mutely.

"He was drafted and went to Europe. He promised to send for me when it was over." She raised herself from her chair and walked across the room. "Were you looking at the one of a young man?" She pointed to a frame close to the floor. "Can you see that it's David, with Goliath's head at his knees? It's bloody! Isn't it? He cut Goliath's head off."

Youthful and merciless, David leaned over Goliath's severed head, its eyes still open and staring at the ground. Kneeling in a puddle of the giant's hair, David had strung a cord around Goliath's neck, as if the head were a dead fish that the boy was preparing to take home.

The old woman smiled. "If you look, David can't be much older than you. Do you know about David and Goliath?"

To the old woman's approval, I recounted the story of the young boy David whose parents had forced him to live outside, watching the flocks and fending off predators in the hope of making him strong. David's parents succeeded, turned their son into a brave boy. Then aware of the risk, they sent him to the battlefield. When David heard Goliath's taunts, daring the Israelites to fight the Philistines, the boy marched out with only a slingshot and a shepherd's bag filled with five smooth stones. Alone together, the boy and giant bickered, each claiming the blessing of his respective god. Then, David aimed for Goliath's head.

The pain must have been extraordinary when the stone sank into the thick skin of Goliath's brow. Still, the Bible makes no mention of Goliath's cry for help to his four brothers who were with him that day. The giant simply fell dead with a thump, facedown in the dirt. David climbed on top of the large corpse, seized Goliath's sword, and decapitated him. Proudly armed with his freshly cut prize, David went to King Saul, who, impressed or intimidated by the boy's victory, made David a prisoner, refusing to allow him to return home. Having prepared their son to survive on his own, David's parents never saw him again.

"Was there anything else?" the old woman asked.

"Not really," I answered. "Except when I told my mom, she said she learned the same lesson as a little girl." I smiled in conclusion.

My host stared for a moment, then caught herself. She leaned to another picture at the center of the wall, this one of a young woman. The subject was sitting at a desk, formally dressed in a crimson coat and a wide-brimmed hat trimmed with fur of the same color. Her head was partly turned, as if someone had just called her name. Distracted from her work, she gazed at her audience, this time an old woman and a little boy.

"My husband said that she was as pretty as I was." The old woman stepped closer to the wall, straining to see what her husband had admired. "When I told him that she looked more like a boy, he laughed and bought it anyway." The girl did look like a boy who had been told to be still and, obeying, waited with a self-conscious smile. The old woman stepped away from the wall, widening her gaze to the album of prints hanging in front of her.

"When the army discharged him, I met him in Paris. We liked the museums. They were cheap. But he insisted on buying up these prints." She motioned through the empty space between her and the wall, then dropped her arm limply at her side. "They're a waste," I said. "What're we going to do? Hang them in every room?"

Her voice shifted to a low mimic. "Oh, we'll have something to remember."

She mumbled back at herself. "Remember? How could you forget?"

Her voice trailed off, and hoping to recapture her attention, I blurted, "Where's your husband now?"

The old woman appeared shaken, then did her best to collect herself. "He died a long time ago."

She never said what had happened to him, and her voice told me not to ask. In a selfish though unintentional act, he had left her to fend for herself, alone too soon. Still, she loved him for what he had given her and forgave him for what he had not. Sorting through her losses, she decided that some things were worth keeping. As she and her husband had planned, she spent the money to have their treasures framed and hung, though they were only counterfeits. She became the custodian of their memory, and in return, memory rewarded her, strengthening her against isolation, contempt, and poverty. She survived every assault her heart could take and proved that kindness was always possible.

I glanced into the darkness outside the window and realized my mother would be looking for me. The old woman noticed. "You should go before your mother gets worried."

At the time, the old woman's kindness was little more than a source of attention and cookies. On the sidewalk, beside the anthill, or sitting in her living room, I never bothered to ask her name or even to thank her. More like the minister's sons than I wanted to be, I took the spare change, the food, and whatever else she offered, giving her nothing in return. Our last meeting had ended. Dismissed, I walked out the apartment door and noticed my mother in the courtyard below.

"Andy, is that you?" she yelled to me. "What are you doing up there? I told you to leave that old woman alone. I've been looking everywhere for you." I tried to apologize, but she ignored me, then led me into the house for dinner. Later that evening, as she turned out the bedroom light and told me to go to sleep, she was still angry with me for having gone off on my own.

IN THE BEGINNING of August, the minister's wife complained about my mother talking to herself in the middle of the night. To placate his wife, he moved us out of the spare room and into their garage. He set up two cots for us and cleared a workbench for our things. But the solution proved only temporary.

Early one evening, the minister walked into the garage and pulled my mother aside.

"It's time you and Andy got going." He paused for the weight of his words to sink in. My mother did nothing at first, just stared at the man. "Hope, we've talked about this more than once." He nodded, looking over her shoulder toward me. She stepped to block his view. "He's seven and a half years old. He's supposed to start second grade in what?—two weeks, maybe three?"

My mother pressed against his chest, standing on her toes to reach his face. "Give us another week," she whispered frantically. "Let me talk to your wife. I'll work it out."

The minister retreated a step, and my mother apologetically backed away, glancing at me and letting the man continue.

"You need to find someone . . ."—he hesitated—"to take him."

The three of us stood in silence. In the back of a garage, I watched a minister struggle with his conscience, then suggest the greatest loss that I could know. Never before had I heard the words so clearly, felt their threat so closely. Behind my mother's back, I waited for her to protect me.

She thought for a moment. Then, as always, she negotiated with the danger and offered the man what he wanted most. "What if we left tomorrow evening?"

The man's face broke with relief. "Thank you, Hope." Then eyeing me beside the cots, he reached into his pocket and pulled out his wallet. "How 'bout fifty? That'll help. You can try one of the motels."

He pushed the bills into her hand, hanging at her side. Her fingers curled around the money, and I turned away.

Chapter Six

⚭

Aㅤll of it seems inevitable, as if my mother insisted on stumbling toward some uncertain yet unalterable fate. Every circumstance seemed to follow a plan that her mind had laid out for her and that she spent months futilely trying to evade. After the minister told us to go, she took to the old neighborhood streets again. Only this time, she found the motel where the county came to take me.

Within days, she lost her job at the beauty school again. Desperate to get it back, she returned to the salon with me in tow. Deprived of a religious benefactor, she pointed to me and begged the owner to change his mind. When the man refused, she became enraged and began screaming at him. He called the police and had us removed.

If I knew how she got money after that, I have forgotten. I can only think that nothing would have been easy, nothing would have been deserved. What I do remember is that the money quickly ran out.

The darkness around us deepened. The voices returned, constantly whispering, some warning, others threatening that they were close. She talked about people who watched and followed me. They were waiting for our moment of weakness; screaming, she begged me to be careful.

She and I were left huddled together in a rented red room, our story rapidly becoming only another in the hundreds that haunted its small space. Whatever clothes we owned were reduced to a pile in the bathtub. We went out only to hunt for food, usually finding it in Dumpsters. During one trip, my mother discovered a cat. Though I argued against it, she insisted on taking it in, telling me that it understood the voices and could protect us. The animal quickly became my competitor. When we found a can of something, my mother insisted that the stray be fed before I was. One morning, she woke up and found me stealing food from the animal. In the single act of violence from her that I can recall, she slapped me, then begged the cat not to leave.

Her vanity disappeared. She bathed less. She wore her clothes to bed. Already thin, she grew thinner. Sometimes, she told me to stay with her. Other times, she seemed not to care. Often, no matter what I said, she seemed confused.

We shared the same bed until she decided that having me sleep in the open room, by her side, was no longer safe. The threat required more than her arms for protection. I was hunted, and she had to be certain that no one would find me. With the voices constantly goading her, whispering in her ears, she realized that I had to be hidden at night, when the danger was greatest.

She inspected our anonymous room, took a pillow and blanket from the bed, placed them on the floor in a closet, then stared at me with sallow eyes and told me to get in. She said not to be frightened by the dark and not to cry, because she would always be just outside. She promised that, with the door closed, I would be safe.

The hours I spent in the closet grew longer as the danger around us increased. I cannot recall a single day of school. I sat, slept, and rested in that box of darkness, until at last, as she had warned, they arrived to take me.

.   .   .

I HAVE FORGOTTEN what we said to each other that warm February morning.

She woke me early and asked me to run an errand. She wanted a pack of cigarettes, handed me a note for them, then told me to go down to the family deli where I had fetched candy bars and coffee for her co-workers at the salon. I pulled on a shirt and a pair of pants, and I laced my own shoes as she had taught me:

"Andy, keep still. Pull the strings from your toes and through the holes on both sides. Now, take one string in each hand and pull again. Not that hard. Cross one string under the other and make a knot."

"Mom, you do it!"

"No, I want you to. Make a loop and hold it between your finger and thumb. Do the same thing with your other hand, and tie both loops together."

"I can't! See?"

"That's all right. Let's try again."

The process was hopelessly complex, and I liked the feel on my feet when she did it for me. But she persisted, knowing that I had to learn it for myself. To this day, I knot my shoes as she explained, and still I get it wrong. My laces constantly come undone, in a quiet, daily reminder of her. I never intended to let her go.

It was a Saturday, and the wide sidewalks were empty. My mother and I had lived around the neighborhood for nearly two years and had often been in the deli together. The owner had known me almost since the day that I had arrived from Chicago. He used to smile whenever I came in for my mother's pack of cigarettes. He always accepted her notes. Yet this time, when I arrived, he was distant. Perhaps, earlier in the morning, a stranger had stopped in and asked about me. Maybe he was afraid that trading cigarettes for my mother's notes had gotten him in trouble. Whatever his reason, he refused to sell me the pack. Though I could tell he was lying, he accused me of writing the notes all along and smoking the cigarettes myself. Giving up, I walked out the door. He told me never to come back.

I began walking back to the motel when a county sheriff's car swung around the corner, slowly keeping pace behind me. I reached the curb, crossed the street, and turned in the direction of the motel. The car followed me for more than a block before finally pulling up alongside me. The deputy rolled down the window and scrutinized me with a steady look.

"Are you Andy?" he asked.

I could have lied or run, but I stood motionless and answered. "Yes."

He told me to get in the car. I opened the back door and obediently climbed in. Together, we drove the remaining block to the motel. As we approached, I saw my mother on the sidewalk. She was in her bra, barefoot, arguing with a well-dressed woman.

The deputy sped up, then abruptly parked in the middle of the street. Forgetting me in the backseat, he ran out to protect the woman from my mother, who was now screaming, inches from her face. My mind raced.

Please, don't hurt her.

Don't argue with them. You told me this would happen.

Leave her alone.

Watching from the car window, I saw the deputy grab my mother's shoulder and shove her away, but she returned with only greater rage. When I saw him reach for her again, for the first time in my life, I raced to protect her. Throwing open the car door, I ran to her. She reached out and wrapped her arms around me, wounded but roaring. Everything left in her thrust forward in that one, ferocious moment.

Then, without thinking, I pulled away. I had tried my best, but I was afraid of the voices, the closet, and the dark. Unlike her, with her blood on the bathroom walls, I needed to survive. I needed to be safe.

Maybe I pulled away because she had so thoroughly prepared me. Like getting me ready for school in the morning, but only more so; she had to get me ready to abandon her when the final day arrived. She understood her little boy and knew that he was not the kind who was made for battles. Preparing me for one, she must have doubted my strength. Yet she knew that I had to go, that I had to be ready to leave, and that I had to be strong. Perhaps she also knew that, when the time came, she would find it hard to walk away and that my strength would be needed to overcome hers.

When she felt my slight tug, pulling away, she let go. The well-dressed woman took advantage of the briefest betrayal and pulled me several feet from my mother. The deputy brushed past me and descended on her. Turning back, I saw my mother pinned facedown on the sidewalk. The deputy's hand pressed on her head, and his knee was in her back, as the social worker rushed me into a waiting car. My head rang.

Please, don't hurt her. Leave her alone.

I HAD NO idea where we were going. As the social worker drove and tried to comfort me, I wondered who had betrayed my mother and me. Who had noticed and called the county? Was it the minister? Did the landlord get back at us for the unpaid rent? Was it my school when I failed to arrive for second grade? Whoever had called, my mother was right. Someone had been watching. I should have been more careful.

The road was a long one, and the social worker chattered through side streets and freeways. Each time I threw out a question, she replied with an ill-fitting answer:

"Did he take her, too?"

"Priscilla will be fine."

"Can she sleep at the motel tonight?"

"Priscilla will come to see you soon."

"Did he let her get her clothes?"

"Priscilla can take care of herself."

All the while, she used the wrong name. Knowing or caring too little about the woman whose child she had just taken, the social worker referred to my mother as Priscilla. My mother hated her first name. She insisted on her middle name, Hope, and no one who knew and cared for her used any other. A small point for an adult. But I was seven years old, beginning a long trip, and only the words Mom and Hope mattered to me. I wish that the woman had used at least one of them.

The county had no particular plan when they took me. They had no place to put me, other than an enormous warehouse where they put other children. As the social worker drove the last road to MacLaren Hall, she outlined a well-rehearsed set of tasks for me. First, I would go to MacLaren. After MacLaren, I would go to a temporary foster home. Then, to a long-term foster home. Finally, I would return to Priscilla. I only had to wait and count each step: one, two, three, and home.

The social worker drove up to a tall fence festooned with barbed wire. At a call box, she rolled down her window to announce our arrival. The car idled as she waited for the gates to part slowly, then she crossed through the barrier and to the side of a large, white building. Gazing through the windshield, she spoke to me. "It's time to get out, Andy."

She stepped out of the car, opened the passenger door, and unbuckled me. She waited for me to move, but I remained still. Impatiently, she put her hand on the roof and leaned into the car.

"I told you, I've got to get going. Come on."

I got out. Silently, she and I walked to a heavy, metal door. She shouted into another call box, giving her name and title. A voice acknowledged us. The door let out a sharp buzz, then a loud click.

Side by side, we entered an empty hall, separated from the rest of the facility by several large doors. The ceiling was high. The gray walls were old and thick with paint. The competing scents of ammonia and soiled diapers drifted in the air. Metal lamps with fat, yellow bulbs hung down, glaring at us, illuminating the room's single embellishment—a bronze plaque, at least half my size, cemented into a wall across from us. From that spot, the sculpted face of a woman of wealth and good breeding reviewed every child whom the county surrendered to her philanthropy. In this great cavern of absence, my life as a foster child began.

The social worker put her hand around the base of my neck and guided me to a low half-wall, where another woman sat, surrounded by files and stacks of paper. The clerk looked up from her desk, glanced at the women, then at me. As the clerk spoke, her words filled the massive hall.

"Is he a drop-off?"

I don't belong here. My mom knows I don't belong here.

"Yes," the social worker answered. Before the clerk said anything, the woman began clicking through a worn protocol. "Last name, Bridge. First name, Andy or Andrew. Allegation, neglect." She paused, looked at me, then added, "No birth date."

The clerk looked up over her paperwork with an annoyed expression. "Mother's maiden name?"

"I have no idea," the social worker answered defensively. "I had the file sent over last week."

The clerk leaned over her desk, pointed her pen toward me. "Well, does he know?"

I stared at the two women dumbly.

Mom, are you still at the motel? Are you alone? Did you ask Carol to help get me?

"The kid doesn't know." The social worker shook her head. "Try using his name, Bridge."

The clerk returned to her papers. After a few moments, she extracted a single, thin folder. Slowly, she read the label aloud. "Bridge. B-R-I-D-G-E." She thumbed through the file and asked, "Did he bring anything?"

"No," she answered. In the skirmish with my mother, the woman had left behind what little I had.

The clerk put down the file and looked at us, waiting, as the social worker bent to speak to me.

"I'm going now."

Please don't leave me here. My mom has to find me before dark. She doesn't have a car. She has to ask Carol for help.

Detecting something in how I stood or the look in my eyes, she reached toward me and gave a rub on my shoulder, before recovering her composure.

"It'll be fine. They'll take care of you. There are lots of children here."

She got up, whispered something to the clerk. Then, turning to get a last look at me, she walked out the door, taking with her my last connection to my mother.

Please don't leave me alone. Please don't leave me here.

Abandoned by the social worker, I looked to the clerk and moved toward the opening that led to her desk. She glared at my intrusion and stabbed her finger at me. "Who do you think you are? You don't get beyond that." She pointed to the half-wall. "Stand right there! Understand me?" She pressed an intercom on her desk, and shouted as if the thing were broken. "There's a pick-up out here." Then she returned to her work.

Several minutes later, another door banged open. A man in a white uniform appeared. The sound of children flooded into the chamber before the door shut behind him.

The clerk looked up. "There he is."

"Where's his file?" the man asked, without looking at me.

The clerk handed him the folder and, ignoring us both, returned to her work. He paused to read the label, bounced the folder's edge in his palm, then tapped me on the back, signaling me to walk with him.

He pointed to yet another door, and we disappeared into a long corridor. I followed him until he stopped at an empty room. "You, stay," he commanded. I froze in place.

He left but soon reappeared with another man. The two of them stripped me to my underpants and weighed me. While I shivered on the scale, they joked between themselves, turning the pockets of my discarded pants inside out. Finished with their search, they looked me up and down, then sauntered across the room to several large bins filled with clothes. Working together, they uncovered a pair of old dress shoes, jeans, and a white T-shirt with MACLAREN HALL stenciled on its back. After handing me the clothes, both men stared in silence while I fumbled to dress myself. Finishing as best I could, I motioned to my abandoned clothes heaped on a table.

"Can I take my shirt? My mom gets mad when I lose things."

Irritated, the man who had led me down the hall stepped toward me and condescendingly shook his head. "Nooo."

I glanced out the window through the heavy grating that covered the glass. The afternoon light was fading, turning the room a yellowish red.

In half a day, everything that comprised a seven-year-old's life had been seized, and no one along the way had thought it necessary to tell him why. In fairness, no one at MacLaren may have known the answer. Yet even with nothing left, I still had a mother and a name. Had they asked, I could have told them.

Mom, it's getting dark, and you're running out of time.

The boys' dormitory consisted of dozens of neatly arranged beds, each with an identical pillow, blanket, and white sheet. The grid accommodated every male child over five years old. A separate, identical room was reserved for girls. Infants and toddlers of both sexes were housed in their own wing. A male counselor sat, feet up, at a desk in the corner. Looking up from his magazine, he examined a clipboard. On it was a hand-drawn map of beds. He pointed.

"Over there, near the middle."

Unsure what he meant, I wandered in the general direction that his finger had indicated.

"Stop! That one. Sit and wait for the others."

He disappeared behind his magazine, adding, "Boys eat in twenty minutes."

Eventually, boys of every age, size, and race began stumbling into the room. All of them were dressed as I was. They were to be my companions, with whom I shared nothing and everything. Divided into groups, we were ordered to stand in lines. Then two men marched us to our dinner.

Onto hundreds of plates the staff dished out a meal of macaroni and fried bologna, which their charges greedily consumed. When we finished, the night shift arrived and another group of male counselors filed us back through the halls to the dormitory.

Standing at the open entrance over the crowd of boys, one of the men yelled sharply, "Bath! Let's move it!" He clapped his large hands several times. "Time for bath! Let's go!"

Obediently, the boys began untying their shoes, pulling off their shirts, pants, and underwear. They walked naked across the room, where they waited to be escorted to the showers. I panicked. I had only lived with my mother; before that, with my grandmother. I had never stood naked in front of one, much less dozens of strangers. When the last boy joined the others at the dormitory door, I remained by my bed, fully clothed.

Mom, why aren't you here yet? You have to come, now.

Standing with the gang of lost, naked boys, one of the men yelled at me from across the room.

"I said, let's move it!"

I froze when he crossed his arms, and in some unknown ritual, slowly started to count: "One. Two. . . ."

I stared at him, silently pleading for an explanation.

"I'm telling you, you better move it. Three. Four. Five."

I had not moved. He nodded to a second man behind him. "I'll handle these guys." Then, he turned toward me. "You take care of that."

The boys left, and the remaining man approached me. I was new, and the rules had to be made clear.

"Let's go," he ordered.

We left the dormitory and passed through several corridors before stopping at a stairwell. He hooked his hand under my armpit and yanked me down the stairs while I grasped at the railing on the other side, trying desperately to hold on to it. We halted at the bottom.

Mom, I need you.

The man dug in his pockets for his keys and reached to unlock the door.

I'll be good. I promise.

He grabbed me again and shoved me down another hallway until we reached a black, windowless room. A bare mattress lay on the floor.

I didn't mean to pull away.

He threw me inside, shut the door, and locked it behind him.

I didn't mean to leave you.

The darkness lasted two days. How long I pounded at the door, screaming to be let out, I have forgotten. Yet I do remember never protesting something as trivial as modesty ever again.

AN IMMENSE, ASYLUMLIKE facility, MacLaren Hall had been built on the arid outskirts of Los Angeles. MacLaren, or Mac, was the closest thing that Los Angeles County had to a public orphanage. Having decided no longer to house foster children at their juvenile hall facility, county supervisors opened MacLaren. However, the supervisors saw no need to change MacLaren's administration and left the county's Department of Probation responsible for the facility's daily operations. Probation officials promptly surrounded MacLaren with a perimeter fence, and for good measure, laced it with barbed wire. Employees were recruited from the existing juvenile hall to run the new foster care institution, to staff its dormitories, and to care for its children. With a keen eye on keeping order, county officials then chose armed guards to patrol the hallways.

By the time I arrived, hundreds of foster children were locked behind MacLaren's walls. The institution's bulging dormitories accommodated the whole span of childhood, from hour-old newborns to eighteen-year-old adolescents. Most were poor. All had been neglected, abused, or abandoned by their families. Labeled unsuitable for public education, MacLaren's children attended an on-site school, where they were offered a curriculum thought appropriate for children whom the county deemed uniformly "slow."

Officials euphemistically called MacLaren a "shelter care facility." More accurately, it was a violent dumping ground. Incarcerated more than cared for, children were forgotten for months before being moved on to foster families, group homes, or whatever else the county could find. Children who were sent back—or as the county described it, children who had "failed placements"—were lost entirely, often institutionalized for the remainder of their childhoods, cycled between MacLaren and an endless chain of temporary foster families, group homes, psychiatric wards, and juvenile detention centers.

Early one morning, several weeks after I arrived, the boys' counselors marched us out to the great empty hall where each of us had entered the institution. As we waited single file, one of the counselors announced that our "court day" had arrived. Then, joking about a new kind of field trip, he swung open the main door and ordered us out. Two buses, normally used to transport county prisoners, idled in the fenced yard. The sides of both vehicles were marked LOS ANGELES COUNTY JAIL, their windows blackened and barred. Several sheriff's deputies, uniformed and armed, impatiently ordered us on board.

Arriving at Los Angeles County's criminal court building, the deputies escorted the convoy of foster boys through several back hallways and rooms, until we halted at a large, empty auditorium. One of the MacLaren counselors advised us "to give our asses a rest" at the cafeteria-style tables, then ordered us to keep our hands in front of us and our heads face down. Again with that familiar chuckle, he reminded us that "a visit to lockup back at the Mac" waited for any boy who spoke or otherwise misbehaved.

I listened as, one by one, the last names of the boys were yelled

around me. Finally, I heard my own. With a knuckle rap on the back
of my head, the counselor signaled me to get up.

One of the deputies led me through a locked door and into a
bustling corridor. Throwing nods and greetings to his fellow deputies
along the way, he prodded his seven-year-old charge between lines of
handcuffed men in jailhouse uniforms who lingered alongside the
walls. Most of the prisoners ignored us, though some stared and a few
grinned. Suddenly, the man stopped and swung open a large wooden
door. Together, he and I entered a courtroom from the back. Unsure
why I was there, I glanced up at my escort, but his dull eyes revealed
nothing.

Then I looked ahead and, for the first time in nearly a month, saw
my mother. With an armed bailiff at her side, she waited at the
wooden railing on the spectator side of the room. She was dressed in
a red paisley blouse that I recognized, and I noticed that she had cut
her hair. The jeans that she wore were new. Behind her, the rows of
court benches were empty. Her expression was blank, and it occurred
to me that she looked tired. I smiled in her direction, and as the
deputy nudged me forward, I wondered if she would recognize me in
my MacLaren clothes.

In the center of the room, two women waited at separate tables.
Both were clad in nearly identical dark blazers and crisp skirts. One
extended her arm, and the deputy left my side. "There's nothing to
be afraid of, sweetheart," the woman whispered. She brushed my hair
from my forehead, and as I squirmed toward the railing and my
mother, she tightened her hold and introduced herself. "I'm your attorney. This won't take very long, I promise, honey."

I tugged again, looking away. "The lady at the next table," she continued, glancing at the deputy across the room while struggling to
keep me still, "she's the attorney for the county. She'll do most of the
talking today." Then my advocate stood, wrapped her arm around my
shoulder, and secured me firmly at her hip.

In front of us, a tiered platform spanned the far wall. From the side, a female clerk tended to a robed man who sat alone, perched atop the monument's summit. An immense seal of the County of Los Angeles hung above them. Clutching files and paperwork, she whispered into the magistrate's ear before retreating into the corner behind him. The stenographer sat to the side, relegated to a tiny desk. Motionless and bored, she looked to be about my mother's age.

Finally freed from his clerk, the judge scanned the room, tapped his gavel lightly. Taking her cue, the stenographer readied her fingers, and the woman at the opposite table began speaking. "Your honor, may it please the court."

The judge nodded, then thumbed through a file on his desk that had caught his attention.

The woman carried on: "The County of Los Angeles requests the continued detention of the child in accord with California Welfare and Institutions Code, Section . . ."

The judge glanced up, still nodding.

Around me, I felt the woman's arm relax. Seizing the advantage, I turned and looked behind me. My mother gazed quietly ahead. The woman pulled me back, then relented a bit, loosened her grip, and let me twist toward the railing. Noticing the small disturbance, my mother's head turned, and from the few feet that separated us, she glanced at me, snagged in the woman's arms.

The lawyer at the other table continued. "The child requires the protective services of the County of Los Angeles."

As I stared into my mother's desperate but tearless eyes, we listened to the county lawyer pound through formalities. Motionless and mute, she had readied me for this moment with lessons for the childhood that she knew would follow.

I need you to be brave for me.

"The county believes that returning the child to her at this time would constitute a . . ."

Be still . . . be still . . . be still.

"Mrs. Bridge continues to exhibit a resistant attitude toward children's services. The County of Los Angeles remains better equipped to meet the child's best interests and safety."

I'll come back for you. I promise. I'll come back.

The judge banged his gavel.

My mother looked away, and I turned to the front of the room.

"Objections?" The man peered in my direction, though even I knew he meant the woman beside me.

"No, your honor," she chirped, giving me a little squeeze. "We have no objections."

"Well then, motion granted," he muttered, glancing at his assistant, who had already risen with new paperwork in hand. As the room watched, he signaled the helper to approach and added, "Child's detention is ordered continued."

My lawyer had kept her word. The proceeding was brief. The whole business was finished in fewer than five minutes. No witnesses were called. No evidence was proffered. No pleas for help were heard. As I was escorted from the courtroom, my mother's stare kept to the space in front of her.

She had not interrupted. She had not cried. She had not run to me. Maybe she was just hanging tough. Maybe, I tried to convince myself, she knew some way to get me back without telling any of them. But there was something more in the room that morning. Something in the sum of details that even a seven-year-old boy could notice: the smart business suits that the women lawyers wore, compared to the paisley blouse and jeans that my mother had chosen; the holstered bailiff, who remained steady at my mother's side, and the lawyer she was never given; the condescension that lingered in the words "resistant attitude" and the indifference in the judge's eyes; the failure of my attorney to say anything at all.

My mother was twenty-four years old, descended from a line of impoverished women, educated to the tenth grade, abandoned by a husband, and plagued with fear. Standing at the judging bar, she must have recalled courtroom encounters from her own childhood. Now, a woman among her betters, she could do nothing more than be still and be judged.

Apart from MacLaren's staff and the other children, I had seen no one in weeks. Yet in my brief absence from it, the world had changed. Trailing back through the corridors to the auditorium where the remaining boys waited their turns, I could not have named the change, but I felt it in the numbness that filled me.

By early afternoon, every boy had been called. The counselors loaded us up, and we returned to MacLaren in the prisoners' bus. Behind the barbed-wire fences and inside the locked wards, I watched children arrive and leave. Though many of my memories of the place have scattered, I have kept some.

I remember that otherwise ordinary activities in the life of another seven-year-old became grotesque events at MacLaren. For breakfast, lunch, and dinner, staff herded us into the immense eating hall, and what had once been mealtimes now became feedings. For bathing, after we stripped, staff marched us naked through MacLaren's corridors to its central showers and tubs, where boys of varying ages grabbed at one another as staff looked on and laughed. For discipline, being sent to a corner meant staying there for hours. Being told to go to your room was replaced with being locked in a basement.

I recall a girl, a year or two older than I was, who bragged about having sex with older boys. She told me to sneak into the girls' shower area during lunch, where she and I could do the same. A younger boy became my friend, until one day, on the playground, he bit me in the face.

Yet mostly, I remember the children whom I avoided, like the blond-haired boy who slept a row or two over, who looked like me but had long wide burns running from his buttocks to his feet, and the teenage girl who sat in the courtyard clawing at her crotch. I watched staff keep their distance too. Though no one explained what had happened, even I understood that those were wounds that only an adult could make.

At first, I hoped for my mother, waited for her to appear. But eventually, I gave up searching for a rescuer. In that death house of childhoods, I did as I was told in silence. Weeks passed before the county noticed that I had withdrawn completely. Alarmed, social workers resolved to find me another placement, no matter how temporary.

CHAPTER SEVEN

∞

ARLY ON A Friday morning, after they pulled me from my
bed, MacLaren's staff stripped me for the last time. Handing me the
soft, dirty clothes that I was wearing when I had first arrived, the two
men led me to the great entrance hall where I had been admitted.
One of them pointed to a chair, signaling me to sit. "I wouldn't fuck
this up if I were you," he warned, then the two of them returned to
the boys' ward.

I had never met the social worker who arrived about thirty minutes later. With me sitting quietly beside her in the front seat, she
drove back across the San Fernando Valley, past North Hollywood
where my mother and I had lived, finally stopping at the dry foothills
of the valley's most westerly corner. The ranch-style home that we
parked in front of was barely distinguishable from the other tract
houses alongside it. As the woman halted at the curb, I stared at the
small lawn planted with spiked yucca trees and the station wagon
parked in the driveway. Stepping onto the sidewalk, I smelled smoke
in the air. The woman and I glanced at the hills behind the house,
then at the field of knee-length grass in front of it.

"I guess they've had some fires," she observed. Then without a word from me, she took my hand, led me to the front door, and pushed the bell. Quietly, she and I waited at the threshold of a stranger's home.

Moments later, a large woman with bleached blonde hair answered the door. She smiled, surveying the two of us.

"Mrs. Leonard?" the social worker asked.

The woman smiled, held her eyes on me.

"It's good to see you again," the social worker continued, still holding my hand.

"Well, I'm glad the two of you could make it." The blonde woman stepped to the side. "Please, come in."

"I'll just be here a minute." The social worker glanced down at me and tugged me inside. "Oh, this is Andy. He's a little quiet."

The woman knelt to me, then, spotting something, threw the social worker an irritated look. "What's wrong with his nose?"

I glanced up at the social worker and pressed against her. In the blonde woman's foyer, I had trouble answering when or why, but sometime during my stay at MacLaren, my nose had begun to bleed regularly and profusely. Left unattended, an infection had spread, and my nostrils had become swollen and crusted with blood.

"Yeah, I saw that too," the social worker replied quizzically. "Looks like one of those kid things."

The blonde woman grimaced, then extended her hand to me.

"Aren't you going to be a gentleman and shake Mrs. Leonard's hand?" the social worker chided.

Cautiously, I lifted my arm. The women laughed, then the blonde one gave my hand a firm squeeze.

"He's seven . . . no, he's eight." The social worker hesitated. "There had to be a birthday in there somewhere. I told you what I knew on the phone." She handed the woman a thin folder. "There's not much more than that."

As I lingered between them, the two women chatted awkwardly for a few moments. "The brushfires come every year," the blonde woman joked, dismissing the social worker's concern about the smoke outside. Smiling back politely, the social worker tapped me on the shoulder to wrap things up. "Well, we shouldn't need the bed for more than a few weeks. A month at the most."

"That's not a problem," Mrs. Leonard reassured her. "We'll put him in my son's bedroom. I've got friends coming next week. We can't have this guy messing in the guest room's sheets."

Reaching for the front door, the social worker told us to have a good weekend, then repeated her promise to return. "You be sure to be a good boy," she called back from the porch toward the foyer. I stared mutely back as she turned toward the front lawn and her car. Then my new foster mother reached over my head to shut the door.

Seeing that I had no more than what I was wearing, Mrs. Leonard drove me to get some clothes that afternoon. Pushing her cart down the aisles of the warehouse store, she shopped more like she was buying groceries than clothes for the eight-year-old trailing behind her. "I think three shirts, two pairs of pants, a pack of underwear, and some socks should do it." She turned toward me, then, digging through several cardboard crates, pulled out what was needed.

Back at the house, she deposited the bags on the floor of her son's bedroom. "You need to change," she instructed me, then waited as I slipped from what I was wearing and quietly surrendered the last of what I had of my mother. She glanced at the dirty bundle of my belongings in her hand. "Thank God. You won't need these things anymore." Then, rushing to the kitchen to start dinner, she left me waiting in the bedroom for her children—two daughters and one son—to get home from school.

Her son, Christopher, arrived first. Four years older than I, he discovered me sitting on the other twin bed in his room. Halting at the bedroom door, his first words were, "She didn't tell me another one of you was coming."

Embarrassed for being an intruder, I looked up at the thick-faced, mannish-looking boy. As he stepped inside, I quickly stood up.

"What are you doing here?" He moved closer, a bit too close. "My mom promised not to put any more of you in my room."

I shifted to the far end of the bed, watched as the larger boy surveyed the space for more evidence of me. "I'm sorry," I muttered to the side of his turned head, trying to think of something to satisfy him, a reason for being where I was. All I could come up with was the same whispered repetition: "I'm sorry. I'm sorry."

He locked his amber eyes on me in that way that an older boy silently tells a younger one, *Don't look for fairness from me*. Then, shaking his head, he spotted the two shopping bags of clothes slumped against the closet door. He reached for them, threw them at my feet. "Keep your shit away from my stuff," he ordered, before dropping his backpack on his bed and heading for the kitchen and his mother.

Unsure what to do, I waited beside the bed, listening as the boy argued with the woman about why she had chosen his room and not the guest room to lodge me. "Well, just tell him to leave your stuff alone," she offered.

"They never leave when they're supposed to," he retorted, moving on to the more general offense of my presence in the house. The front door opened, and the foyer filled with the voices of the boy's two sisters. Stomping across the floor, the boy bitterly repeated himself for the benefit of everyone now in the kitchen. "They never leave when they're supposed to. Never." Then the front door slammed, and his voice disappeared.

A few minutes later, the older of the two girls leaned through the bedroom door to get a good look at me. Six years my senior, tall and heavyset like her mother, Jessica introduced herself with a smile before scurrying back to the kitchen to help with dinner. Then Becky, the family's youngest and gentlest child, appeared. After asking my age, she rattled off with a grin, "If you're eight . . . I'm ten, Christopher's twelve, and Jessica's fourteen. Everyone's two years apart, which means you'll have to fit in."

Yet the arrival of her father was another indication that Becky had

been wrong. Round-faced with glasses and a comb-over, Mr. Leonard
worked as an electrical engineer for a nearby defense contractor. He
came home in the early evening, then listened to his wife explain that
an eight-year-old had arrived from MacLaren Hall that afternoon. He
waited as she retrieved the boy from their son's bedroom. Meeting me
for the first time, he glanced at me, shook my hand, and, without a
word, sat down in the living room to the evening paper. That was the
extent of his welcome. From my first day, Mr. Leonard was clear. He
would tolerate me in his house, but I should expect nothing more. I
would be his wife's concern.

PUT TO BED that first night, I lay mute in the darkened room, listening to the quiet house, and quickly turned my head. Across from me
in his own bed, Christopher breathed heavily in his sleep. Beyond
him, the bedroom door stood open.

Maybe he arrived from the fires that smoldered in the hills or the
smoke that hung in the air. Maybe he came from the fear that hunted
a little boy. Whatever the reason, he required only the night and my
sleeping mind to return. And now, inside, he prowled the house, forcing his way through my thoughts as they gathered in unknown rooms
and halls like clouds of minnows in an all but dead pond. Patiently,
the Night Man searched for the boy who was their source.

He moved nearer, the hallway creaking beneath his weight. Until
finally, his black shape paused in the open door to the room. In the
faint light, he carried the silhouette of a man in workman's clothes.
He rested against the door frame, his sloped shoulders weighted with
heavy-knuckled hands hanging lifeless at his sides.

I tried to be still. But as swaths of time passed, the stiller I was, the
more I felt the sheets tenting over my bare feet and legs. An itch plucked
at my shoulder and crept down my back. Slowly, thoughts crowded into
my head, until one managed to slip through and swim away.

From the threshold, the Night Man's eyes darted suddenly into the room. He stared at me as I lay in the bed, wrapped in the green light of the room's curtains. He gave a last look down the hall, then entered the room, stopping only a few feet from me.

"I've been looking for you," he said casually, unconcerned that he might wake someone and be discovered. "You know not to hide."

He stepped closer and glanced across the room at the Leonards' sleeping son. He grinned and turned back to me.

"I know you're awake."

He kept his stare on my closed eyes.

"I know you can hear me," he added lightly.

The bed sank and the blanket pulled tight at my waist. He leaned over me, and I felt his hot breath in my ear. "Open your eyes." He and I both listened as the Leonards' son rolled over, turning away from us. "You know me," he continued. "I've come for you. Open your eyes."

Then, as he did on nearly every visit, he raised his large, rough hand to my face, covering my mouth and nose, pressing harder and harder, cutting off the air, until his coarse palm dangled in the stream of thoughts and fears that swam through my head. Finally, seizing a random bit of mind, the Night Man smiled in triumph, lifted his trophy to the dim light, looked down on me, and whispered, "Look at me! See what I can do!"

I woke with a jolt, the pillow sticking to my face and neck, the sheet tangled in my legs. I stared into the night and felt the darkness push back at my eyes. Though the Leonards were only as far as a bedroom down the hall, no cry from me could hope to matter in the rooms of a house that would never be my own. Silently, I listened for the danger, but only heard the heavy breathing of the Leonards' sleeping son.

Be still. I remembered my mother's voice. *Be still.*

IT WOULD TAKE more than that Friday night or the weekend that followed, but time at the house confirmed that foster children were very much a matter of Mrs. Leonard's concern. My foster mother was born shortly before the Second World War in Tallinn, the capital of the newly independent Estonian Republic. The daughter of a policeman and a seamstress, she had a decent life until the Nazis invaded the Baltic states, arrested her father, then packed her parents, brother, and her onto a train for southern Germany. She was eight years old when she arrived at the Nazi slave labor camp outside Dachau. Her new masters pulled her from her parents and brother, then transported her to a satellite camp that the Germans had specially constructed with children in mind. There, she survived alone for nearly four years until General Patton's Third Army arrived early one spring morning, shortly after her twelfth birthday.

With Germany's defeat, she and her family were rescued from their captors, only to remain in a string of new camps built by the Western Allies for "displaced persons" unwilling to return to their newly communist homelands. They wandered German soil, applied to immigrate to country after country, and, declined by all, finally compromised on the United States. After the years of death, starvation, and drift, she despised the Russians for stealing her home but tolerated the Germans for taking the childhood that she could live without.

She was sixteen when she arrived in the United States. She mastered English with only a slight accent and found Mr. Leonard, an American from Minnesota, to marry. Yet she remained an unrelenting immigrant, remodeling her house into a Baltic freedom shrine. She adorned rooms with maps of her forsaken nation. With plywood, she crafted coats of arms, complete with oak leaves, acorns, and lions. She designed and cut tiny Estonian folk costumes, then glued them to the bodies of stripped Barbie dolls.

Reaching middle age, she told her husband that she wanted more than what her own children could offer. She wanted children who had lived as she had as a child. She wanted children who knew fear. With her husband's permission, she called the county's foster care department. She returned the package of forms that came in the mail.

When the social worker arrived at the house with more forms and questions, she described her childhood, then told the woman that she was willing to take the county's "worst cases." She submitted to fingerprinting and a criminal background check, then several months later, she received her license. Soon after, she possessed the children that she had wanted, the children that she said were so much like her. But now she was an adult, and like the commandant she remembered as a child, she possessed all authority.

THE MONDAY MORNING after I arrived, Mrs. Leonard drove me the three blocks to Elkhart Elementary School. In the school's main office, a secretary named for a saint, Mrs. Augustine, resisted admitting a young boy with no school transcripts or medical records.

"You don't even know if he's had his shots?" Mrs. Augustine protested. She leaned over the counter, gave me a quick once over. "God knows what he's got."

Yet, having fought the same battle before, Mrs. Leonard insisted. The records could take months to arrive in the mail, longer if the county social worker insisted on bringing them personally, or never at all. When the morning bell rang, the school's secretary and my new foster mother were still squabbling. Only after Mrs. Leonard made it clear that she would spend the whole day, if necessary, did the woman finally relent.

Using the thin file that the social worker had left behind, the two women filled out as much of the paperwork as they could. Mrs. Augustine took Mrs. Leonard's word that I belonged in the second grade, but insisted that I be vaccinated within the next two weeks or as soon as the county stickers entitling me to free medical care arrived.

"Do you know any doctors who take them?" the woman inquired.

"Not my own kids' pediatrician," Mrs. Leonard answered. "But I know someone I can use."

When they finished, Mrs. Augustine gave Mrs. Leonard a handful of mustard-colored tickets that entitled me to free lunches. Mrs. Leonard tore off one, told me to hand it to the lady in the cafeteria during lunch with the other children. Then promising that she would be back in the afternoon, Mrs. Leonard left me in the school office.

My first morning at a new school, I waited alone to be escorted to a classroom. I had not been in school, or at least in a public school, for nearly a year. Other than at MacLaren, I had attended none of the second grade. Most importantly, I had not been in school since losing my mother. I had not been in school as a foster child.

By the time I was taken to meet my new class, morning recess was about to begin. From the blacktop's edge, I saw nothing different in this clutter of monkey bars and swinging rings. I recalled the jump-rope spaces where the girls played and the kickball courts where the boys competed. Watching the throng of children, I remembered that their screams and cries meant little. Then, as I knew would happen, I caught the eyes of several classmates.

The first of their inquiries were easy, ones that I had answered many times:

"What is your name?"

"Is this your first day?"

"What grade are you in?"

Then suddenly, their simple questions began demanding impossible answers:

"Why did your parents move here?"

"Do you have brothers or sisters?"

"Where are you from?"

I wish that it had been harder. I wish that someone had told me something else to say. I wish that I had been better than just another eight-year-old boy. I denied my mother and put the Leonards in her place. I have forgotten the details of what I said, though I must have claimed the Leonards' daughter Becky and son Christopher as my siblings. They went to Elkhart Elementary too. Nothing fit together neatly, but it was easier than I might have thought. Christopher never spoke to me, and Becky could be avoided. On the playground that morning, I cobbled together a family of lies. Then behind them, I hid the woman I wanted most, the one I desperately prayed would return.

When the recess bell rang, my second-grade teacher waved me over from the playground. She was prim and gentle. She pulled me to the front of the room and introduced me to the class before sitting me among them. After several claps for silence, she doled out stacks of picture workbooks, then asked the class to open them to their assigned page. She handed me a pencil and eraser, laying a piece of lined gray paper in front of me. Eyeing my closed workbook, she opened it to the proper page. As the class murmured around us, she whispered the instructions above my head, patted me softly on the shoulder, then moved on.

I stared at the simple workbook and its collection of colored drawings of a factory baking bread. I had already forgotten what the teacher had told me. But from my classmates to the left and right, I could clearly see the assignment: I was to copy the bakers, the ovens, and the loaves. After what seemed like minutes, I looked up from the empty paper. I watched as the teacher crouched from child to child, helping each of them move along. Like the playground outside, the classroom felt familiar. I remembered Mrs. Nagami, glanced at the door and at the long narrow window like the one through which my mother's face had once appeared. Then, I returned to my work, picked up my pencil, covered the paper in empty rectangles, and claimed they were loaves of bread.

At noontime, I threw the meal ticket away rather than stand with it among my new classmates. Later, I would learn to watch the lunch line dwindle before rushing to the window just before it closed, avoiding humiliation but also eating. Though it irritated Mrs. Leonard, I was relieved when the school eventually stopped offering free lunches to foster children altogether.

I forget why—perhaps I had picked at it—but just after lunch that first day, my nose began to bleed again. Rushing to me with a handful of tissues, my new teacher tried her best to halt it. Yet the blood continued streaming over my lips and down my chin. Panicked, the woman called the school nurse, who arrived at the classroom in minutes. After shuttling me to her office, the woman sat me on the examination bench, briefly peered up my swollen nostrils, then reached for the telephone and told Mrs. Leonard to come get me.

Arriving at the elementary school hours before her appointed time, Mrs. Leonard was annoyed. When the nurse informed her that the school refused to take me back until I was taken to a doctor, she grew even angrier. Still, the nurse refused to relent. Finally, Mrs. Leonard ordered me to her car, then said nothing on the way back to her house. More than a week passed before the county stickers arrived. Several more days passed before the doctor agreed to see me. I returned to school at the end of the month, staying for the remainder of second grade.

Without explanation, the social worker who dropped me at the house fresh from MacLaren broke her word. She never came back to retrieve me. Christopher was right. I never left when I was supposed to, and though no one had bothered to inform me, a slow countdown had already begun.

School years, birthdays, holidays—none of the usual markers in a child's life are measured in eighteen-month intervals. Yet, as I learned, few markers matter more to a foster child than the end of his first eighteen months in care. I had started fourth grade and was nine years old when my eighteen months elapsed. At a hearing that I never attended, a judge again reviewed my detention under Los Angeles County's care, examined my "best interests," then redefined me in the eyes of the law. I was no longer a temporary foster child but a permanent one. Mrs. Leonard's license was only for temporary placements, and my change in status would have normally required moving me. I had seen babies, toddlers, and teenagers come and go within those first eighteen months at the house, and I had suspected the same would ultimately happen to me. Yet, whether for love, money, pity, convenience, a mix of them all, or something else entirely, the Leonards agreed to change their license, if only for me. For the time being, they agreed to keep me.

Suddenly I was different from the other children who arrived at the house in the mornings, evenings, nights, and afternoons, and who left within days, weeks, or at most, a few months. I stayed. Like a survivor on a life raft, not wanting to be there but having nowhere else to go, I remained. And in those earliest months, sometime after the Leonards' stewardship changed from temporary to permanent, I remember two great occurrences in my life. The first was the arrival of a foster boy named Jason. The second was the return of my mother.

CHAPTER EIGHT

～

"JASON! GET OVER HERE."

Impatiently demanding his presence, Mrs. Leonard motioned in wide circles, as though she were directing traffic with one flabby arm, while cradling a camera in her other hand.

I kept my distance, perched on the sandstone diving rock overlooking the pool's deep end. Beyond the rippling water, I watched Jason step from the shallow end, anchoring his foot on the pavement and carefully avoiding a toy boat that lay at the pool's edge. As the olive-skinned, thin-shouldered boy drew nearer to Mrs. Leonard, I lowered my head to the water. As if uninterested, I sagged my arms at my sides trying to remain ignored while I continued to spy.

"I said, get over here. Now, young man!" she yelled again. "And get that balloon out of the water before it clogs the drain."

The boy scuttled closer, clutching a pink birthday balloon against his side, then waited for our foster mother to step from the sliding glass doors that overlooked the backyard. Jason had arrived shortly after Christmas, and the Leonards seemed to like him. Now several months comfortable with the house and its family, the boy eagerly accepted the role of freshly crowned ten-year-old and patiently waited for Mrs. Leonard to mark his birthday coronation with a photograph.

March was a cold time—even in the San Fernando Valley—for two boys swimming in an unheated pool. Above us, a gray blanket shrouded the sky, and after a dry winter, the faint smell of smoke drifted in the air as a fire wandered somewhere in the hills at our backs.

Lingering half-naked and soaked at the pool's edge, Jason must have felt the day was colder still. His oversize trunks sucked at his thighs, and water ran down his legs in countless streams that converged in a single flood around his feet. His teeth clacked, and his body prickled with goose bumps while Mrs. Leonard ignored the chill and tinkered with the camera over her ample belly.

By the time Jason arrived, Mrs. Leonard had recounted nearly all of her childhood to me. As if they were fairy tales, she narrated gruesome accounts of people, places, and happenings that I had never heard of. Holding me in her lap, she pulled me in closer. Then whispering in my ear, she began her stories with the soft reminder, "Unlike my own children, Andy, you and I both know what it means to go hungry."

From the concentration camp outside Munich to her tract home in the San Fernando Valley, Mrs. Leonard's journey had been laden with rage. Her voice seethed with hatred as she described what it had been like to be taken from her home and parents, to be forced to steal food and to eat grass, and to applaud with the other camp children as she watched the Allied soldiers hang the guards and commandant. Unlike anything I had heard from my mother, Mrs. Leonard spewed anger as she described how the Russian communists seized what was left of her home.

Yet, as I had already learned, and as I suspected Jason would soon learn, Mrs. Leonard's rage did not require the thought of a German officer or Russian soldier. A foster child could summon it as well. A lapsed chore, an uneaten vegetable, or an unmade bed was invitation enough. Well before my own tenth birthday the month earlier, I had known the fear of having an all-powerful woman yank me by the arm or heave me by the ear across a room. I had felt the isolation of being ignored or referred to in the third person for days at a time in a house that was not my own.

And that day by the pool with Jason and me, if the camera had turned itself on our foster mother instead of us, the picture would have revealed a frightened girl who had eaten herself into omnipotent obesity. Her form sloped with fat, as if the hungry belly she felt as a child had refused to be satisfied. Sheer size endowed her with terrifying confidence in front of children. She had an intuition for invisible wounds, and she loved the feel of swift, final judgment.

At last finished with her photographic adjustments, Mrs. Leonard looked to Jason. "All right, make a smile." Her face disappeared behind the translucent cyclopean eye. "A bigger one. And hold that balloon still! I don't want the thing to blur."

Jason tightened his grin, while Mrs. Leonard fumbled for the button. Finally, the camera clicked, exploding a useless flash of light across the boy's face and chest. Without a word, she dropped her hand to her side, surveyed him up and down, and walked back inside.

EARLIER THAT GRAY morning, I woke to Mrs. Leonard yelling my name from down the hall. "Andy, rise and shine. Now!" I recognized her figure at the door as she flicked on the ceiling light above me. Jason stood at her side smiling, waiting for me as I got up. Mrs. Leonard took the lead, and the three of us walked down the hallway, through the kitchen to the family room, where her husband and three children were already waiting.

The sun's overcast light barely lit the large room. The strands of a burnt-orange shag carpet, occupying the center space, were meticulously combed with the carpet rake that Mrs. Leonard used for special occasions. A bookcase with the *World Book Encyclopedia*, along with piles of Mr. Leonard's *Scientific American* and Mrs. Leonard's *Psychology Today*, loomed beside a large picture window overlooking the front yard. Dieffenbachia plants climbed to the ceiling, their wide leaves dust-free from the home brew of sour milk and water that Mrs. Leonard gave us to polish them. The walls were hung with pink balloons and streamers, and an old, cake-smudged HAPPY BIRTHDAY sign was taped to the wall.

Avoiding the carpet, I cautiously made my way to the edge of the sofa next to the Leonards' children. Jason gingerly walked to the stool and table. A large, elaborately wrapped box waited, surrounded by Hershey bars and scattered M&M's. Jason sat down, admiring the loot, before looking to Mrs. Leonard across the room. She nodded and smiled. Taking his cue, Jason lifted his gift and tugged at the bow.

"Careful with the tape," Christopher yelled out.

"I know," Jason snapped back, aware that Mrs. Leonard reused the paper and ribbons. He smiled in her direction. "I haven't ripped anything." Sitting on a stool, he picked away at the tape to please her.

Finally, he lifted the lid and sucked in an excited breath. He shifted his head toward Mrs. Leonard and, returning the box to the table, jumped from his perch to the sofa. She gripped him into her and, with his face pressed in her hair, he muttered, "Thank you. I never had a better birthday."

"Oh, I know, sweetheart," she answered, then caught my eyes just as I looked away. "You know, we thought about keeping it until Christmas."

"No, please don't." The boy protested, clinging to her. "I love you," he whispered.

Mrs. Leonard laughed. "I love you, too." Then she pushed the boy away.

He leaned toward Mr. Leonard and extended his thin arm. "Thank you," he said, manfully shaking Mr. Leonard's hand.

"You're welcome, Jason. Don't forget the card."

The boy glanced at the table, spotting the sealed envelope beside his still half-opened gift. He quickly returned to the stool, extracted the card, then looked up and grinned. "For a good son," he read the inscription aloud.

I glanced at Christopher, as the teenage boy rolled his eyes then yelled confidently across the room, "Why don't you show us what it is?"

Jason plunged his hands inside the box all the way to his elbows, struggling to pull his gift free. He caught a piece of falling tissue as it drifted toward the floor, then freed a plastic cargo boat from the remaining wrappings and ribbons. The boat's deck teemed with fragile cranes, tiny crates, and dozens of molded people to manage its freight. He cradled the imaginary world in his lap, looked out at the family, and smiled. "This is the best birthday I've ever had."

When the morning was over, Jason and I unstuck the streamers from the walls and, side by side on the couch, rerolled the reels tightly for the next birthday to arrive. As I stared at my fingers, stained from the crepe paper, Jason chattered on about the day, the party, and how lucky he was to have the Leonards.

Other than birthdays, the family room had only one other exceptional use. In clear view from the kitchen, the space complied with court orders that required parent visits to be observed. Court mandates governed every child-parent encounter with the level of monitoring corresponding to the threat that the court determined a mother or father posed. Children whom the county placed at the Leonards' were almost uniformly allowed to see their parents only under Mrs. Leonard's surveillance from the kitchen or in her seated presence.

In the room where Jason would have met his mother, had she ever come, he took the gift that Mrs. Leonard offered in her place. I considered what the Leonards' son surely knew as he watched Jason on his stool.

You're not their son, I thought, glancing at the boy beside me. *It won't last.*

"ANDY!" MRS. LEONARD yelled from the kitchen into the family room, where Jason and I sat. "Go get dressed for your mother. She's *supposed* to be here today."

The county was never good with details. In an unexplained contra-diction, only after the court deemed me a permanent foster child did it grant my mother the right to see me. Also unexplained was the court's unusually lax provision that allowed my mother to sit with me outside Mrs. Leonard's view. The court's other stipulations, however, were more typical: My mother could see me once a month for a single hour, at the Leonards' convenience, and if she was late or wanted to resched-ule, that month's visit would be forfeited automatically.

For my mother, the court's order must have amounted to: *He's not yours, but you can see him*. For Mrs. Leonard, it was an affront: *You let her in my house*. For me, it was simpler: *She's come back. She's come back*.

That day was among the very first of my mother's visits. Outside the house, I waited for her to pull up in her light blue Falcon. Kick-ing at the clumps of crabgrass that had invaded and nearly conquered the front yard, I thought of Jason. Alone on the lawn, waiting for my mother, my real mother, I hated Jason for giving Mrs. Leonard every-thing that she had wanted. On my birthdays, when I smiled politely and thanked the Leonards, I did it only because I had to. No matter what the Leonards offered, nothing would ever be enough for me to surrender my mother. That morning, I was sure that Jason had it wrong. Even after months of absence, I was sure that a mother could not be replaced. I knew that without her I would be lost.

When she finally pulled up, I ran into the street and around to the driver's side, watching her through the window as she parked. With barely a hug, I rushed her inside, hoping that no one had noticed the unfamiliar young woman in dark sunglasses, wearing a skirt that hugged her thighs and exposed too much of her bare legs.

Visits were never easy. She and I sat together awkwardly in the bedroom, surrounded by judgments in a stranger's house, quietly ig-noring the past and the present, pretending about the future.

She always brought a gift. When we had lived together, she never came home with presents. With so little of her motherhood left, however, she had few other weapons in her war with the Leonards. I

remember a Hot Wheels set, a stuffed elephant, even a banana-seat bicycle with broad handlebars that barely fit in the trunk of her car. On
Jason's birthday, she brought a small truck.

"Thank you for my toy," I said, fidgeting with it in my lap.

"I got it at the drugstore. Maybe next time I come we can go together," she offered.

I thought of the drugstore down the street from where we had
lived and of my mother and Carol, laughing through the aisles, trying
to outdo each other's pranks. I also remembered the court order that
barred her from taking me anywhere with her, even into the Leonards'
backyard. Still, I pretended for her, as she was doing for me. "Going
together would be nice."

She smiled, and I hugged her. I told her how pretty she looked.
She mentioned a new apartment that she had and a bedroom that
waited for me, all the result of a new job. She asked me how school
was, if I had made friends. I smiled back, blankly answering, "Everything's fine."

When our scheduled time had nearly passed, I looked to the bedroom door, where Mrs. Leonard was waiting in the hallway. Her face
forced into a smile, she tersely called me from the bedroom.

"She's had her hour," she hissed, glancing at my mother on my
bed. "She's got five minutes, then it's the police. Do you hear me?"
She waited for my nod. "Get her out."

I returned to the room to negotiate, trying to think of something I
could offer or say.

"What did she want?" my mother demanded, locking her eyes on
the door frame.

I thought for another moment, then blurted the only thing that
seemed left, "I love you, Mom."

In the kitchen, Mrs. Leonard ordered her children to set the table,
then ignored Becky when she asked when my mother was supposed
to leave. I glanced at the bedroom window, imagined Mrs. Leonard

retrieving her husband from the garage. I thought of him bursting into the room, angry that my mother had stayed past her hour. If she argued with him, she might defend herself briefly, but I knew that, in the end, she would be cornered and lose.

"If you don't go, she'll get her husband," I whispered, avoiding her face and looking at the floor.

"So?" she snapped.

I could hear lunch being put on the kitchen table. Then I said what I had seen, not at the Leonards', but before.

"If you don't leave, they'll hurt you."

"No one's *ever* going to hurt me," she muttered, angrily reassuring herself as much as me.

"She said she'd call the police," I confessed.

She paused, considering the threat. "All right, I'll leave," she relented finally. Looking me in the face, she brushed aside my hair. Her hands were rough, her nails bitten raw. She lifted her slender arm, exposing the thin scars that lined the underside of her wrist. Softly, she kissed me on the head before beginning her familiar good-bye. "Be a good boy for Mom. Be sure to do what they say. And promise not to cry. . . ."

"Andy! Get down here," Mrs. Leonard's voice intruded from the kitchen, pointedly ignoring the fact that my mother was still down the hall. "What're you waiting for, a written invitation?" Then she grumbled to one of her children, "He's always a problem when she visits."

". . . and don't forget we love each other. You're my only boy."

"And you're my only mom," I whispered, concluding the pact.

I watched as she reached for her purse and coat, then strode out of the room without looking back, giving no promise of when she would return. On the bed with the new truck in my lap, I listened for her to pass across the tiled foyer, hoping that she would not notice the kitchen table set for lunch without her, or the birthday cake that Mrs. Leonard had surely laid out for dessert. When the front door slammed, without an argument from her or a threat from Mrs. Leonard, I was relieved.

"Andy, now!" my foster mother yelled again.

I jumped from the bed, rolled the truck deep beneath it, and ran to the bathroom to wash my hands for lunch.

IN THE KITCHEN, the family surrounded the table. Mrs. Leonard had laid out a pot of baked beans, cooked with brown sugar and sliced hot dogs, Jason's half-eaten cake to the side, a pan of lime Jell-O slathered with a homemade Thousand Island dressing. I ate quickly, then asked Mr. Leonard to be excused.

On the pretext that "boys need sunshine," Mrs. Leonard barred Jason and me from the house most afternoons in what amounted to a child lockout. I had two choices—sitting in the front yard, talking with Jason for hours, or swimming in the backyard and ignoring him. I walked to the bedroom and put on my trunks.

Anticipating our hunger during our afternoon exile, Mrs. Leonard made provisions. As I walked through the kitchen on my way to the backyard, she handed me an extravagance that she had enjoyed as a Baltic child, *koogel-moogel*.

A breeding ground for salmonella and general revulsion, the treat required little preparation. Retrieving a plastic coffee mug and metal spoon from the kitchen, she meticulously separated an egg, plopped the yolk into the cup, dropped in a handful of sugar, and sent me out with it. Smashing the sugar into the raw yolk produced a viscous, whitish-yellow substance that Mrs. Leonard insisted would keep us nourished and entertained for the afternoon. Alone in the backyard, I walked to the far end of the pool and dumped the glop into the yucca plants that lined the Leonards' pool.

Though Mr. Leonard regularly hacked back the yucca's thick stems, the severed shoots only produced new siblings that tangled with each other, competing for sunlight. On industrious days, the man climbed up his wobbly ladder, then spent hours stripping the plants of their sword-shaped leaves, stretching for the tallest ones that towered even above him. Fortified by my *koogel-moogel* droppings and hardened by the chemical assault of chlorine from the pool, the plants resisted as long as they could. Hours later, at last stripped to their cores, the yuccas stood bare, a pile of twisted bones.

The Leonards lined the lip of their pool with rocks stuck together with globs of cement. As their home was being built, they drove into the surrounding hills and quarried the rocks themselves. They made dozens of trips, splintering rock from the mountains, pitching the plunder into the back of their station wagon. Mostly, they took hardened brown clay that, in the summer heat, sucked up a child's wet footprint in seconds. But they also found burgundy-colored prizes that were craggy and sharp, absorbing nothing. Ever the engineer, Mr. Leonard bragged that these iron-hard chunks had come from lava that had exploded from the hills, scalded the ground, and frozen into what he and his wife had snatched and planted around their pool.

With the correct pressure and speed, several of these rocks were sharp enough to cut the bottom of a wet, slippery foot. Beside the pool, with Jason still inside the house, I disturbed the water, as if to test its warmth, but then lifted my foot and pressed it against a chosen red stone. As I trusted it to, the stone produced a deep, clean slice. Nothing was sloppy. I did only what my foot could sustain, containing and making safe what would otherwise have been dangerous. In the seconds that it lasted, the heavy slicing was wonderfully selfish. The moment tolerated nothing but itself in my head. Everything stopped for it, allowing only a tender, rushing calm.

A Band-Aid would have been useless, and asking for one would have meant surrendering the wound, its creation, and its pain to someone else. The next day, my white socks would absorb the blood in a red stain the size of a half-dollar. In the warmth of my sneakers, the wound would give me dominion over a world that had taken

everything else. The gentle, mindful pain would be mine alone, sepa-
rating me from the Leonards, their children, Jason, the birthday party,
the now, the past—everything.

On Jason's birthday, unsure if my mother would ever be back, I
prized the wound I made, offering it as a clandestine gamble. I told
myself that, if I made the cut long and deep enough, my mother
would rescue or at least return to see me. I could ransom her, as she
had desperately ransomed me years before. If she never came back,
the wound would be my silent offering to us, as mother and son.
The cut might eventually heal and disappear, but another could always be made.

Startled by the sound of the sliding glass door, I turned to see Jason
in his swimsuit, smiling, with his birthday boat in one hand, a pink
balloon snug under his armpit, and a cup of *koogel-moogel* in his other
hand. For a moment, we stared at each other, alone.

"It won't float," I warned him, breaking the silence. He looked
confused. Pointing at his toy, I clarified from across the pool. "It's not
a real boat. You'll just sink it, and she'll get mad at you."

Still, he insisted the thing was as good as it appeared. Delicately setting his cup to the side, he began arranging dozens of plastic parts
around the deck and cabins. As I watched, he climbed into the shallow end, waded waist-deep into the pool's center, and launched his
toy. The vessel glided a few feet, crossing into the deep end, but it
soon began taking on water, then quickly sank, sending its Lilliputian
passengers and cargo plummeting to the pool's floor. I looked at him,
half smiling in vindication.

"Go get it before she sees," he implored me, extending his arm
over the water to catch the few pieces that were still floating.

"You did it. You get it."

He dipped his head but quickly reemerged. Panicking, he glanced
back and forth between the pool and the glass door to the Leonards'
living room.

"Hurry up! Andy, get it for me!" he whined.

"All right. All right. Just shut up," I shot back. "Or they'll hear you."

Heels first, I jumped into the deep end. The water flushed over the ripped skin of my foot, locking in the pain but cleansing the incision in feathers of drifting blood. I scooped up the dozens of pieces from the pool's floor and returned them to Jason, who sat on the steps, quickly arranging and drying everything beside him.

Finished, I lifted myself to sit at the pool's far edge just as Mrs. Leonard intruded through the glass door, camera in hand.

"Jason! Get over here."

She'll see the wet boat in a puddle by the pool.

"I said, get over here. Now, young man!"

He should never have tested the thing in the first place.

"And get that balloon before it clogs the drain."

He's afraid I'll tell her.

"All right, make a smile," she commanded.

Jason trembled on the pavement as Mrs. Leonard fiddled with the camera. The bulb flashed, and she walked back inside. Jason returned to the pool steps, ignoring me.

That day, I swam from afternoon into night. While Jason sat in the shallows, grinding and spooning down his yolk and sugar, his legs dangling in the distance, I lingered in the deep cold, drifting in his echoes. Watching him from below, resisting the water's effort to lift me as long as I could, I slipped my fingers through the narrow slots of the steel drain, taunting the creature that I imagined waited below to snap off a finger or, drawn to the faint taste of blood from my foot, break out and drag me down and away through the pipe. Then, unable to hold my breath any longer, I surged upward, gasping and sucking in air, before plummeting all over again.

As I kept to my end of the pool, Jason kept to his. I asked him nothing about his birthday, and I was relieved when he asked me nothing about my mother's visit. Things were easier that way—neither of us had to acknowledge that both occurred in a foster parent's house.

Around us, the water lapped against the rocks, and in the empty space between us, we left the truth undisturbed.

After darkness descended that evening and Jason had gone inside, Mrs. Leonard opened the sliding glass, and listening as she approached, I slipped below one last time. Her black, formless shape appeared above me, squatting at the edge of the water, shadowed by the lights that stretched from the house to the pool.

"Andy! I said, get out. Now! I know you can hear me!"

The shouts smacked at the water's surface, bouncing one, two, three times, gradually losing strength, descending through the warmth, then the cold, and finally, like a shower of stones, landing on the pool's floor in a quiet muffle. Under the water's deep shelter, I screamed back, the pool filling my mouth, flooding my throat. Yet at the end of the day, the watery cold, now black, had patiently waited to swallow whatever I had left to force from my lungs. Only empty air rose to the top, briefly disturbed the surface, then escaped into nothingness.

Come back. Come back. Come back.

At last surrendering to Mrs. Leonard's orders, I sat alone by the pool. My skin tingled as water steamed from my body. My eyeballs, stinging from the chlorine, splintered the glow of the streetlights into dozens of captured stars. The skeletons of the stripped yuccas lay heaped next to me in cluttered silence. In the distance, brush fires devoured the hills around the house.

The flames sprouted from nowhere, fed by dead heat and dry grass. First came the smell of smoke, as heavy clouds of it built, filled the air, then blew from the hills to the house. Waiting and looking hard enough, I saw glowing streaks of fire that crawled the ravines in thin lines, like streams of red and white clotted magma. Embers followed, lifted in the heated air, drifted from their birth, extinguished, and descended on the house in exhausted ash. Finally, sirens screamed in the distance, first one crying voice, then a chorus. Until, slowly, the darkness emptied and was silent again.

With one leg dangling over the water's edge, the other across my lap, I examined the wound I had made. The thick skin of my foot was soft, white, and clean from the water and chlorine. I fingered the slice, spreading it to expose deep red flesh and tearing at its edges. As I shivered from the cold, my thoughts focused on my foot and the single source of pain that now returned, to the exclusion of every other.

CHAPTER NINE

∽

As HE HAD shown me at his birthday party and then reminded me again and again, Jason was different from me. Jason never wanted to leave.

Jason spoke to stay. With a gravelly rasp in his voice, he launched into conversations. He delighted in attention from the Leonards and their three children. He laughed at their jokes, while I was afraid to smile.

Using whole vocabularies that I had abandoned, he said things like "my house" and "my room," while I maneuvered conversations to avoid them. Without invitation, he called the Leonards Mom and Dad, while I refused both words and insisted on using their first names. Going for broke, he put everything on the table in a single bet. He embraced the Leonards, saying, "I love you," and when I saw it, his affection for them embarrassed me.

Each month, the county checks arrived, a payment for every foster child in the house. Delivered in the afternoon mail, the envelopes were unmistakable, with their light blue Los Angeles County seals and mechanically stamped postage. For hours, the checks lay on the kitchen counter, strewn among the bills and advertisements, waiting until Mr. Leonard walked home from work.

To Mrs. Leonard's cry, "Daddy's home," the three Leonard children, along with Jason and me, doing as we had been told, ran to the kitchen to greet him. Muttering back his hellos and sorting through the stack of mail, Mr. Leonard spotted what had come from the county, slipped his finger through the sealed flaps, ripped and spread them apart. With a smile, he extracted two checks—one for Jason, one for me—held them between his fingers, kissed his wife, then walked back to their bedroom for a shower before dinner.

All of a childhood arrived in each envelope, covering everything that the Leonards were obligated to provide: a bed, food, clothing, an allowance, and any random purchases that might be required. Like scratches on a wall marking our increasing heights, the stipends grew with our ages according to an established schedule. If special circumstances arose, the Leonards could ask for more. If an envelope was late or went missing in the mail, they called and complained. Yet Jason claimed more than what the checks could ever reimburse. Jason claimed a family that would never be his.

Less than a month after his birthday, another social worker visited the house. This woman arrived with a fifteen-year-old girl in tow. With Jason and me peeking in from the kitchen, the woman sipped coffee with Mrs. Leonard in the family room while the girl sat off to the side.

"Her name is Jenny. She has been in foster care since she was twelve," the social worker announced, ignoring the girl, who nervously glanced around the room. "She's been nothing but trouble, gone through more placements than even I know." The woman shook her head, disgusted with her young charge. "Now she's got herself pregnant."

Though it meant packing her house with three foster children in addition to the three of her own, Mrs. Leonard accepted the girl. When the day came for the abortion that the county had requested, Mrs. Leonard had it done in the morning. With Jenny's pregnancy finished, Mrs. Leonard returned to her afternoon housework. That day, watching Jenny through the sliding glass door, I wondered what there was to cry about as she sat at the edge of the pool. Mrs. Leonard kept her in the house for a few more weeks. Then one afternoon, in the spring of fourth grade, before Jason and I had come home, the county came and took the girl away.

Jenny's disappearance alone should have been lesson enough for Jason. With ease, quiet, and speed, she had gone missing. Still, Jason ignored the lesson. He continued declaring his place in the family, claiming security where there was none.

Jenny had not been the only child to arrive and leave. Neighbors visited, often praising Mrs. Leonard for taking in children like Jason and me. On more than one occasion, as he and I watched, Mrs. Leonard lifted a book from a small desk beside the kitchen table, pushed aside the plates of cookies and mugs of coffee, and shared her scrapbook of the county children who had come and gone.

She gave each child a page, taping a picture at the top. In her ornate script, she wrote the child's birthday and any details she felt were worth keeping. She noted where the children had come from—their parents, another foster home, a group home, a hospital, or MacLaren. She noted children who had pleased her and those who had not. She recorded what they had endured at the hands of their parents or others. Then, like an obituary, each entry ended the same: The child was gone on such and such a date.

Around the kitchen table, Mrs. Leonard kept the worst of the details secret, but not much was required to tempt and satisfy the circle of voyeurs. Occasionally she prefaced her remarks with, "Did I ever mention that I lived in a camp as a child?" Then quickly, she answered herself, "Oh, I must have," before smiling, inviting her guests to pull closer, then launching into stories of enduring loss.

"This was Jade," she began. I looked over her shoulder and saw the photograph of a small girl with soft, dark curls and glasses, lying on the floor. "She was one of our first." One woman leaned across the table for a better look. "Her mother gave her up, and we thought about keeping her." Mrs. Leonard continued. "But the social worker said it was a bad idea. You know, adopting a black baby." Chewing cookies, both guests mutely nodded.

She moved on to another page, another picture. "Matthew. Now he was sixteen when we got him. Got in all sorts of trouble," she lamented. "Handsome, don't you think?"

"He is good-looking," one woman answered. "What was wrong with him?"

"We left him alone one night to take Andy and the kids out to dinner, and when we got back, he'd put his fist through a wall." She swivelled in her chair, then pointed toward the end of the kitchen. "Right there, next to the door."

Matthew had shown me attention. Tall, skinny, and blond, he had been in foster care since he was a baby. He had taught me how to make homemade tattoos by blowing the ink out of a ballpoint pen, dabbing a needle tip into the glob, then stabbing it into his skin, a quarter inch or so deep, holding the pattern as steady as he could. He had blotched out his name across several inches of his forearm and had covered both biceps with an amalgam of blue and black peace signs, crosses, swastikas, and unfinished strokes.

As I stood beside Mrs. Leonard, my mind leapt to Matthew's defense. *He didn't break through the wall. He just sort of dented it.* But I said nothing out loud to correct the exaggeration.

"My God, what did you do?" the same woman asked.

"Well, we had to call the county. What do you think?" Mrs. Leonard retorted. "I'm not sure where he ended up, maybe MacLaren. Who knows what happened after that." She glanced at Jason, then me. "Children need to be accountable for what they do."

The two women said nothing.

"Did we ever talk about Lindsey?" Mrs. Leonard continued.

If they had, the story could never have grown cold. "She was nine, and she arrived in a full body cast. She wouldn't fit through the bedroom door. We had to put her in the family room."

I remembered the odor of Lindsey's rotting cast as it aged and soft-ened with her sweat. I was also nine years old when a social worker and two sheriff's deputies toted Lindsey into the house. Hiding in the hallway, I eavesdropped on Mrs. Leonard talking about her on the telephone. Lindsey's father had taken to raping her, and after she be-trayed him to a teacher, he beat her with a bat, breaking her arms, legs, ribs, and back, but leaving her skull intact.

A woman at the table looked over the half-wall that separated the kitchen from the room where the family watched television in the evenings, apparently trying to imagine a nine-year-old girl encased in plaster.

"How did she take a bath?" the woman asked, still peering into the next room.

"The kids and I had to wash her down with a sponge. Talk about a mess!" Mrs. Leonard paused, shook her head in disgust. "The county allowed her father to visit, as long as he stayed ten feet from her."

Before Lindsey's father arrived, Mrs. Leonard ordered me to my room and told me to pull the drapes over my bed. I did as she said, but when I heard the man's footsteps coming up the pavement, I turned to the window and glanced outside. Spotting me, the man threw me a peekaboo sort of grin. He and his girlfriend stayed for an hour. I waited for another half an hour, then left my room. Walking into the family room, I found Mrs. Leonard scrubbing the white Naugahyde couch where the man and his girlfriend had sat talking to Lindsey, who had been placed on a backyard lounge chair beneath the picture window on the other side of the room.

That night, lying in my bed, I thought of Lindsey's father, how he had discovered me spying from the window, and the secret that he and I now shared. Though I had done it once already to ward off the other man who arrived in my sleep, I double-checked the window latch, resecured the wooden stick that blocked the slide from opening, then tugged the curtains together as tightly as I could.

Several weeks later, the doctors cut Lindsey out of her casing and sent her back home to her father.

Done with Lindsey's story, one of table guests indulged herself. "How did you get these two little guys?" The woman smiled at Jason and me. I shifted my gaze, then was relieved when Mrs. Leonard turned to Jason.

"You came just after New Year's. That was almost six months ago." She shook Jason gently by the waist. "Right?" He shrugged but said nothing. "Oh, he's playing shy."

Then Mrs. Leonard looked at me, wrapped her arm around my backside, and pulled me closer. "Andy. We've kept you now for over two years." I watched as she glanced back at her guests. "You should see his mother . . . if she comes. Hope! Before they took him, they'd find her walking the streets at night, shrieking like a banshee. They'd arrest her, and then she'd be back at it in a couple days." I squirmed and she squeezed me tighter from behind.

"The social worker said they found the two of them in a motel in North Hollywood. Little thing had been hiding in a closet, eating cat food off a plate on the floor." She sipped her coffee, broke off a piece of cookie. "Some people shouldn't be mothers." Around the table, the two women nodded. I began fidgeting.

Mrs. Leonard shot me a look. "Stop bending your thumb like that!" She shook her head at the women. "He has got this nervous thing he does, twisting his thumb to his wrist. He'll sit for hours doing it. The social worker said he picked it up at MacLaren. I think it was with Hope."

It was a ten-year-old's compulsion, and the social worker was right. I had started it at MacLaren when my seven-year-old joints were still soft. Using my left hand, I took my right thumb, pressed it counterclockwise into my palm, and forced the digit flat against the wrist below it. The slightest anxiety was sufficient cause. Over time, the joint extended, creating a large notch and making it impossible to lay my right hand flat. No one ever asked why I kept doing it, or what was wrong. No one ever asked if holding my hand would help me stop.

Mrs. Leonard reached for my hand and pressed it on the table. "Look what he's done to the joint, the way it sticks out. The doctor said it was nothing." She paused, surveying her guests. "You know, both of them get Medi-Cal. The county gives them better medical care than my own children get. My husband's right, we live in a welfare state." Slowly, I slipped from her grasp.

Mrs. Leonard flipped through page after page describing a procession of children, whether they had pleased or disappointed her, and where they had gone, if she knew. While Jason and I looked on, each child's loss became the stuff of kitchen prattle. When the afternoon waned, the neighbors got up, sighed as they looked at Jason and me, and announced that they could never bring themselves to do it.

Still, Jason persisted.

THE LEONARDS' HOUSE was a maze of rules. Some rules were typical. Mrs. Leonard forbade children from chewing gum or whistling inside. She expected children to remember words like please, excuse me, and thank you. Other rules were less typical. Citing the ever-present Russian threat to the United States and to her home, Mrs. Leonard forbade the color red from everything—furniture, clothes, Christmas ornaments, even food when possible. Mrs. Leonard disapproved of dimes, because they portrayed Franklin Delano Roosevelt, the American president who had handed the Baltic states to Joseph Stalin at the end of World War II. The violation of any rule, typical or otherwise, was inevitably compared to what Mrs. Leonards' Baltic compatriots were enduring under the communist horde. Accordingly, a child who reached too far at the dinner table was acting like a "Russian pig," and one who interrupted an adult conversation was behaving like a "pinko."

Another house rule was that the guest room was strictly reserved for visitors and foster children. Dozens of children had used the room, though its white laminated desk, bookshelf that reached to the ceiling, and queen-size bed had never been designed for a child. A large closet occupied an entire wall, and Mrs. Leonard used the space to store old towels, stained bedsheets, and junk from lawn sales.

The Leonards were avid collectors. Saturday mornings, they toured the neighborhood yard sales, bartering, buying, and loading up their car with things that no one cared to keep but could not bear to throw away. Usually, by early afternoon, the Leonards returned to admire their orphaned bargains—a ceramic owl to go with those already displayed in the dining room, clothes for their own children or Jason and me, half-dead plants, or toys for upcoming holidays and birthdays. On weekdays, when there were no garage sales, they drove around the neighborhood on garbage nights, digging through people's trashcans. They were always especially proud of these treasures that they nabbed for free. Yet regardless of its source, everything found refuge in the guestroom's half-wanted clutter.

Mr. Leonard's salary as an electrical engineer must have been enough to sustain the family, but he and his wife were always on the lookout for ways to bring in extra cash. For several months, they tried breeding rabbits in the backyard. The animals were sold alive or, on occasion, butchered for food by the Leonards themselves in an abandoned playhouse they had built for their older daughter, Jessica. Hundreds of the rodents resided and multiplied in dozens of low-slung wire cages behind the pool, until an anonymous neighbor called the Health Department and complained about the swarms of flies that feasted on their droppings.

Mrs. Leonard spent years describing how rude the inspector had been and how his behavior was only proof that we were living in danger of approaching "communistic" rule, which she inevitably linked to treachery by Senator Edward Kennedy, who she insisted was secretly aligned with Fidel Castro. Yet, threatened with fines and possible prosecution, the Leonards surrendered their rabbits, selling as many live ones as they could before slaughtering the remainder. Unaware of what husband and wife were doing, I accidentally interrupted them in the playhouse. Mr. Leonard yelled not to come in, but I was already at the door. The two of them stood together, covered in blood, a pile of skinned carcasses in the corner.

In place of the rabbits, Mr. Leonard applied his talents as an engineer and transformed the garage into a private television-repair shop. Left alone to find something to occupy her excess energies, Mrs. Leonard resolved to turn her rummaging into a homegrown business. She increased the intensity of her travels to garage sales and her patrols through neighbors' garbage cans. She returned with trash bags stuffed with stained blouses, outgrown jeans, shoes, socks, and discarded but perfectly useful household items. She placed free advertisements in *The Recycler,* a local flyer distributed at news kiosks, 7-Elevens, and liquor stores. Almost immediately, strangers began arriving at the house in search of a good deal.

Pantyhose were a particularly popular item. As Mrs. Leonard explained incredulously, certain neighbors had the wasteful habit of discarding nylons after only a single leg had been snagged and ruined. With an eye for profit, she collected pairs of the closest-matching colors, cut off the bad legs, then taped the remaining shanks together at the crotch. She called the new sets her Mix and Match Collection. Yet her capitalist flare burned brighter once she understood the value of specialization. She decided that household goods had to go, and when she examined her remaining inventory, genius struck: One man's garbage could be her haute couture. If she combined single articles of clothing into larger outfits, she could charge a premium. Around Halloween, she added wigs and hats to transform her simple outfits into entire costumes of crap that she sold at a hefty profit.

Business was brisk, and Mrs. Leonard bragged over dinner that she could sell anything. What not even she could sell, she offered to her own children and me. Though we did our best to decline, an all-out refusal risked pricking her anger, and we accepted what we felt we had to. Whether they came from the neighbors' trash or elsewhere, she deemed some items too special for wearing around the house. She strictly reserved long pants for school and short pants for play. Long pants were more likely to rip at the knees, and as Mrs. Leonard said, laughing, "Skin heals, but cloth takes a needle and thread."

As business grew, she expanded her weekend purchases and late-night garbage raids to include homes beyond the immediate neighborhood, a fact that relieved me somewhat, knowing the clothes that she offered me to wear were less likely to be recognized. However, the Leonards' younger daughter, Becky, was not as lucky. The family next door had not escaped Mrs. Leonard's midnight rummaging. The father was an ophthalmologist, while the mother taught at a local private school. Their son was roughly Becky's age, and when she reached her teenage years, Becky's crush on the boy became obvious. One afternoon, shortly after she had entered ninth grade and I had started seventh, she and I were sitting on the front lawn with the neighbor boy when he noticed that the shirt she was wearing had once been his. Laughing at his discovery, he exclaimed that he recognized the stain that had caused his mother to throw it out in the first place. I watched as the girl bravely denied that the shirt could have possibly belonged to him, arguing that she too could have purchased the same item and was just as capable of spilling spaghetti sauce on it as he was.

With me already in Christopher's room and with Jessica and Becky sharing a room of their own, only the guest room remained when Jason arrived. For weeks, the room had been quiet, waiting for another lost child. Younger children had had trouble finding the bathroom at night, and although they tried desperately, they were unable to control their bladders, humiliating themselves in the sheets and on the floor. The smell of urine, sour and old, lingered in the guest room's mattress. Mrs. Leonard sprayed vinegar on the bed and carpet and eventually began ordering deodorants from industrial catalogs. Yet nothing masked the scent. Finally, she resorted to keeping the door closed, abandoning the room and its rancid air until the county delivered another child.

In the hour before Jason arrived, Mrs. Leonard cleared a closet shelf to make a space for him—no child had ever asked for more. Sooner or later, she might throw away the garbage; but the child would almost certainly go first.

Still, Jason ignored his guest-room status and wanted to stay. He and I never discussed it, but he wanted the label that I never did. He wanted the safety that he believed would come with it. He wanted to be called permanent. I think the Leonards thought of keeping him for his efforts.

At dinner, Mr. Leonard required the children to hold their freshly scrubbed hands over the table for his inspection before eating. He ordered children who failed his test to walk around the table, extend their hands to him again, and remain still as he rapped their backside with his hand or a burnt kitchen spatula. As much as an hour before dinner, Jason would ask Mrs. Leonard for a clipper to begin cutting his cuticles and digging at his nails.

"If you only use the hot water, it makes your fingers soft," Jason pointed out, as he stood at the bathroom counter with his palms pressed flat in the sink. He lifted his pink hands from the scalding water, and I watched as he shoved the curved point of the clipper's small, metal file under his nail and began poking. He winced but continued.

"It hurts, but after a while you can do it." Finished with one finger, he proudly extended it to me, displaying the skin he had managed to scrape out and had left at the nail's edge in a pulpy, reddish lump.

"If you make them bleed, just keep washing them," he explained, moving on to the next finger. "You have to get the blood out, or it looks like dirt when it dries."

I regularly bit my nails, which only enraged the Leonards. "You're just defying us," Mrs. Leonard snapped, as I waited beside her husband with my hands in front of me. Lifting the spatula, Mr. Leonard glanced up at me. "Good show, mister. You keep that up, and we'll just do it again." Trying to hide my habit, I also began soaking my hands under searing water, carving down to the quick, making space to cut away the nail's ragged edges. Yet, my attempts were rarely successful.

"Didn't I do a good job?" Jason asked, as Mr. Leonard leaned over the table and examined Jason's short fingers, cherry red from the bathroom.

"Yes, Jason. You got them good and clean." Mr. Leonard spared Jason the swipe across his backside. "Let's be sure to see the same tomorrow, young man."

After dinner, in front of the television, Jason made a nightly habit of quietly crawling into Mrs. Leonard's ample lap.

"Oh, Jason. It's my time now. My show is on," she answered, pulling her body around him to see the screen and patting him on the back.

Yet Jason stayed. Folding himself into a ball of pajamas, skin, and bone, he pressed deeper into her embrace, muttering sleepily, "Hold me. Take me. Keep me."

CHRISTOPHER ADMITTED TO opening the door. It was late, and he had been the last one to bed. By sheer chance, Mr. Leonard was away, testing a weapon system in the Arizona desert. Other than her own children, Jason, and me, Mrs. Leonard was alone in the house.

The night was quiet when Christopher thought he heard something at the window above my bed. He was frightened at first, lying still, thinking what to do, hoping that the disturbance was only the wind or maybe just a bad dream. Yet whatever was there refused to go away. Finally, he slipped from his sheets, crept across the darkened room, paused at the drapes to confront what was on the other side of the glass, but then thought better of it and turned toward the hall. Quietly, he walked past the living room and peered out at the night from the safety of the kitchen. Seeing nothing, he cracked open the front door, which suddenly shoved at him as my mother pushed her way inside.

She had to have known that there was not much time. Still, according to Christopher, she was calm, politely asking if I was sleeping, reassuring him not to be afraid and that she would not be long. As she entered the darkened bedroom, I woke. She turned on the desk light, gently said hello, then sat on the bed beside me. She told me not to worry, that she would be gone before anything happened. She glanced at Christopher, who ran to retrieve his mother. In the time that it took Mrs. Leonard to arrive, my mother possessed the moment entirely. She asked silly, motherly things. Was I ready for school in the morning? Did I remember the school where I went when we lived together? Why did Mrs. Leonard insist on cutting my hair that way? In the brief quiet, she proved that no matter how a judge, a social worker, or the Leonards defined her, she remained my mother. She was as I remembered and as I wanted her—confident and strong, there for me alone.

She looked to the door and smiled at the sound of the house waking, readying itself to overcome us. We listened to Christopher pleading at the end of the hall. "She only wanted to see him. I didn't know it was her." Together, my mother and I waited for Mrs. Leonard to appear.

For a moment, Mrs. Leonard froze and stared at the two of us from the bedroom threshold. Then she exploded into the same scream, again, again, and again: "Get out! Get out! Get out!" She shoved Christopher to the side, and the teenager retreated to the hallway where his two sisters and Jason had gathered to watch. "Get out!" she screamed with each step as she approached the bed.

My mother glanced at her briefly, wrapped her arms around me tightly, and whispered fiercely several times, "You are my boy. Remember, you are my boy." Then she got up, strode past Mrs. Leonard, and left.

When the front door shut, Mrs. Leonard lingered before marching out to secure the locks. Her three children followed, leaving Jason behind at the bedroom threshold. He stared at me, and in that moment between us, something reminded me of MacLaren whenever we saw another boy called from the line because an aunt or an uncle had unexpectedly arrived. How we eyed the boy when he came back, wishing that we had been the one to have been claimed, if only for a few minutes. Staring back at Jason in the doorway, I felt good for being the one who had been claimed that night, for being the boy whose mother had searched him out and had found him. Without a word, Jason ran down the hallway to join the others.

"Andy!" Mrs. Leonard screamed from the far end of the house. "Get down here now."

Slowly I put my feet on the bedroom floor and, in my pajamas, walked toward the noise. Passing through the kitchen, I saw the two girls tugging at the family room drapes, then found Mrs. Leonard, Christopher, and Jason in the living room. The boys were on their knees, double-checking the wooden bars that secured the wall of sliding glass doors that looked out onto the backyard. Mrs. Leonard paced back and forth, convincing herself that something was staring back at her from the motionless shadows.

"She's right there." She pointed at the glass. "Right there, next to the pool."

Christopher glanced up, surveyed the darkness around the unruffled water. "There's no one out there, Mom."

"Really?" she roared sarcastically. "Tell me, what imbecile let her inside in the first place?" Eyeing my reflection in the glass, she turned. "Were you just planning on standing there like a stick all night?"

"No," I whispered nervously.

"Is that all you have to say?" She marched past me, continuing to secure the house. "Maybe we should all just sit and wait until she busts in again. Would you like that?"

With his mother out of sight, Christopher stood up. Jason settled on his haunches. The older boy looked at the two of us and whispered to keep his voice from escaping the room, "Looks like one of you won't be here much longer." His mother's voice on the kitchen phone interrupted him, and we listened as she asked for the police.

Then Christopher pushed his way past me to join his sisters in the other room. Avoiding Jason's eyes, I stared into the backyard.

Over two years had passed since I had been taken from her, and with a judge branding me a permanent foster child, my mother had to have known that the county had no intention of giving me back. That night, despite what Mrs. Leonard told the police, my mother had not come to steal me. Had she wanted to, there had already been plenty of opportunities—after or before school, around the neighborhood, or during a scheduled weekday visit when Mrs. Leonard was certain to be alone. The police took over an hour to calm Mrs. Leonard as she cried hysterically, claiming that my mother cleverly knew that her husband was away, and that she was still outside, watching. Yet my mother's purpose that night had been simpler. Defying the boundaries of fifteen-minute telephone calls and one-hour visits, my mother had done what so many do every night—checked on her son as he lay in his bed in the dark.

The next morning, I woke thinking that she could not have left me for good. I remembered her earliest promise, the one that she had made in the shadow of a white clapboard house across from the emptiness of a plowed stretch of farmland—that she would be back, that if I waited long enough, if I were a good and patient boy, she would return to find me. In the quiet of every morning that followed, I waited. And on dawns that felt too lonely, I repeated the secret refrain that she whispered in the chaos of that one evening.

I am her boy. I am her boy.

Chapter Ten

⧜

AFTER THAT NIGHT, something changed in Jason. With three weeks left in June, he began anxiously, even insistently, asking Mrs. Leonard what was going to happen at the end of the school year. Trailing her through the kitchen, refusing to accept her vague replies, he quizzed her in dozens of different ways. "Am I going to go to summer school? Can I pick my own teacher for next year in fifth grade? What do you do for Christmas?"

Listening from the bedroom, even I could hear the one unspoken question that repeated itself underneath the slew of Jason's inquiries: "Are you keeping me?" Alone at my desk, my face reddening at the embarrassing reminder of my own uncertainty, I quickly got up and shut the door.

Several days later, Jason learned from Christopher that he had belonged to the Indian Guides program with his father when he was younger. That evening at dinner, the ten-year-old looked at Mr. Leonard over the table and asked, "Dad, do you think you could take me?" Bewildered that the question could even be posed, the man looked dumbly at the boy. I held my eyes on my plate, waiting for the silence to pass and the subject to change. When the conversation finally resumed and I looked up, Jason was still staring at the man.

During our afternoon exiles to the pool or the front yard, he and I had never talked much. But now I noticed that he had begun wandering off alone. Hunting for him on a hot Saturday afternoon, I found him at the side of the house, under the Leonards' bedroom window, hunched and perspiring in the dirt, clutching a handful of Popsicle sticks.

I recognized the sticks from school. The playground coach had given them to us to make jewelry boxes. Doing as I was told, I had pasted the sticks together, one over the other, and finished the wooden box and lid. Though the young teacher had told us to take the gifts home to our mothers, I had no idea what to do with mine. The idea of giving the project to Mrs. Leonard was unbearable. Carrying the box back from school, I stopped at a neighbor's house, rushed up the steps to the porch, dropped the gift at the front door, and ran back down to the street.

Apparently Jason had kept what he made. Maybe he had even planned on presenting it to Mrs. Leonard. But in the end, not even he had the strength to replace his mother so completely. Sorrow weakened him, and he pulled the project apart.

Making room for me, Jason stood up. With the two of us blocking the narrow pathway, I knelt to examine his new work. Against the house wall, the broken sticks from the playground now marked row after row of graves with rounded wooden tops. Twigs fenced and protected the necropolis. I looked up at Jason standing behind me in the sunlight.

"Did you bury anything?"

"Mostly bees and flies. I found the dead flies under the windows, and the bees drowned in the pool." He rested his hands on his hips and surveyed his domain.

I scanned Jason's tiny graves, the size of thumbprints, lined in a dry grid, one after another. The cemetery was better than the plastic toy that the Leonards had given him for his birthday. This creation invited curiosity, pleading with me to come closer, to look again. Was everyone buried alone, or were there families lying together? How many people filled the space? What were their names? Had any died as children? Gazing down, I showered my own imagination on the flat earth, before glancing up again at the boy behind me.

"I saved a spot for my mom and sister. See?" Jason pointed toward two sticks in the middle of the square of earth. The little plots beside the house were the only mention he had ever made of his family.

My eyes returned to the ground, but suddenly hunting for mistakes, I got up and pulled away. The mounds of dirt were too big for his grave markers, I noted. Cemeteries had grass and trees. More than that, no two headstones were ever exactly alike.

"Who cares about bees and flies?" I asked caustically, then giving him no time to answer, quickly added, "You're not supposed to be here. They'll find out, and she'll get mad."

Ignoring me, he sank to his knees. Pushing several Popsicle sticks deeper into the ground and straightening others, he managed a soft retort. "So what?"

I looked down the narrow path. Afraid that the Leonards might hear us through their window, I glanced at Jason crouched at my feet, then began stepping away. "It doesn't look like anything," I snickered under my breath. "You better not let her see it."

Jason had to have known the risk he was taking in choosing the side of the house. The long, cramped walkway was crowded with junk that Mr. Leonard had collected from his repair work. Mrs. Leonard complained about it endlessly, calling it a fire hazard. At spots, the debris barely allowed enough space for a foot to pass. Jason's graveyard might go unnoticed for days, but its discovery was inevitable.

I had found safer places for my secrets. After school or on weekends, I disappeared for hours into the wide field that faced the house. Cornered by two roads and bordered at another side by a swaying line of eucalyptus, the tract of empty ground stretched for acres. Thick grass covered the earth, reaching as high as my knees. Walking deep into the green felt like wading through water and left only a narrow, broken trail in my wake.

Flat on my back, I was immersed completely, aware of only grass and sky. I remember the watchful crows, dozens of them, flying on heavy wings, pushing their own way through the air, black and confident. They swooped and glided over me, cawed raucously at one another, but somehow always knew enough to land together. With their dark and glassy eyes, they surveyed immeasurable distance, always protecting the bit of ground and sky that they claimed for themselves.

There, alone in the grass, I remembered my mother's promise: "Don't forget that I can always find you . . . that I'll always know where you are."

Staring at the crows above, I whispered back, "Then where are you? How could you have let this happen?"

The field would have protected Jason's creation of Popsicle sticks and dirt, but he longed for discovery. Along the side of the house in half secrecy, Jason confronted his loss, then dared to do what I refused to do. He left his pain visible, exposed.

THE MONDAY MORNING after I had found Jason crouched in the pathway beside the house, he and I left for school as we always did. We carried lunches in paper bags on which Mrs. Leonard had written our names in an elaborate script that always drew unwanted attention. Shoulder to shoulder, we walked the sidewalk in front of the neighbors' house, then rounded the corner. We stopped there, reached over the low brick fence, and fed their dog the sandwiches that we had carried with us for a few hundred feet. The dog's name was Rusty, and his skin hung on his bones.

Before Jason arrived, the neighbors had stopped by the Leonards' to show off their new puppy, fresh from the veterinarian, with a clipped and taped tail.

"He wasn't what we wanted," the woman neighbor complained,

as I sat cross-legged on the kitchen floor with the puppy in my lap. "We wanted something bigger. The shop said he'd grow to your knee and weigh about fifteen pounds." She grimaced. "He won't scare anything. But we were tired of looking from shop to shop and hunting the paper. So we settled on this one."

Mrs. Leonard and the two neighbors paused to consider the puppy and me. Finally, Mrs. Leonard shook her head and snickered, "Well, you get what you get, I guess."

Listening, I stayed quiet as I held the animal and hoped he would behave.

Over the months, Rusty grew out of being a puppy. Whenever I stepped into the Leonards' backyard, the dog managed to hear me. Within minutes, he began his sharp bark, calling at me from behind the yard's cinderblock wall.

Jason and I felt sorry for Rusty. The dog was perpetually hungry and always snapped at the food that we offered, nipping our fingertips with his teeth. That particular morning, his hunger got the better of him, and, overwhelmed by the sandwiches and attention, he jumped his fence. Once outside, he began wandering the street, confused about where to go next. While I just stared, Jason yelled at me to chase after the dog and not to let him run away. Jason and I dropped our backpacks and, after a few tries, managed to corner and catch Rusty by the collar and drag him back to the house. We scrambled as we lifted him up and over the fence, our combined strength barely sufficient to get him back in his yard.

"Do you think anyone saw us?" I asked nervously, not knowing exactly who I meant.

Jason grinned brightly. "Not unless you're counting the dog."

He laughed, and I smiled at his joke. If either of us were given a dog, we promised each other, we would love it better and never leave it outside, alone.

Then, as I did every school morning since Jason had arrived, I turned on him. "I'm going." I walked a few yards, until, conscious of his presence behind me, I snapped around with a sharp stare. "I told you . . . stop following me." I watched as he clutched his backpack and halted. Ignoring him as best I could, I hurried down the block, watching for him from the corner of my eye and staying ahead of him the whole way to the school's gate.

From the beginning, I had been relieved when the school put Jason in another fourth-grade classroom. After that, I made sure that he and I always arrived separately. During the day, I never looked for him.

In the early chill of morning recess, I hid, shivering in the boys' restroom, wearing a dirty windbreaker that reached to my knees and was expected to last. I had no idea where Jason ate lunch. Did he sit with the other children at noon? Or had he discovered a secret place like the one I had found, away from the lunch area, where I crouched with my hands around my knees, between the bushes and a classroom wall? I never asked. No one asked.

Jason was an uncomfortable bridge between the Leonards' house and the elementary school, between what I knew about myself and what others could never know. He and I were not brothers, not even friends. We may have lived in the same house, but his name was different from mine, and the Leonards were not our parents. Jason threatened to expose the truth about me, about my mother, about all that had happened. If classmates felt responsible for fights and divorces among their parents, I felt responsible for even more. I was the boy who had not listened to his mother's warnings. I was the one who had not helped her. I was the one who had pulled away. By my tenth birthday, my life had grown thick with lies, too thick to include anyone, least of all him.

I never heard Jason's responses to the impossibly simple questions from classmates about where he had come from or why he had arrived in the middle of the school year. He may have spoken honestly, though I doubt it. I imagine that he answered the questions with a lie and a smile, convincing himself that he was telling the truth or that he could make a new one. When the school day was done, and the afternoon bell released us, I never waited for him. Even that afternoon, with only a few days left in school, I was careful to walk back to the house alone.

Whether rescuing a dog that we had tempted into the street or collecting the pieces of a capsized toy from the pool's floor, Jason and I shared small moments of chaos, then parted. Our own childhood disasters had brought us together in the first place, and we were overjoyed by the chance to fix a problem that had not outgrown us. Saving Rusty from the street was a rare moment of honest affection between two boys who shared so much and so little. Alone on an empty sidewalk, we understood each other. He told me a joke and made me smile. Briefly, we captured what it meant to love something: "To never leave it outside, alone."

After that morning with Rusty, what I remember most is Jason's absence.

THE SAME DAY that Rusty jumped his fence, somewhere on the three blocks between the Leonards' house and the elementary school, Jason disappeared.

By late afternoon, Mrs. Leonard had called the police, and they came in crushing force. Preparing for her guests, she laid out Kool-Aid and snickerdoodles on the kitchen table. Like everything else, she baked in quantity, tripling or quadrupling recipes into enormous piles of egg and sugary dough. Rolling hundreds of gluey globs between her palms, she smashed the balls against baking pans, leaving the imprints of her fingers to bake and harden. Scraping the burnt edges over the sink with a knife, she complained that the oven was too hot. The task took hours, but the cookies lasted for weeks. The Kool-Aid was ready in seconds.

Sweating in black uniforms and the early summer heat, dozens of men invaded the house, coming and going as they pleased in a thuggish hunt for the boy. Radios blared broken conversations. Black shoes left scuff marks on the kitchen floor. Flashlights glanced through closets, under beds, into the crawl space beneath the floorboards. Officers swarmed the backyard, then spread across the neighborhood. When Jason failed to turn up, more squad cars swung up to the house, crowding the street, their headlights pointed into the front yard.

Then came the helicopters, hovering over the field across the street, pounding the air like huge, predatory flies, threatening the spot where I hid from the Leonards some afternoons. Spotlights swept over the tall grass to the sound of Jason's name falling from the sky. Everything was noise. Sheer force would prevail and smoke out the boy who had run away.

When a cluster of men circled and questioned me, Mrs. Leonard stood among them, watching me with her arms folded. I was the other foster boy, so I must have seen where Jason had gone. We went to the same school. We were in the same grade, lived in the same house. We walked to school and back together, didn't we? Surely I had seen him during the school day. Had I helped him run away? I stared back at the men, frightened, able to tell them the only truth that I knew: that I had no idea why or where Jason had gone.

After several hours, Jason's exhausted pursuers seemed to realize that both the search and the boy were unnecessary. The thump from the helicopters faded, the mass of squad cars dispersed. The last policeman in the house used the Leonards' telephone to call Jason's mother, telling her to contact them if he turned up. Mrs. Leonard thanked him with a plastic bag stuffed with cookies, offered him more Kool-Aid, which he declined. With a last look at me, he shook his head and reached for the front door.

"We'll do what we do with the others," he remarked to Mrs. Leonard, stepping onto the porch. "We'll issue the arrest warrant for him. Sometimes we find them, sometimes we don't." He straightened the hat on his head, then turned to join his partner, who was already waiting in the car.

No anguished relatives appeared on television, begging for Jason's return. No one worried that he might have been taken. If anything, over the course of the afternoon, the Leonards had grown increasingly irritated with him. Jason would not be any further inconvenience. He had disappeared on his own, and if he were lucky, he would find his own way back.

With the last of the officers gone, Mrs. Leonard told me to rub the scuff marks from their shoes off the linoleum. She cooked a late dinner for Mr. Leonard as I crawled across the kitchen floor, dabbing a dishcloth in lighter fluid and erasing the black rubber marks at her feet.

About a week later, a single squad car drove up to the house. An officer got out and escorted Jason inside. Jason had spent nearly three days hiding, but no one had been looking for him. With nowhere else to go, he showed up at his mother's place. She let him stay for the afternoon, but by nightfall, for whatever reason, she telephoned the police and told them to come get him.

The Leonards called to tell the county that they would keep him, but only until another foster-care placement was found. Listening from the bedroom door, I needed no one to tell me not to do what Jason had done. I knew not to run. I knew it from the parade of social workers, who knew little more than my name and age, and from the parade of lawyers and judges, who knew even less. I knew it from the children who came and left the house as though they belonged nowhere at all. I knew it from Mrs. Leonard's taunting response when one of the other county children or one of her own threatened to run away: "Go ahead." There was a mistake in thinking you mattered and a terrible penalty for demanding to be claimed.

A week after Jason returned, over a bowl of breakfast cereal, Mrs. Leonard told him that he would be leaving in a few hours. He and I were still in our pajamas. She grinned with anger, recalling the embarrassment that Jason had caused her and her husband. She must have known before that morning, but she had waited until the last minute to hurl the secret at him. From across the kitchen table, I glanced at Jason, who sat shaken into stillness, revealing nothing but the tremor in his hand, still wrapped around a spoon.

"I suggest you get moving, mister," Mrs. Leonard added. "You won't try that stunt again."

Jason spent the morning in the Leonards' guest room, where he had lived for nearly six months. He laid his belongings across the bed and floor. He folded and packed what was his—several new shirts and a pair of pants, along with the cargo boat from his birthday, all of which he had acquired while living at the house. Mrs. Leonard brought him several trash bags for his things, though one bag was enough. In the middle of packing, she came into the room and surprised him with a stuffed toy.

I looked in from the doorway and watched him laying his clothes inside the bag. "Why did you run away?" I whispered.

He glanced at me blankly. "What?" he asked, though I knew that he had heard what I said.

"Why did you run away?" I repeated.

He dipped his boat into the trash bag, then answered, "Because."

I retreated to my bedroom and, alone, finished his sentence in my head: *Because you thought they'd come running after you.*

Shortly before noon, a woman whom Jason had never seen before arrived to take him to another home that he had never known. Like the social worker who had taken me from my mother years before, this woman carried awesome, anonymous authority. Her shoes, skirt, and blouse were matched to modest imperfection. Her manner was crisp and professional as she and Mrs. Leonard exchanged pleasantries. Her words were brief and practiced, nearly mechanical. The woman had met the Leonards before, when she had come to get other children from their house. Still, she declined Mrs. Leonard's offer of coffee.

"Where is he?"

She looked at me, apparently thinking that I might be Jason. Caught in the woman's sight, I froze.

"Oh, the boy you want is in the guest room," Mrs. Leonard explained. "Everything's ready to go."

A long hallway divided the bedrooms on the right side of the house. Along both walls, Mrs. Leonard had hung family photographs of her own children, Jason, and me together. I followed the woman and Mrs. Leonard, as they walked silently down the hall. Inside the room, Jason had been well prepared. He was freshly bathed and clean. His hair was oiled and neatly combed. His shirt was tightly tucked into his beltless pants. Yet he fidgeted with his fingers.

"Did you get everything?" the woman asked.

Standing anxiously beside the plastic bag that contained all that was his, he nodded. "Yes, ma'am."

The stranger inquired further, in a parental tone, "Have you said good-bye and thanked everyone, like you're supposed to?"

"Yes, ma'am, I did."

He quickly looked to Mrs. Leonard, and for the first time since he arrived at the house, I heard him use her proper name. "Thank you, Mrs. Leonard, for letting me stay." Then he held his smile as she tersely answered, "You're welcome, young man."

Jason was cooperative, still trying to please, hoping somehow to overcome the circumstances around him. I think he thought that someone might still save him. At this last moment, he seemed to think that someone—someone who loved him—might still step forward and change everything.

The woman motioned the boy toward her. He took a step, and she rubbed her hand on his back as if to say, "This will only hurt a little." Then, with the smooth ease of a scalpel, she excised him from the house.

The woman's small car was parked on the street. She strode quickly across the middle of the lawn, leaving Jason to trudge behind, struggling with his trash bag of possessions. She opened the trunk, put Jason's bag inside, and unlocked the passenger door for him. Jason climbed in and sat down, looking at his feet. The woman latched the seat belt across his lap. Taking care not to catch a hand or finger, she slowly shut the door. Other than a quick glance out the window, Jason fixed his eyes on the space ahead.

Jason's taking was nearly silent. No one fought for him. No one cried out and said it was wrong. No one said they would remember him. No one admitted that he had meant anything at all. As at the scene of some roadside accident, no one knew what to do, except to stare at the victim and at his pain.

Mrs. Leonard gave a stiff smile, exposing her thick teeth. She waved perfunctorily. Abruptly, before the car had pulled away, she walked back inside. Standing alone, I waited for the car to turn the corner, watching as the two figures inside shrank, then disappeared.

In that speck of time, standing there at the curb, I understood what Jason and I shared. He and I were foster children, and we would never be far apart. I could have been in that car as easily as he was. Like him, I could expect no more than watchful bystanders. My mother had given me my one extraordinary act on a Saturday morning in the street, when I had pulled from her arms. There would be no more courageous, exemplary acts on my behalf. No one but she would ever again step forward to claim me.

Chapter Eleven

❦

After Jason left, more foster children arrived at the house. Social workers dropped off babies of every size and color. By the middle of fifth grade, I had learned to cradle the heads of the most fragile infants, to change their diapers, to feed and burp them, then to rock them tenderly asleep.

Though I have forgotten if there was a reason, mostly girls flooded through the house. A sixteen-year-old named Susanna arrived. I hungered for Susanna's attention, and she encouraged me to read. I checked out books from the school library. My favorites were Roald Dahl's stories of young boys who found rescuers, like *James and the Giant Peach* and *Charlie and the Chocolate Factory*. Susanna wrote poetry and helped me enter my own little poem in my school's writing contest, for which I won first prize:

> The lion that we see
>   is as proud and fierce as can be.
> Yet, he sits behind his bars
>   and dreams of jungle nights with stars.

Then, like the other children from the county, Susanna was suddenly gone.

Some of the children frightened me. An angry, dark-haired girl took Susanna's place. Threatening to cut her wrists, she locked herself in the bathroom one evening. Listening to the girl's screams from my bedroom, I rocked on my bed, remembering my mother hurting herself in our own bathroom years before. This girl stayed less than three weeks.

Around the beginning of sixth grade, a pair of blonde sisters arrived. One girl was seven, the other was eight, and their father had molested them both. On the way to school, next to Rusty's fence, the seven-year-old explained sexual intercourse between a man and a little girl. From Lindsey in her cast, and from MacLaren before that, I had known that evil of that kind existed. But hearing it directly from someone who was even younger than I made it more horrifying than I had imagined. For the remaining weeks that she and her sister were in the house, I did what I could never to be alone with either of them.

Among the boys, I remember only a few. A teenager who was a year or two older than the Leonards' fifteen-year-old son arrived, but he spent most of his time alone. Several boys around Jason's age also came. None of them stayed as long as Jason had. None of them made the claims that he had, to the house or to the Leonards.

Around the end of elementary school, as best as I can recall, foster children stopped coming. Mrs. Leonard never said anything to me, never warned me in advance. She simply left me to notice. Yet, once I had noticed, I was too frightened to ask what had happened, or more importantly, why I alone remained. When her neighbors and children inquired about the emptiness of the house, she simply replied, "Because this is my time."

From Mrs. Leonard's sharp stare across the room, I understood what I needed to know. I was a twelve-year-old boy who had overstayed his visit. No one said when my mother would come back, whether they would help her, or whether she would be left to do it alone. But this was the house that she knew, the address that she could find. This was the place where she had left me last, and of all places, this was the one that she and I still shared. I had to wait. I had to hold on as best I could.

BY THE END of elementary school, Mrs. Leonard's time for other foster children may have ended, but the time for her rage had only begun. The most insignificant annoyance could rouse her anger, and once provoked, her emotions became impulsive, spasmodic. Two years had passed since my mother had burst into the house in the middle of the night, and I now watched as my foster mother became as unpredictable as the woman whom she had replaced.

I learned quickly that anything could provoke her wrath. I might have forgotten to empty a wastepaper basket or to wring out a washcloth after taking a bath. I might have scuffed her kitchen floor with my rubber sneakers or left a pair of balled socks on the bedroom floor. I might have made an expression that amounted to a twelve-year-old's challenge. Or I might have committed no offense at all.

Around the house, I competed with her own children to find things that might appease her. Saturday mornings when she left for garage sales, I rushed about the house with them, to dust, vacuum, and scrub whatever I could. When she returned, I understood that the child who showed the least would be the most vulnerable. As the youngest and smallest in the house, I was the one who nearly always came up short. Each weekday morning before I left for sixth grade, I rubbed her shoulders and back as she read her newspaper. When she had dinner guests over, I volunteered to deliver elaborate meal prayers, thanking God and her for all that both had given us.

When Mrs. Leonard's rages did come, the matches were hardly even. Weighing a spindly seventy pounds, I stood four foot nine against her five foot ten, two-hundred-plus pounds. She lorded it over me, bending to meet my eyes, squinting her own in fury. Digging into my arms or grabbing at my face, she screamed that the foster child in front of her was ungrateful, lazy, obnoxious, confrontational, stupid, and undeserving. With her hand at my ear or at the base of my neck, she pulled me to the floor and through rooms.

In those moments of hate, an intimacy existed between her and me. The Russians, the children's camp outside Dachau, and the insatiable hunger that she had endured at last found their object. Every brutality, every savagery that she had known found its satisfying release. Refusing to forgive the vulnerability she had suffered as a young girl, she imposed it on me, then did her best to show me how it had felt. Yanked alongside her, trapped as much as she was by her rage, I was the foster boy whom she would not abandon. I was the child with whom she shared the most.

During one fit, she tossed me across the kitchen, ripping away part of the back of my ear. The tear was small, but the shock on her face was unmistakable when I sheepishly revealed it to her the next day. Alone with me in the bathroom, her immense body bent over my bony frame, she dabbed the wound with antiseptic. "Seriously, Andy, how *do* you manage to do these things?" she asked, as the iodine dripped from my chin down the sides of the sink. I looked up at her in the bathroom mirror, shrugged, and smiled stupidly. She glanced at me, her expression somewhere between an apology and denial.

Later, in my mid-teens, she adopted subtler but more potent tactics, attacking my ears only with spitting screams. Weekday afternoons, before the foster care department shut its doors for the day, she often reminded me that my county social worker could still be telephoned. "Just who do you think the county will believe, mister?" she asked, her hand resting on the kitchen phone. "What do you think happens when a child's case file is labeled 'defiant'?" She reserved evenings, nights, and weekends for the threat of MacLaren Hall, its seven-day, twenty-four-hour staff, and the "emergency placement" bed that waited for me.

On more than one occasion, like one of my nightmares, she woke me in the middle of the night. Flipping on the bedroom light switch, she informed me that she and her husband had had enough, that they had called the county, and that it was time for me to pack my things. As I staggered out of bed, she explained that a social worker would pick me up in the morning and take me back to the facility where I had come from. Before the sun rose, I dressed and collected what I could fit into my school backpack, though I remembered that children were forced to surrender whatever they had with them when they entered MacLaren's gates.

Shortly after dawn and before breakfast, Mrs. Leonard reentered my room and found me packed, dressed, and waiting on my bed. Her ritual continued. She would, she announced, allow me to go to school but she would use the day to decide exactly where I would spend the remainder of my childhood. When I returned from school in the afternoon, she would let me know whether I was staying or going. But never during the day did I break down, divulge the secrets that I had spent years protecting, and tell a teacher, student, counselor, or stranger about the judgment from a foster mother that awaited me in the afternoon. Approaching the Leonards' house at the end of the school day, I looked for the stranger's car parked at the curb, trying to see if Mrs. Leonard had made good on her threat and someone had arrived to take me.

Normally, Mrs. Leonard made a point of confronting me at the doorstep, making me ask permission to be let inside. In the same kitchen where she chatted with her neighbors, she required my abject apologies. Oral testimonies were usually insufficient. She claimed that she could only believe that I was genuinely sorry if I showed her, by begging for her forgiveness on my knees.

Giving in would have ended or at least shortened the ordeal. Yet I always refused, only prolonging Mrs. Leonard's verbal demands. She extracted exquisite explanations. Precisely why was I sorry? What had made me such a selfish boy? Why had I forced her to endure my intolerable misbehavior? I pleaded with her, offering whatever answer

I imagined might please her. Prior to granting me her mercy, she challenged me to list the reasons why I should continue to live in her house and why I was appreciative of her and her husband.

Occasionally, I challenged her more, refusing to stand and submit. Around the middle of sixth grade, I returned to the house in the afternoon. Quietly closing the front door, I heard Mrs. Leonard's footsteps thumping toward me from down the hall. When she blocked the way to my bedroom, I halted. With Becky and Christopher still riding their bikes home from junior high and Jessica at the senior high school even farther from the house, I was alone with her.

She stomped toward me, grabbed me by the back of my neck, and pulled me to my bedroom door. Barefoot and naked beneath a loose dress, she held me against her side. "Do you see that?" she demanded, then shoved me deeper into the room. "I said, do you see that?" She paced to my desk, snatching up a wet wad of clothing that she had deposited there. Returning, she clasped her hand around my biceps, shook me to ensure that she had my attention, then jabbed the wet lump against my chest.

She released me and waited as I unfurled what I had done. The day before, while tending to a model car with a bottle of glue, I had smudged the frayed legs of my cutoff shorts. Now, in my shaking hands, I held out the cutoffs, which had evidently gone through the wash once already. Instantly, I rushed to apologize.

"Sorry?" she screamed, jerking the shorts from my hands. "You think sorry works, mister?" She glanced at the gummy, finger-width lines, then seized me by the head. With me bent and stumbling under her hand, she dragged me out of the bedroom, then down the hallway and into the kitchen. "Sorry? You think you're sorry?" she bellowed through the empty house.

Arriving in the kitchen, where she had prepared the rest of her performance, I watched as she reached for a scrub brush from the counter, then crammed it into my hand. "No, I'll decide when you're sorry." Grabbing a waiting bucket, she threw the glue-sullied cutoffs inside. She thrust it toward me, and a cold wave of soapy water splashed across my face and down my shirt. With me clutching my cleaning tools and the house around us quiet, she paused and glanced out the kitchen window, then cocked her head at me with a questioning grin. "Why do you think I need you?"

Twelve years old, wet and frightened, I stared back at her cement eyes. Wanting to cry but refusing, I placed the bucket at my feet. *There had been someone who needed me,* I thought to say. Then, as if my mother and I were in that kitchen, confronting her substitute together, I shot back with what I had long known.

"You need me, because you like this."

Her face swelled, but before she could speak, I aimed again for the tender marrow of her rage. "What you're doing, right now, feels good to you. Doesn't it?"

Convulsing in response, she rushed for the safety of the kitchen telephone. "Last time I checked, mister"—she frothed, pawing through a drawer for my social worker's number—"you were the one whose mother went mental."

As the piece of paper shook in Mrs. Leonard's hand, I picked up the bucket, then went to the backyard and scrubbed the shorts until every smudge of glue was gone.

Years passed before I realized that Mrs. Leonard never actually called the county and never intended to have a social worker take me. Indeed, my social workers rarely came, anyway. During my first year with the Leonards, a county worker checked on me once every couple of months. But with the arrival of fourth grade and my ninth birthday, the county's visits dwindled to once every six months. In junior high school, annual visits had become the norm, the worker changing with each. By high school, the visits had ended almost entirely. When I finally asked Mrs. Leonard why my social workers had stopped coming to see me, she sniggered back, "I guess that's what you call being in a permanent placement."

Even if the social workers had come and spent time with me, what was I supposed to say? That Mrs. Leonard had a temper and yelled at me? That she shook me by the arm and pulled me by the ear? They praised her when they arrived, thanked her for being such an accommodating foster parent. They dropped children off, then swept them away without explanation. If they had believed me and responded, where would they have taken me? Back to MacLaren or to some place that I had never seen? In the end, social workers offered no protection. If anything—knowingly or not—they were simply weapons in Mrs. Leonard's arsenal.

When I challenged Mrs. Leonard, I never felt accomplished or brave. I trembled with fear. I never forgot that she could summon the county when she chose, and within hours a car could appear in front of the house ready to take me. Yet I was doing only what I thought I needed to do, defending my mother and myself as best I could, telling the world—even if no one beyond Mrs. Leonard's kitchen could hear—that I still knew that none of this was right.

Her own children warned me, "Why can't you just shut up? You'll only make it worse. She'll just single you out again." They themselves tried desperately, yet even they were not safe from their mother's rage. Confronted by it, they were mute, compliant when necessary. I had once seen Becky fall to her mother's feet, begging for leniency and forgiveness. Without the strength of someone else to defend, of another memory to hold, the woman's own children were more vulnerable than I was, because, unlike them, I understood where she ended and I began. Long before I arrived at MacLaren Hall or the Leonards' home, I had been taught what was right and what was wrong, what was sane and what was crazy, what was love and what was not.

OUTSIDE HER HOME and her private realm of foster care, Mrs. Leonard was exquisitely vulnerable. On the street, in a grocery store, in front of her own house, she was like a fat pinkish crab freshly plucked from its shell. People laughed, pointed at, or did worse to her. I saw it, and she did too.

At the end of sixth grade, my elementary school marked the leap into junior high with its Annual Culmination for Parents and Departing Students. The invitation arrived in the mail addressed to "The Parents of Andy Bridge." Dutifully, Mrs. Leonard and her husband announced that they intended to go.

"I want you in that suit of yours, young man," Mrs. Leonard called out from the kitchen after breakfast on the morning of the ceremony. "You better have hung that thing up."

The valued article of clothing, which Mrs. Leonard had awarded me, was a boy's orange three-piece leisure suit trimmed with heavy white stitching. Its origins were unknown. I wore it with a clip-on tie in blue and brown stripes, a button-down shirt in yellow and green, and a pair of black vinyl dress shoes with gold buckles.

"Did you hear me, young man?" Mrs. Leonard yelled again. "I'm not ironing that shirt a second time."

"I'm putting it on." Still in my pajamas, I tugged the suit's jacket and pants off the plastic hanger, then tossed both on the floor. I dropped to my knees, reached underneath my bed for the dress shoes.

"Don't forget the belt," she reminded me.

I ignored her, racking my head over what I had done with the misplaced shirt.

"I said . . . ," she paused, waiting for my reply.

"I won't forget," I grumbled back, tugging at an overstuffed dresser drawer, digging out the belt and my pair of brown socks. Returning to the closet, I spotted the shirt balled in a dusty corner. I snatched the item from the floor; its cloth was as wrinkled as a raisin. Crouched on the floor, I frantically wasted several minutes stretching at the collar, hoping that the body and arms could be hidden under the vest and jacket. *No good,* I thought. I gave the collar a final once-over, then looked up and saw Mrs. Leonard watching me from the bedroom door. My eyes welled with tears as I feebly lifted the shirt toward her.

"Oh, Andy," she grimaced. "Why can't you ever hang things up?" She marched toward me, shook her head, and pulled the shirt from my hand. I offered no excuse. She let out a reprimanding snort, held the shirt by its shoulders for a good look at the damage, then reached down and tousled my floppy hair. "Put on your pants and shoes." I watched from the floor as she left the room. "Andy, I'll be back in a minute. Let's just hurry up, OK?" she called warmly from the hallway.

I had had other reprieves from her anger, and hoped that this one would not be my last. Her rage was not always present, just always possible. I did as she said, pulled and zipped up the pants, slipped on the belt, then the shoes, and waited on the edge of the bed.

Several minutes later, she thudded back toward my bedroom and waved the crisp shirt through the doorway like a flag on a hanger.

"Thank you," I whispered, reaching for it. She smiled from the threshold and watched as I wrapped and buttoned the warm shirt around my chest. Finished, I looked up at her.

"Done?" she asked. "Well, aren't you just about the most handsome sixth-grader that I've ever seen?"

I looked down at myself, then glanced up at her smile. "Thank you."

"Well, you better get going." She motioned with her arm toward the hall. Halfway through the door, I felt her hand fall on my shoulder. I turned and she looked me in the face. "We do care about you," she whispered, pulling me closer to her.

Without thinking, I wrapped my arms around her sides. I held her because I was twelve years old and needed to hold someone. I had pulled from my mother's arms to survive, and if only for a moment in that bedroom, my survival seemed to depend on clutching this woman, regardless of who she was.

"It's hard to believe, you're graduating from sixth grade, getting ready for junior high school. . . ." She sighed over my head, as I pressed deeper into her warm belly. She squeezed back—a little too tight—while I clung to her with no intention of letting go. "Aren't you my little millstone?" She tapped her hands on my back, signaling me to let her loose, then led me onto the front porch.

"We'll see you later," she called from behind. "And stop worrying about that shirt," she scolded. Dressed in my orange suit, I turned and faintly smiled. She gazed at the late-morning sun before looking down at me. "Trust me, Andy. It's gonna be a good day."

Though I had kept variations of my old habits, I had become braver at school. During morning recess, I no longer hid in the bathroom but lingered in the school library or, when a teacher let me, stayed inside my classroom. Even though the free meal tickets had ended, I avoided the lunch tables, eating off to the side. I refrained from talking about home, never mentioned the Leonards or my mother. With my secrets carefully secured, school became a haven, and I had begun to succeed.

In fifth grade, I attracted the interest of Miss O'Malley, who made a point of commenting kindly on nearly every piece of schoolwork that I did. Then in sixth grade, at Miss O'Malley's request, my new teacher had me tested. Able to concentrate and score well, I was retracked from "delayed"—barely able to trace loaves of bread from a second-grade workbook—into an enriched curriculum.

More important, I began making friends. I was drawn mostly to outcasts, to those classmates with few friends themselves. Too timid to introduce myself, I always waited for someone to come to me.

During a sixth-grade recess, a fellow classroom lingerer approached me for the first time. Her name was Rachael Mackenstein. She was a studious girl with a small round face and a tuft of red, woolly hair. She wore a pair of old, thick, square glasses that resembled a set of ice cubes dangling in front of her eyes. She was unusually pale by California standards, and deep blue veins webbed around her neck and thighs. Rail thin and beleaguered by scoliosis, she lugged a spine brace that ran from her skull to her pelvis. A wrapping of headgear obscured her smile.

I liked Rachael for her gentleness. When classroom projects were doled out and students paired up, Rachael always waited, knowing that I would go unchosen and the teacher would be left to match her with me. She was patient, never selfish about claiming credit for projects we did together. She could not have found it easy, befriending a boy with so many secrets. When she asked me about my family and where I lived, she must have found it odd that the answers never quite fit. Still, she came as close as anyone at school had come to knowing me. And though I know she meant well, she could not have understood how a simple act of kindness could disturb my delicate balance of lies.

With barely a month of sixth grade left, to please Mrs. Leonard, I had chosen a final social studies project chronicling the history of the Soviet Union's territorial domination and its ever-expanding network of Siberian slave camps. I had titled the assignment "Freedom: Soviet-Style" and had only a few more camp locations left to designate. I had convinced Mrs. Leonard, a talented artist, to help me finish my poster-size map of the sprawling Russian empire to accompany my essay. My efforts had even secured her promise to draw several hapless inmates accompanied by a sadistic guard. Absorbed in my work, I ignored the doorbell when it rang through the house.

"Andy," the Leonards' younger daughter screamed from the foyer, drawling out her words. "You have a little visitor."

I listened from my bedroom desk, confident that it was a hoax and that no one knew where I lived.

"Oh, Andy," Becky repeated herself. "Someone's here to see you."

Relenting, I pushed away Joseph Stalin's biography and walked to the front of the house. In the middle of the foyer, Becky was grinning beside the door, opened only a crack. "Well, haven't we got a surprise for you," she exclaimed, then threw open the entrance to reveal Rachael waiting on the porch.

"Hi, Andy." Proud of surprising me, Rachael grinned.

"What do you want?" I grabbed the edge of the door, shielding the inside of the house.

Unaware of the depth of her intrusion, she teased me. "Oh, Andy. Don't be mad. Aren't you going to invite me in?"

"No. I'll see you tomorrow," I answered, then quickly tried shutting the door.

She giggled, blocking the way with her foot.

I struggled for several seconds, listening as she laughed and yelled at me through the gap. Then the ruckus did what I feared most. It summoned Mrs. Leonard from her evening television program. With her at the edge of the foyer, I froze. The only sign of Rachael was her sneaker wedged in the door.

"Andy, we always open our door to visitors," Mrs. Leonard scolded from the kitchen entrance. I waited a moment, hoping that either the girl on the porch or the woman in the hallway would retreat. Both held their ground. I cracked the door a few more inches. Mrs. Leonard's stare bored into me, demanding that I widen the entrance entirely.

Beneath the lintel, Rachael beamed. She and Mrs. Leonard exchanged glances, then with Mrs. Leonard's silent permission, the girl waited for me to retreat and stepped inside the foyer. To Mrs. Leonard's approving nod, the girl said, "Thank you, Mrs. Bridge."

I turned to my foster mother, my eyes mutely pleading.

"It's Leonard . . . Mrs. Leonard," the woman corrected. Then glancing at me, she headed back for the family room and the television set.

I turned to Rachael, my mind consumed by the name that she had just heard and the confusion I saw briefly pass through her eyes.

"I wanted to say hi." She grinned as if she had shown up at any other classmate's house.

With Becky spying from the living room, my face filled with anger and hurt. "Hi," I muttered back and went quiet, still worrying what she might do with the Leonards' name.

"I just wanted . . . ," the girl stammered, then noticed my hand return to the door. "What's wrong?" she asked.

I said nothing, only widened the door a bit.

Rachael stepped to exit and, grazing my cheek with her headgear, turned and kissed me.

The anger in my face strengthened.

Noticing my icy expression and wrongly assuming that the peck on my cheek was the true violation, the girl frowned and walked out the door.

Twisting the lock and ignoring Becky, who cackled in the living room, I walked to the bedroom. Sitting at my desk, feeling guilty and lonely, I stared at Stalin's mustached grin. I never really cared much about Rachael's kiss. Years would pass before I would even recognize that it qualified as my first. Twelve years old, overcome by secrets, and alone in my room, I missed the friendship that I had rejected at the Leonards' front door. The next morning, when I returned to school with my map of Russian domination tucked under my arm, Rachael and I ignored each other, though for different reasons. She ignored me to protect a secret kiss, and I ignored her to protect a secret past.

Now, weeks later, dressed in my orange leisure suit and prepared for the last day of sixth grade, I walked through the school's gates. The administration scheduled the ceremony for a quarter past noon, and the younger students had been sent home for the summer before the tar playground had grown soft from the heat. My classroom was on the top floor of what everyone called the New Building. The structure's first floor was reserved for fifth graders; its second floor, for sixth graders. A wall of windows gave a sweeping panorama of the school's grounds.

Above me, the heavy numbered clock on the classroom wall pointed to just past noon. The blackboard was sponged clean from the night before, yet, gliding my fingers down the long metal track below, I had still managed to collect three ridges of yellow dust. I looked down at my caked fingers then reminded myself not to get any on my pants.

"They're coming," a boy suddenly screamed like a sentry at his post. My well-dressed classmates stampeded to the windows at the back of the classroom. Shoving aside those whom they knew they could, they scaled the tables and chairs, leaning over the window sill—as close to the glass as school rules allowed—and before the clock could move, they were alert and ready for the parade of parents below.

Among the rows of empty desks, Rachael sat reading a book. From the other side of the room, our teacher looked up from her own desk, limply chiding, "Class, please." Frustrated with no result, she joined the line of onlookers. I returned to the chalk dust.

"There, that's my dad," the same boy called out proudly. "You can see him. He's just inside the gate." Behind me, the throng swarmed at the glass, spotting and claiming mothers and fathers as they crossed onto the playground. I glanced at the floor, noticing a line of chalk across my thigh. With my attention divided between the bustle and my pants, I rubbed at the slender chalk line, widening it into a smear. "Yeah, I see him," another boy yelled over the commotion, acknowledging his friend's claim. Now hunched beside the chalkboard, I lathered my pants with a bubbly glob of salvia. The mark deepened. *It's not coming out,* I thought, frantically inspecting my pant leg. *She's not gonna like that.*

Over my head, a girl's shriek abruptly jolted across the room. "Whose parents are *those?*"

I rose in time to watch the mob uniformly push itself in the direction of the girl's accusing finger. The clamor shifted to laughter. Peering over the jumble of shoulders, my teacher let out a surprisingly girlish squeal. The woman quickly covered her mouth, but she had already emboldened several boys to join the jeering. I glanced at Rachael, who looked up from her book just in time to see me as I began navigating the empty desks. At the window, I looked down on the yard, panned the school grounds, and finally sighted the two of them.

Mrs. Leonard and her equally large husband had made it about a quarter of the way from the gates to the lunch area. Arm in arm, their heads high and backs stiff as lampposts, the two had strayed slightly from the procession and looked to be headed straight for the New Building. Mrs. Leonard had selected a deep bluish-green dress, which was nearly normal. Yet in the roasting sunlight, the color exaggerated her girth and her makeup made her face appear unusually pasty. For footwear, she had chosen her familiar white, wooden, single-strap shoes—one of the few pairs that did not hurt her feet. Whenever she wore them inside the house, they pounded over the kitchen linoleum like two little hammers. For her husband, she had chosen work boots, flood-high jeans, a green flannel shirt, and protective straw hat.

"Boom, boom, boom, boom," three boys began chanting in unison as the Leonards moved closer to our building, unaware that an audience above was dissecting their every move. "Boom, boom, boom."

Not to be outdone, one of the class's better-looking boys seized the moment, trumpeting like an angry elephant on an African desert, swaying his arm through the air like a trunk. I stared at the little opportunist.

Everyone hates you, I thought. *I've seen you lick off your retainer after you're done eating.*

As the handsome elephant boy returned to the window, I eyed the crisp collar of the burgundy dress shirt that his parents had clearly bought him for the day's ceremony and the freshly cut hair at the nape of his neck. In my orange leisure suit smeared with chalk, I felt a pang of jealousy at what his parents had given him.

Paste eater, my mind jabbed at him as I turned back to the window.

"So, whose parents are they?" a redheaded girl asked from the far side of the glass. A self-proclaimed teacher's pet, she whined uncontrollably whenever she put her hand in the air, then shouted out the answer as if there were a risk she would not be the chosen one. The budding, pimply inquisitor climbed down from the window, then cast a suspicious eye at our row of classmates. "Well?"

From across the room, I looked at Rachael, who had put down her book and was nervously glancing in my direction.

"Yeah, whose are they?" another girl chimed in. The two little sets of dark, probing eyes scanned the room, then rested on me. Laughter echoed through the wall from the classroom next door. I thought of Mrs. Leonard's hug as I had left the house that morning. *She even asked Mr. Leonard to take the day off to come,* I remembered. Caught in the two girls' gaze, I considered claiming the parents who had never really claimed me, but turned away.

Wordless, Rachael looked on.

A boy broke loose from the line and began parading through the rows of desks. Imitating Mrs. Leonard, he clasped both hands on his hips, arched his back, and jutted his chin in the air. Stopping periodically in front of a desk or a classmate, he bowed his head, looking down his nose like some kind of misplaced queen. The boy had it exactly right. With a sixth grader's precision, he ignored Mrs. Leonard's ridiculous dress and shoes, cast aside her foolish husband. Instead, he aimed directly for her pitiful pomposity, piercing her clumsy guile and exposing the fear beneath it. The class erupted in laughter, and confident that the Leonards could have belonged to no one among us, our teacher clapped in approval. A second round of laughter pealed through the room.

Below the window, to my classmates' delight, Mrs. Leonard had now bent over the drinking fountain next to the boys' restroom. Mounted at an eleven-year-old's height, the spigot was far too low for any adult, forcing her to squat, clutching her dress over her backside. The boy next to me shifted from his elephant's screams to the slurping sounds of an overgrown fly. Satiated, Mrs. Leonard rose and was followed by Mr. Leonard. He lifted his hat, exposing his sunburned scalp, then tucked the hat between his knees and sucked at the trickle. He straightened himself in front of his wife. The class howled as she wiped his mouth with her finger, then rubbed the excess on her dress.

From across the room, Rachael stared at me as my face filled with shame. From the quiet in her eyes, I saw that she knew who the show outside the window was all about. The woman who had refused to be called Mrs. Bridge had arrived. With the class roaring around us, twelve-year-old Rachael showed me what a friend was supposed to do. Steadfast in her chair, she stayed loyal, said nothing. Thinking of the story, I remember what I wish I had said then. *Thank you, Rachael Mackenstein.*

AFTER THAT LAST day of sixth grade, Rachael and I parted. She attended a better junior high because her parents refused to send her to the one nearby. Along with several others from the neighborhood, they arranged a car pool to a more distant campus. The Leonards chose convenience, having their own children and the children from the county bike to the closer—though less enriching and more violent— Kepler Junior High School, down the road.

As I continued with school, Mrs. Leonard's vulnerability outside the walls of her home only intensified. The smallest outings left her exposed. When she and her husband took us out for dinners, I watched the hostess snicker as she seated us at a center table, aware that a booth would never be ample enough for Mrs. Leonard's girth. With the waitress rolling her eyes, Mrs. Leonard ticked off her precise order: a chef's salad, Thousand Island dressing on the side, extra croutons and jack cheese, and a Diet Coke. Inevitably, the meal arrived with one or more of her requirements violated. The dressing was not in a plastic tub but slathered on top, the croutons were soft from the refrigerator, or the cheese was less than two solid handfuls. Reviewing her plate for us, she made it clear that each imperfection was an intentional affront. Multiple exchanges between her and the waitress ensued, until the croutons returned crunchy enough and the jack cheese avalanched over the edge of the bowl. As one demand followed another, Mrs. Leonard's eyes reddened, both from rage and tears. Still she persisted, too embarrassed or too hurt to stop.

On one especially painful afternoon, she fetched me from the nurse's office at my junior high. As we walked the block to where her car was parked, three older boys trailed behind. The oldest of the group, really more of a young man, ran in front of us, barking with feigned enthusiasm, "Excuse me, ma'am."

Mrs. Leonard foolishly stopped.

"My friends and I were thinking of running away to join the circus. Can you tell us where it is?"

Mrs. Leonard stoically pressed forward.

"'Cause we just heard that the fat lady rolled away." The boys howled at our backs. I dared not look back at them, and Mrs. Leonard's face held steady. She was especially quiet during the drive back to the house.

When her own children hatefully whispered about her, confiding that she was embarrassing, even crazy, I was smug. "She's not in my gene pool," I replied. Even alone, I mocked her, mimicking her fat waddle in the bathroom mirror. *She deserves it,* I reassured myself, looking back in the mirror. *She doesn't belong to me anyway.*

Yet, as much as I tried, part of me grew to care about and even love Mrs. Leonard. Though I refused to defend her, I was vulnerable to her occasional kindnesses. She threw birthday parties for me, she included me in family vacations, and she sometimes let me keep the change when I ran to get something for her from the grocery store. Still, over the years of a childhood, her kindnesses amounted to little more than moments. If she had not been so frightened, so filled with anger, and so capable of cruelty, I might have eventually substituted her entirely for my real mother. I might even have gone along with foster care's fictions, done my best to ignore the checks that arrived in the mail, the social workers that could drive up to the house at any time, the children who had come and gone. With only a bit more from Mrs. Leonard, I might have claimed her as my own. I might have surrendered Hope entirely.

CHAPTER TWELVE

SHORTLY AFTER THE start of seventh grade, a note arrived for me in the mail. The thin greeting card, separated from the bills and flyers, had been left on the kitchen counter for me to find when I came back from school. Sweating with my backpack still on, I stared at the old-fashioned script, then flipped the envelope and read the back flap. I would have never remembered the street but instantly recognized the city, the state, and most of all, the name: K. Reese, Chicago, Illinois.

With my heart pounding, I clutched the card in my hand and hurried to my bedroom down the hall. "Grandma, Grandma, Grandma," I whispered to myself, sliding off my backpack and sitting on the bed. Carefully, I tugged at the flap and broke the seal.

The card's cover was a cartoon of Snoopy on his doghouse. A collection of empty thought bubbles drifted above his head. Inside were the printed words, "Thinking of you." In her handwriting below was the note, "Grandma loves and misses you. XOXOXO, Grandma."

I stared quietly at the card, turned it over, and read the printing details on the back. The note was short, but my mind quickly made up the rest. I imagined Grandma Kate scanning the racks of a card aisle, picking out the very best one. Paying for it and its heavy envelope, she pulled a bill from the large purse that she always carried. I imagined her walking up the four flights of stairs to our apartment, unlocking the row of dead bolts and the doorknob, then, once inside, sealing the entrance back up. She sat at the kitchen table, across from the door that led to the balcony and trash chute. Then, beside my empty chair, she thought of me and wrote the few words that arrived at the Leonards' house. As an adult, the card would have seemed insufficient, the short handwritten note even odd. But as a boy, I was accustomed to filling empty spaces with memories. Grandma Kate's card was simple but did what I needed. It assured me that someone else was keeping those memories too.

That evening, I approached Mrs. Leonard in the family room. As the television yelled from the corner, I waited for a commercial. "Did you see the card for me in the kitchen?"

Ignoring me, she reached for the *TV Guide*.

"Do you know how my grandmother got the address?"

She shrugged, chuckled at something in the magazine.

I waited a moment longer, then, knowing to give up, returned to my room.

After that first card, more cards arrived on the kitchen counter. One came for Halloween, another for Thanksgiving, then one for no holiday at all. All of them had the same or similar note followed by a string of hugs and kisses, then the signature, "Grandma."

On a Saturday morning in December, just before my seventh grade broke for Christmas, Mrs. Leonard shook me awake and told me that I had a telephone call. As I trailed behind her into the kitchen, she pointed to the unhooked phone on the table, then headed into the family room. With my bare feet on the cold linoleum floor, I sat down, picked up the receiver, and groggily spoke. "Hello?"

"Andy, sweetheart, is that you?" she quietly asked.

"Yes, Grandma. It's me." The chill in my voice surprised me. The phone went quiet.

"My goodness, you sound so . . . grown-up."

I was nearly thirteen years old. Almost to the day, eight years had passed since she had finally given in to her daughter, Hope, and boarded me on an airplane for Los Angeles. The five-year-old's voice that she remembered had cracked and begun falling away.

"Oh, did you get Grandma's cards?" Her own voice faltered, as the sound of tears spilled into the line.

I glanced across the kitchen table, eyed Mrs. Leonard reading the Saturday paper in the family room. Pressing the receiver against my mouth, I whispered back, "It's all right, Grandma." I waited for her to catch her breath. "I got your cards. I promise. Everything's all right."

"Are the people that you're staying with good to you? Grandma's sorry she misplaced you."

"Yes, Grandma." I answered as well as I could. "They're good to me. They're very good to me."

"You know you can write me back if you want." She smiled over the line. "Did they tell you you can write?"

"OK," I answered calmly, as my mind ran through the list of "theys" that she could have meant. "I promise to write."

The conversation paused for several seconds.

"Well . . . even on Saturdays, long distance calls get expensive. You remember Grandma doesn't have too much money."

"I know." My eyes warmed as I watched Mrs. Leonard reach for her coffee.

"I'm sending you something for Christmas," she quickly added. "So you watch for it, all right?"

"All right, I'll watch for it."

"Grandma promises to call again. I love you."

Then, when I thought she was about to say something else, she fumbled with the receiver and hung up. For a moment longer, I held the phone, pretending that the call had not ended. Except for Mrs. Leonard rustling the morning paper, the house was quiet.

"Bye," I finally replied to the nothingness and slowly hung up. Then, hoping Mrs. Leonard would not look my way, I walked lightly across the kitchen floor, down the hallway, and back into the bedroom. I glanced at Christopher in his bed, then crawled into my own.

The sheets warmed around me, and I thought of sitting on the airplane in Chicago, warning Grandma Kate that she had to go before we took off. Crouched in the aisle next to me, she had told me to remember her, to mind my mother, to be a good boy. That morning, after her call, I wished that I had told her that I had done all three things that she had asked of me. But even more than that, I wished that I had also told her just how badly I had been misplaced. I turned, and facing the wall, waited for sleep to replace the loneliness.

As Grandma Kate promised, her package arrived a few days later. She had gone to Wrigley Field, where she and I had never gone together. She bought a present for a boy she loved but no longer knew—a baseball with the autograph of every Cubs player that season. Inside the card, she wrote that she loved me, then added a postscript that she hoped the gift would do for both Christmas and my birthday.

All I knew about baseball was that I was bad at it. Neither Mr. Leonard nor Christopher had any interest in teaching me to throw or catch a ball, and I had seen the humiliation of other boys who tried learning on their own in junior high. Grandma Kate could not have known that, when given the choice at school, I ran laps around the fields to avoid lining up for teams, and at the house, I swam alone in the backyard pool to avoid everything else.

Spotting the baseball on my desk, Christopher snatched and tossed it in the air. "Like you can throw a ball," he snickered. As I leaped for it, he teased me with it, lifting it back and forth above my reach. Threatening to hurl the ball against the bedroom wall, he waited for me to retreat back into my chair. Grinning, he took a closer look before bursting into laughter. "You call these things autographs?" He held the ball under my nose. "They're not even real. They're a bunch of rubber stamps." He dropped it in front of me, then left the room.

I never needed Christopher's observation. The moment that I

opened the package, I saw that the signatures were nothing more than a clutter of copies. Worse, the ball came with a printed warning not to throw or hit it, because not even it was real. In the years that followed, I was never tempted to lift the ball from its plastic cup and test it outside. The ball would have fared no better on the front lawn than Jason's boat had fared in the backyard pool. Yet I kept the counterfeit ball on my desk carefully framed in its case, and when I examined its identical gray signatures, I was reminded that I had come from someplace that was worth remembering, and that I still mattered to someone.

BY THE TIME the Leonards' younger daughter, Becky, dashed for the kitchen telephone at the other end of the house, it was already on its fourth ring.

"Leonard residence, may I help you?"

I glanced up from the typewriter on my desk and out into the hallway. My backpack lay on the floor, stuffed with untouched eighth-grade homework, and as the punishment required, the bedroom door was open. From the corner of my eye, I noticed Christopher lift his head from his own desk. Around us, the house was quiet, while Becky listened to the caller.

"Oh, yeah. She's here. Lemme get her." Another moment passed as the girl pressed the mouthpiece against her chest. "Mother, it's Andy's social worker on the phone."

Panic stabbed at my stomach. Without thinking, I looked at Christopher, who gave me a dead stare, then turned his back and hunkered over his book. I punched out another sentence.

"Mother!" the girl screamed. "It's Andy's social worker!"

Ping. I reached to swing back the roller's metal return. "All right!" Mrs. Leonard thundered back from her bedroom down the hall. I glanced at the digital clock, whose glowing red numbers now read 3:52 P.M. I had another hour and forty-eight minutes of typing to go.

Throughout seventh grade, my transition from elementary school to junior high school had gone reasonably well. School was all that I had. Against the backdrop of an absent mother and her brutalizing replacement, I had no other claim to mattering or being different. If Mrs. Leonard made good on a threat and I went missing, I never thought that my teachers would run after me and track me down from wherever I had been put. Still, I studied to be seen and noticed, if only for the moment. I did what was asked of me, finished homework, and studied for exams, hoping that if I were taken, I would at least not disappear, entirely unknown.

Then, more than halfway through eighth grade, I had stumbled. I got a D-plus in typing. Though the course was only an elective, Mrs. Leonard was furious with the mark and invoked her "grade rule." For each letter grade lower than a B-minus, the rule assigned a child an hour of study per day in that subject until the next report card indicated that the grade had been lifted to that minimum threshold. During the school week, study time commenced in the afternoon, following Mrs. Leonard's Estonian lessons—the outcome of which determined eligibility for an after-school snack of lukewarm Kool-Aid and stale snickerdoodles. On weekends, studying could begin anytime, provided it was completed by five o'clock in the evening.

Raising an F to a B-minus could be mathematically impossible. Yet, the failing child would still be consigned to three hours of study time in that subject alone every day for the remaining fifteen weeks of the semester, regardless of subsequent performance or even a teacher's attempt to intervene on the child's behalf. One of Becky's math teachers had once called to convince Mrs. Leonard that the rule was unlikely to produce better test results and that he would work with the girl to improve her mark. Mrs. Leonard thanked the man for his efforts, then invoked the rule nonetheless.

Still, Becky had been only occasionally penalized by the rule. Bullied by her mother the most after me, the eight-year-old girl, who had welcomed me to the Leonards' house when I first arrived, reassuring me that I would fit in, had now grown into a sullen and lonely sixteen-year-old. Following one especially vicious encounter with her mother, Becky had gone to her father, asking him to intervene. Apparently, Mr. Leonard said something to his wife. The following day, in a fit of anger, Becky's mother cornered her alone and told her never to put herself between her mother and father again. After that, Becky had begun spending time sitting on a stool, hiding in her darkened bedroom closet. Closest to me in age, she and I lingered in the same house silently apart. She generally performed just well enough at school to avoid her mother's fury, then came back in the afternoons and said little to anyone.

The Leonards' older daughter, Jessica, had been spared the rule entirely. When I entered junior high, Jessica had already graduated from high school and begun her first year at UC Riverside. I remembered her mostly for her success in pleasing her mother, cleaning the house, finishing up chores then volunteering for new ones. Six years my senior, she and I never had a close relationship, though her good grades had been something that I noticed in elementary school. Among a dearth of role models, she had been at least a distant one. The grade rule had not even existed until the year after Jessica's high school graduation, when Christopher's academic performance had prompted its enactment.

Since the day that I had arrived, Christopher and I had shared his bedroom. He never forgave my presence, and the last thing he wanted to be thought of as was my older brother. Physically, he was my intimidating opposite. Four years older, muscular, dark-haired, six inches taller and fifty pounds heavier, he bulked above my bony frame and blond head. Christopher was a bully who preferred to use "faggot" and "asshole" rather than my name, and more than once I felt the dull slap of his hand against my temple or the sharp stab of his knuckles into my kidneys. Yet when his mother finally told him to leave me alone, he did. Instead, he pointed me out to his friends, who eagerly took up the slack, waiting for me as I made my way back from school. On one occasion, an older boy whom I had never seen before pulled his car up alongside me, parked, then followed me across the length of the field in front of the Leonards' house, kicking me in the thigh and reminding me that he was free to do whatever Christopher could not. As my eyes reddened with fear, his parting words shot to the core of my loneliness. "What's wrong? Little pussy misses his momma? She's not coming back for the shit she dropped."

When I reached eighth grade, Christopher was in twelfth, and his grudge against me had iced into late-adolescent hate. In place of the intimacy of two boys sharing a bedroom, a threatening maturity existed between us. Like hostile boarders, Christopher and I went to bed at different times, ignored each other when we woke, made a point of dressing when the other was not in the room. He frightened me most at night, when I slept across from him, alone.

Tinkering in the garage with his father, Christopher spent as much time as he could outside the house. Yet he never escaped his mother's grade rule and the hours that it confined him to his room or the kitchen table under her watchful eye. That second semester in eighth grade, I may have gotten a D-plus in typing class, but Christopher had come home with a string of three D's and one C. After several years of successfully doctoring his report card, he had been caught that semester, his last of twelfth grade. Across the bedroom from me, slouched at his desk, the seventeen-year-old's study time had been set at seven hours per day, seven days per week. Only a few months shy of his high school graduation and moving out of his parents' house, he chafed under the rule. That July, when he did move out, he left the digital clock that his mother had given him sitting on his abandoned desk.

Because of my "obnoxious attitude and school-based performance," Mrs. Leonard had informed me that I was to "study" typing for two hours every day. She had carted out a battered mechanical typewriter from the guest-room closet, set it on my bedroom desk, and told me to commence. Then, observing my mute confusion, she snatched up a pencil and a piece of white paper. A moment later, she slapped a handwritten note on the desktop next to me.

"Now is the time for all good men to come to the aid of their party!" I read to myself, before repeating the sentence aloud. *Sounds like some kind of communist slogan,* I thought, looking up for guidance but expecting another concentration-camp story.

"That's how I learned to type," she snapped.

I've never seen you type anything. I glanced quickly at my fingers and the cascade of rounded black keys, their white-painted symbols yellowed with age. She rolled a sheet of paper in, and waited for me to start.

Trying not to peek, I began pounding at the ancient keyboard. As Mrs. Leonard surveyed my progress, I produced three versions of the practice sentence, half of the strokes resulting in ink blobs rather than letters. "Well, you've got plenty of time for practice, young man," she snorted before leaving.

"Mother, Andy's social worker!" Becky screamed again from the kitchen.

Ping. I reached for the return again, then looked out the bedroom door just as Mrs. Leonard marched past. My eyes darted back to the keyboard, and I quickly continued striking at the keys.

Mrs. Leonard grabbed the phone from her daughter. Ping.

"Hello? Holly?" I had never met her, but clearly Holly was my newest county caseworker. Mrs. Leonard thudded across the kitchen floor, tugging at the snarled telephone cord behind her. Ping. "I'm just fine. How are you?" She let out an effusive laugh that tumbled down the hall and into the bedroom.

She knows I'm listening, I thought, pushing on with my task. The house echoed with the machine's faltering clack. Ping. I looked down, shoved back the handle, then continued hammering away. Ping.

"Well, I'm so happy you called back. . . ."

Why had Mrs. Leonard called in the first place? Why was the woman calling her back? I kept pecking.

"That's wonderful. What a great opportunity for him," she nearly shouted. Ping. "You know, I've been trying to get him out of the house. . . . Oh, he's fine." She lowered her voice to a whisper while she dug for a pen from a kitchen drawer.

I pounded harder at the keys, filling the void. Ping. Ping.

Mrs. Leonard spoke up again. "Oh, Holly, thank you so much. . . . Yes, I'll be sure to tell him. . . . That's right. . . . Oh, you, too. . . . Bye, bye." Just as his mother hung up, Christopher glanced over his shoulder and sneered at me.

Ping. Ping. Ping. My exhausted fingers halted and the house went silent. I looked at the page. The first few inches were fine, arguably legible. But below, the sheet of paper had slipped on the spool, caught in the teeth along the side, then jammed behind the metal guide. Stuck in a single spot, the keys had punched through the paper while the ribbon spools had faithfully advanced. The red-and-black ribbon lay in the well, tangled and knotted.

That evening, after I finished my typing for the day, I dug into my teacher-assigned homework. Mrs. Leonard appeared at the bedroom door, glanced briefly at her son's back, aware that he had hours of studying left to go, then turned to me.

"Oh, Andy. Your social worker called this afternoon," she announced innocently, pretending that I could not have heard her conversation.

"What did she want?" I asked.

"She and I both think that it's time you get a job. For the summer, at least."

She's never even met me.

"OK." I nodded.

"Fourteen-year-olds need a work permit. You can get one at the employment office." She paused. "Work is an important learning experience. Not to mention getting you off that allowance."

The county pays for my allowance.

I kept nodding.

"The address should be in the telephone book. You need to ask for the county's foster-care employment program."

After a month of avoiding the trip—and Mrs. Leonard's reminders—I rode my bike to the California State Employment Office. The building was a low, redbrick structure with a large, empty parking lot and a small crowd loitering outside.

A woman perched on a tall chair behind the counter greeted me with an empty smile.

"Hi." I grinned back, mistaking the smile for friendliness.

She waited.

"Would you know where I could get a work-permit application?"

Apparently mute, she pointed to a line of teenagers across the room.

I glanced at the clump of teenagers, then at the straighter though growing line of adults behind me. Leaning over the woman's counter, I whispered, "Can you also tell me where the employment program for foster children is?"

She stared back quizzically.

"You know, the special jobs for foster kids. Kids that the county has," I clarified.

"I know what a foster child is, sweetheart." The woman's dead smile dropped. "We don't have any work program for them."

Dread crossed my face. I could hardly ride back to the Leonards' house empty-handed. "No, I'm sure there's a special program," I whispered again.

The woman bent to meet my eyes. "No, young man, there isn't," she hissed.

"Yes, there is," I persisted.

"No, there isn't."

"Yes, there is."

The man behind me pushed closer.

"No, there is not a special program for *foster children*!" she snapped.

"Shush," I shot back instinctively.

The woman straightened herself against her chair, crossed her arms, then looked down on me. "Who told you about the foster children's work program?" she asked loudly.

"My social worker from the county," I mouthed, hoping for mercy.

"Who?" she repeated, keeping her distance.

I looked at her, my eyes pleading.

She waited. The man behind me cleared his throat.

"My social worker from the county," I mumbled, looking down at the counter.

"I'm sorry. I couldn't hear what you said, young man."

I looked up at her, and as she required, repeated it louder. "My social worker from the county."

The woman's smile resurfaced. "Try the same line as the work permits." She glanced over my shoulder at the man behind me. "Next."

At the head of the second line, the clerk excused me for not having brought my birth certificate, issued me a work permit, and instructed me to proceed to another desk for the foster children's employment opportunities.

No one was waiting at this last stop. Inside a cramped office cubicle, a balding man with an exhausted face motioned me to sit down. I explained myself, and thankfully, he was familiar with the program that I was there for. He took the work permit, then bent to open a drawer and placed a plastic box of index cards on his desk between us.

"Is there anything in particular you were interested in?" he asked, resting his hand over his treasure chest.

I shrugged, smiling weakly at him.

"Oh, come on. There must be *something* you're good at. Something that interests you." He grinned encouragingly.

"I don't know," I answered, then glanced at the box and saw that his hand had not budged.

I thought of school and my teachers. I had kept up with my reading as the foster girl Susanna had encouraged. I borrowed lettered volumes from the Leonards' *World Book Encyclopedia*. When one stormy Saturday and Sunday had kept me out of the pool, I had managed to learn everything about every topic that began with the letter *M*. Having saved up my $3.50 weekly allowance, I rode my bike to the closest mall and bought an $18 hardbound *Norton Anthology of American Poetry*, though most of the poems were tough for a fourteen-year-old to understand. Over time, I had acquired every J. D. Salinger paperback at the bookstore and consumed his stories about the Glass family living in New York City. I admired the youngest of the Glass boys, Zooey, who was slender and of average height like me but handsome and easygoing in ways that I would never be. Zooey was an actor, and I wished for the brothers he had, who promised that if he ever did anything at all beautiful on a stage—even something nameless—they would arrive solemnly at the back door dressed in rented tuxedos with bundles of snapdragons in hand.

I looked at the man across the desk. "Sometimes I think about being a lawyer or an English professor."

"Well, well, young man." He smiled defensively, then gripped the box, turning the pinks of his nails white.

"It doesn't really matter," I added, anxious and embarrassed.

"Well, let's see what we have." He snapped open the lid and, after passing over several prospective openings, pulled a card from the container. "File Clerk, Los Angeles County Department of Probation," he announced like a caller at a bingo game. He glanced at me, then joked, "You don't have a set of wheels, do you?"

"Just a bike." I smiled politely.

He thumbed further into the stack. "Bill Collections Trainee." He looked to the side, wrinkled his nose to push up his heavy glasses, then silently mulled over the open position before shaking his head and moving onward. "Emancipation Specialist, County Department of Children's Services—says it's a *summer fellowship*. Now, that sounds like potential to me." He tapped the card on the box and looked across the desk. "Could be a résumé builder. What do you think?" He shrugged. "I guess you're already in foster care."

I waited, staring dumbly.

He slipped back the card, then a moment later piped up with his own proposal. "Hey, did you ever think about joining Reserve Officer Training Corps? You know, ROTC."

"I'm in junior high school," I clarified.

"Oh, we get a lot of foster kids joining the military. Besides"—he hunched toward me paternally—"maybe your school's got a Junior ROTC? Ever ask anybody? Learn a trade, get a free bed, eat a hot meal. Government pays for it all."

I looked back at him. "I already have that."

The man frowned, then descended back into his search. He flipped through several more cards, reviewing some silently, calling out others. Finally, he drew my match from the box. "OK," he declared, "a kid like you has gotta like sunshine."

I nodded.

Smiling with success, he tugged out a notepad from a stack of folders, scrawled the necessary details, then tore off the sheet. "Reseda County Park and Recreation Area, June 28, eight A.M., Park Superintendent Stansky," he announced. "Don't be late."

With eighth grade over, I was excited about my first summer job, and when the morning arrived, I left the house with plenty of time to spare for the hour-long bike ride to Reseda Park.

A shallow pond about the size of a football field dominated the park's landscape. A strip of yellow sand ran the circumference, and beneath several oil slicks, the water sustained a thriving undergrowth of heavy brown-green slime and a school of stocked catfish. On the morning that I arrived, a dozen or so shabbily clad men were already crouched at the water's edge, rods in hand, worms and buckets at their sides, reeling in a meal.

I chained my bike next to the adobe-style recreation center, walked around it twice, then finally located and opened an unlocked door.

Creeping along the walls of a darkened basketball court, I came across another door leading to a string of well-lit but empty classrooms. Superintendent Stansky was nowhere to be found. I meandered back outside and tried several service buildings, all of which were locked. About to give up and bicycle back to the Leonards' house, I tugged open the door to a concrete shed and found a man squatting over the rotary of a tractor lawnmower. As I stepped inside, he shot me an irritated glance and promptly returned to his work.

"Superintendent Stansky?" I asked nervously.

The man ignored me and began furiously striking the mower's blades with a wrench. Around the two of us, the clanging throbbed against the concrete walls. He lifted himself and, glowering at the machine, contemplated his next assault. He coolly paced to the apparatus's side, shook his head, then suddenly kicked the seat with his boot. The mower wobbled for a moment, but quickly regained its balance and stared back at the two of us. Defeated, he threw his wrench to the floor and turned to me.

"Are you the kid the county sent?"

I nodded, faintly smiling at the idea of touring the park's grounds behind the wheel of a mammoth slicing machine.

"You're late." He grabbed the employment envelope from my hand, tossed it on the workbench, then walked to a metal closet and threw me a pair of county-emblazoned overalls and an orange safety vest.

"I'm sorry," I muttered, trying to pull the man-size uniform over my sneakers and street clothes. Wrapped around me, the overalls' waist hung well below my hips and the legs puddled at my feet.

"Work started at six A.M." He tapped his wristwatch with a greasy finger, then walked to the back of the shed, retrieved a broom, a burlap bag, and a metal tin taped to a stick. Marching out the front door, he waved his hand for me to follow. With me trailing behind, he strode into the morning sunlight. Under a fat oak tree, he halted unexpectedly, and as I tumbled against his backside, he grunted, then began scouting the ground's spotty lawns.

"What are we looking for?" I asked from behind him.

He ignored the question, cocked his head toward something in the distance, before quickly pacing forward, implements in hand. After another fifty yards or so, he stopped and glanced at his boots.

"Do you see that?" he asked. Clutching the waist of my uniform, I ran to catch up with him.

"What?" I asked apprehensively, still scanning the park. "You mean the lake?"

"No, *that!*" He raised his voice, then stabbed his finger toward the grass.

I looked down.

"Do you have any idea what that is, young man?"

"I *think* so."

"Canine excrement," he pronounced scientifically, motioning me to examine it.

I bent my knees and peered closer. High on a thicket of crabgrass, a modest-sized pile of dog poop slumped. I stood up, nodding at his analysis.

Keeping his eyes on me, he pressed the broom to the ground, then adroitly flicked a single turd into the tin scooper and tossed it into the sack. He handed me the tools of my new trade, then waited as I fumbled to scoop up what remained. Thinking I had already done reasonably well, I looked up and smiled. But Superintendent Stansky was not impressed. He shook his head at the obvious incompetence of a new apprentice. "You'll get better," he concluded, then waved toward the rest of the park and walked away.

Far worse than the impoverished fishermen who angled dinner from the central lagoon, dog owners had become the park's greatest nuisance. From seven A.M., when the park officially opened, to nine P.M., when it closed, hundreds of piles of canine feculence accumulated on the lawns. With a bit of extra money in the foster-care budget and a public necessity to be met, a career opportunity for the county's children had been born. Equipped with pooper-scooper and broom, and protected by blue county overalls and an orange safety vest, from six in the morning to three in the afternoon, I was to patrol the grounds, clearing the park's lawns of sacks of dog shit.

For the next three weeks, I woke at half past four in the morning, left the house by five, then arrived at Reseda Park, ready to nudge the grass clean. With the slightest flick, I could dispose of anything from the confident crappings of a mighty German Shepherd to the timid droppings of a trembling Chihuahua. I watched all of them crap. Bag and poop-tray in hand, I could discern the guilt in a dog's eyes as it self-consciously glanced to the side and shifted its weight to its hind legs. Within a matter of days, I had developed my own eye for excrement. Under the summer sun, I could spot a solitary pooh that rested yards away. Of course, the bigger the dung, the bigger the dog—anyone knew that. Yet the most common, least remarkable piles could reveal darker secrets. Strings of grass hinted at intestinal aliments, bits of upholstery signaled loneliness, and an earring or a string of beads revealed revenge. But then there were those most intriguing craps, dug out from the bushes or shoveled up from under a tree—the ones that were too large to have ever come from under a dog's tail. These turds were not specifically detailed in the job description, but as Superintendent Stansky always said, "When working for Los Angeles County, you've gotta be prepared for surprises."

When I described my responsibilities to Mrs. Leonard, she praised my new occupation as "a first step toward inducing good discipline." Neither she nor her husband was pleased when I asked for permission to quit.

"Don't you want to save some money?" Mr. Leonard looked at me incredulously from the garage door. "You could buy a stereo."

I considered the minimum wage that I was earning and the pounds of dog shit that it would take to accumulate such a sum. "No, I don't need a stereo."

On the condition that I would not spend the summer in the house, the Leonards allowed me to call Superintendent Stansky and resign

from my county position. On my own, I got another job bagging
groceries at a local supermarket, where the pay was better and the
work cleaner.

When the summer was over and ninth grade arrived, I told a few
classmates about my three weeks with Superintendent Stansky, the
pooper-scooper, blue overalls, and orange vest. I complained about
riding my bike in the summer's morning chill and again in its afternoon heat. In the school corridors, I mimed Stansky, then myself
hunting down a poop, and with a smart aleck's brave face, I laughed at
the farce with the kids around me.

Laughing was easy. The harder part was keeping myself from believ-
ing what that job had implied. In the same position, another fourteen-
year-old might have laughed more genuinely, confident that he meant
more to the world and to those around him than his ability to clean
up after the public's dogs. But, unlike other boys, I needed proof that
I mattered. Left to myself, I was running short on reasons to claim
that I meant anything at all.

That year, I did better in school than I had ever done before. I
never feared Mrs. Leonard's grade rule again.

CHRISTMAS CAME IN ninth grade, but nothing arrived from
Grandma Kate. When school started again with no news from her, I
worried but kept quiet. Then, at the end of January, two weeks before
my fifteenth birthday, I found a letter on the kitchen counter. Retreating to my bedroom, I nervously tore the envelope open:

"Dear Andy," the leaf of notebook paper read. "Hope you didn't
think Grandma forgot you. Have been given permission to see you.
Been saving and not making calls. Should have enough for a plane
ticket in the spring. God willing. Pray for Grandma and for your
mother. She loves you. XOXOXO. Grandma." My eyes ran through
the blue ballpoint script, halting at the same lines each time: "Pray for
Grandma Kate and for your mother. She loves you."

Relieved that Grandma Kate was all right, and anxious for her visit, I stared at the two vague sentences, clarifying them with words of my own: "Pray for Grandma and your mother . . . *because I heard from her. She called or wrote or visited. She said that everything was OK. She talked about you. She remembered you.* She loves you . . . *and she'll be there soon.*" Smiling at the note, I folded it neatly, then tucked it under the baseball that had arrived two years earlier.

That last winter of junior high was a dry one, and when Grandma Kate arrived in late May, the faint scent of smoke had drifted from the tinder-lined canyons to the Leonards' house on the valley's floor. She flew in on a Thursday morning, and rushing home from school to meet her, I found her on the Leonards' courtyard swing, alone in the sweet-smelling air.

Lifting herself slowly, she waited for me beside the front porch steps. "Grandma came like she said she would." She grinned, arms hanging at her sides. "Grandma came."

"I know." I approached her. "I know you did."

If she had seemed old to me when I was five, she seemed frail now that I was fifteen. While my voice had descended into the resonance of a young man, hers had collapsed into the quiver of an old woman. Her hair was solid gray; not a strand of black was left. Her eyes lay bedded in folds of tired skin. Though she had kept her slender frame, her spine now bent at the base of her neck. That day at the Leonards', she was only fifty-five years old, yet time hung heavy on her. No one now would have confused her for my mother, as they had ten years before.

Outside the house, I hugged her carefully. Then, not yet wanting to go inside, I guided her back to the wooden swing. As her daughter and I had done years earlier when she had come to visit at the Leonards' house, Grandma Kate and I sat, unsure what to say. Still, I was glad that she was there and that she had kept her word. That evening, I wished her good night as she went to the guest room, and, delicate as she was, I felt safer with her there just down the hallway.

Back from school the next day, I expected to find her on the porch but the swing hung empty. With no sign of her, I paced through the kitchen, then hustled to the guest room, where I was relieved to see her blue suitcase still open beside the bed. Glancing through the living room's sliding glass door into the backyard, I spotted her beside the pool. From behind the glass, I watched as she gripped her Bible. Then, feeling guilty for spying, I slid open the door.

If she heard me, she did nothing but continue whispering her prayers. Over the last day, the smoke must have bit at her lungs as it did mine. With me only steps behind her, her voice sounded nearly frantic as she begged for God's mercy. She could not have known how much she sounded like her daughter confronting darkness years ago. When my shadow alerted her, she turned, startled to see me. Her expression softened, and she reached for my hand.

"Grandma missed you," she whispered.

"I missed you too," I whispered back. Then we sat and said little more until Mrs. Leonard called us in for dinner.

Mrs. Leonard treated Katherine with kindness, something she had not shown Katherine's daughter. Mrs. Leonard never explained why, and I was simply relieved to see her rages briefly disappear. On Saturday—the last full day of Katherine's visit—the Leonards drove us to Descanso Gardens, an oak- and camellia-lined estate that the county had purchased from a newspaper tycoon decades earlier. The trip took us across the valley, and as Mrs. Leonard chatted with Grandma Kate, I stared out the car window. The off-ramp to North Hollywood, where Hope and I had lived, approached and then disappeared behind us, and I thought to say something but changed my mind. Heading back, I waited for the same off-ramp to appear as Grandma Kate clutched a flower that I had plucked for her from the garden's grounds.

The next morning, only hours before her plane was to leave, she and I sat alone in the guest room.

"Do you still use the landlord's phone on the stairwell?" I grinned at her, proud of my memory.

"Oh, no, sweetheart, Grandma moved years ago." She leaned closer with a mischievous smile that reminded me of the younger woman who had lobbed snowballs at me on the street. "Is that the smudge of a mustache coming in?"

I looked bashfully away and let a moment pass. "Do you still keep up with the Gordies from across the way?" I piped up.

She glanced at me quizzically and considered the question. "You mean Helen and George?"

"I guess. I always called them the Gordies."

"Well, I think Helen had a stroke or something. And, George . . ." She trudged through her mind. "Honey, I don't know what happened to George. Why do you ask?"

"No reason," I answered quickly, embarrassed that I had held on to too much. I waited another moment, then blurted, "Have you talked with Hope?"

She looked surprised for a moment. "You mean your mother, right?" she gently corrected. "You need to call her your mother."

I waited for an answer, said nothing.

"No, sweetheart, I'm sorry. I haven't heard from her in over five years."

Silently, I counted the years, realizing that she had last spoken with her daughter when I had, sometime around that night when she had shown up at the Leonards' house.

Grandma Kate whispered, "She remembers you. I know she remembers you, sweetheart."

I gave her a blank smile.

"Mothers don't forget," she said firmly, as though she were defending herself as much as her daughter for having lost a child. "Mothers don't forget."

I watched as she leaned for her suitcase, slid it closer from the corner of the bed. *Why had I waited until now to ask?* I thought. She pushed down against the top, struggled to force it over the loose bundle of clothes. *Why did it take you so many years to find me here, alone in this angry woman's house?* She branched her thumbs over the clasps, snapped each of them shut. *Will you just remember me? Or will you come back again?* Finished at last, she cupped her hands on her knees and turned her head to mine. *Grandma, will you take me with you?*

A moment passed. She ran her fingertips across her brow. Then in the quiet of her half smile, I recognized her answer, though I heard it only in my head: *No, Andy, I can't take you.*

She straightened herself, bent to lift the suitcase from the bed. "It's time to go," she whispered from the middle of the room. With her shoulders lopsided from the weight at her side, she plodded a few steps toward the guest-room door. "Can you give Grandma a hand with this?" I nodded, rushed toward her. Then, grasping the thick handle, I felt her hand slip away.

We walked down the hallway, past the bedroom where I slept. Over two years had passed since her first card had arrived, and not one social worker, lawyer, or judge had bothered to ask what I thought of her return. No one had sat down with her or me to tell either of us what could be done to help with phone calls or visits, to explain if she and I had any right to each other. She paid for her own trip to see me that spring, and later, when she could afford a telephone, I paid for the calls I made to her on her birthday and on holidays. Whatever we had together was left to the collective resources of a teenage boy in foster care and his impoverished grandmother who lived two thousand miles away. That last morning, I may have been too frightened to hear the words, "No, Andy, I can't take you." She may have been too frightened to utter them. But, in the end, it never really mattered all that much. Because neither of us had any idea how to get to "Yes, I can."

We drove to the airport, and standing in the terminal, I watched as her plane lifted into the gray sky. As much as Grandma Kate loved me, and as much as she may have wanted to, she could not rescue me. As for that other rescuer, I used her first name, Hope, because I missed her too much to call her Mom out loud. But I waited for her just the same. "Mothers don't forget," Grandma Kate had said. Perhaps I should have admitted that their children do not forget either.

CHAPTER THIRTEEN

❦

I WAS LONELY. Years had passed since I had seen her.

"But you have to know where she went," I pressed the woman behind the battered counter.

"Young man, I told you I don't remember. And if I did, I couldn't give it to you without her permission."

"Her name was Miss O'Malley. Nancy Marie O'Malley," I emphasized, using my old teacher's first and middle name as though she and I had been friends. The woman looked down to the floor in frustration. "She taught me fifth grade, here," I continued. "She liked me. I'm sure that she'd want to see me."

We stared at each other across the counter. I was not leaving easily.

"All right, just give me a minute." The woman relented, throwing out a gentle grimace, emphasizing that she was doing me a favor. "I hope you know I could get in trouble for this."

"Thank you." I smiled back and watched as she disappeared down a hallway.

I looked around the office that I remembered as a small boy. Beyond the long window, the lunch tables were empty. It was past four in the afternoon, and school had been out for hours. The row of file cabinets against the far wall had not moved in the years since I had seen it last, though an extra one might have been added. Behind the counter, the room's greatest feature remained its two large desks placed face to face—the one closest to me belonging to the woman who had just marched down the hall and the other to her office companion, who had already left.

Though I doubted that the woman recalled it, on my first day at Elkhart Elementary School, she and Mrs. Leonard had argued about admitting a foster boy with no school or medical records to show for himself. Eight years later, I had begun high school and the same woman had begun old age. Finally, she emerged from the hallway and stepped back to the counter with a slip of paper in hand. "Cathgate Elementary." She smiled faintly. "Do you need the address?"

"No, that's OK!" I answered, erupting with happiness and turning toward the office door.

"You know, Andy . . . ," the woman called out.

Hearing her use my name for the first time, I stopped and looked back.

"It is Andy, isn't it?"

I smiled in acknowledgement.

"I do remember you." The woman leaned over the counter as she had done the first time that she saw me, a boy fresh from MacLaren Hall. "I remember the first day that you were here." She smiled, omitting the other details, which she apparently had not forgotten.

"I remember you, too." I paused, before adding, "Mrs. Augustine."

"How are you? I mean how have you been doing?" Her work day over, she rested her chin on her hand, then waited.

I thought about the truth for a moment, but gave the answer that I was sure she wanted. "I'm great. I just started high school. They put me in all the advanced classes."

"Still with Mrs. Leonard?"

"Yeah."

She nodded and smiled again. "That's good."

"Yeah," I answered, before enduring an awkward pause. "Well, I gotta go. Thanks for your help." I held up the note that she had given me, then reached for the door.

I took the way through the empty schoolyard, walking by the old bungalow where Miss O'Malley had taught fifth grade. *She'll be glad to see me,* I reassured myself, strolling out the school gate. *She liked me.*

Cathgate Elementary was familiar and not far from the Leonards' house. From my high school, I estimated that a bike ride would take forty-five minutes, maybe an hour at most. Still, I would have to leave classes by midday and arrive no later than half past one to get there before the elementary school closed.

The Leonards would never approve, much less provide the necessary permission slip to leave early. So, the night before my planned visit, I sat down at my bedroom desk with a notepad, pens, pencils, and a sample of Mrs. Leonard's handwriting. For several hours, I practiced her commanding script. Freehand or traced, the best of my forgeries resembled something from the notebook of a gum-snapping seventh grader more than the stationery of a forty-something woman. *You'll never get away with it,* I thought, frustrated.

Then the solution, elegant and simple, stumbled into my head. *Just be honest.* Hooky was a charge of "unexcused absence." To escape the indictment, a written or verbal excuse, free of deception, was required. I pulled out a piece of paper and, in my most mature handwriting, carefully wrote:

"Please excuse Andy Bridge from class before lunch today. He has an appointment to go to. Sincerely, Andy Bridge."

The note contained every required element. It was handwritten. It offered an excuse. It was clean of deceit. I was Andy Bridge and had claimed to be no one else. Holding my prize to the light, I smiled proudly at my work.

The next day, after fourth period, I appeared in the high school's attendance office with my contrivance in hand. For the first time in years, someone with the last name Bridge had signed a school document on my behalf. The secretary scrutinized the note, eyeballing me several times like one of the Soviet border thugs Mrs. Leonard described. My hands began to tremble.

"Are you coming back this afternoon?" she grunted.

"No, ma'am. I'll be gone for the remainder of the day," I answered formally.

She took a final look at the paper I had produced. "All right, you may leave."

Slowly and deliberately, I paced out of the office. Then, out of the woman's view, I rushed down the hall and across the campus to retrieve my bike. It was only a quarter past noon. I had plenty of time for the ride to Cathgate.

Sometime around Thanksgiving in fifth grade, I had started arriving at my elementary school early, patiently waiting on the bungalow's steps for Miss O'Malley to arrive. She was slender, even pretty, and kept her dark hair stylishly short. The first time, she seemed irritated to find a young charge waiting for her without an explanation. She invited me inside, instructing me to sit at my desk and stay quiet. I did as she told me, eyeing her as she walked through the classroom, getting ready for the day. After several mornings, she let me sponge off tables that the night janitor had missed, and even sometimes let me run to the school's main office to get her mail or retrieve some supplies. On an oath of confidentiality, she once allowed me to add up scores from her grade book, though I was sure that I had gotten the totals wrong. Eventually, my lingering expanded into the afternoons, and when we were alone, she called me her "little genius."

Though she could hardly have thought of herself as one, Miss O'Malley was a confidante or as close to one as I could manage. She was a morning-and-afternoon companion, reliable in ways that mattered most. She never asked about my family the way that classmates did. She never expressed any desire to follow me home to the Leonards' house, much less appear at their front door. Limited to the confines of the classroom's walls, our friendship felt safe. Warmth and praise came from doing well on tests and book reports. When she challenged the class to see who could name all fifty states on a map of outlines labeled with blanks, I saw to it that I was the first. Then, when she did it with the state capitals, I did the same again. She was tender in ways that could be trusted, in ways that no peer could ever be. Before the others arrived, and again when they left, she listened to the silence from the boy who lingered, and she never demanded any more, never said that the quiet was not enough.

She'll be glad to see me, I thought, riding through the flat suburban streets on my way to see her that afternoon. *She liked me.*

As planned, I arrived at Cathgate just after one o'clock. School was still in session, and I easily found my way to the main office. The woman behind this counter—the third gatekeeper in my odyssey—quickly volunteered Miss O'Malley's classroom location, once I explained that she had been my teacher and fibbed that she had asked to see me. I walked to the room in the center of the school and tapped on the door. No answer. Cautiously, I cracked the entrance open and poked my head inside.

The room's scent wafted toward me, a mix of tempera paint, lead pencils, chalk dust, and sweat. The walls were heavily decorated, as they had always been when Miss O'Malley had taught me. At their tables, an assembly of children promptly glanced up from their sheets of gray paper. Miss O'Malley turned from the front blackboard to look at the intruder at the door.

"May I help you, young man?" she asked, her expression a bit confused.

"Miss O'Malley," I whispered.

She stared a moment longer, apparently trying to place me. "Yes?"

"Miss O'Malley," I whispered again, my eyes reddening.

"Andy?" she asked disbelievingly. "What are you doing here?"

I stood still, unsure what to say.

"He sure is big," a blond-haired boy suddenly yelled, accustomed to children and adults at his school, but nothing in between. His classmates laughed.

"David!" Miss O'Malley scolded him, then quickly returned to me. "Is that you, Andy?"

"Yeah, I thought I'd stop by to visit." My voice quivered.

"Is there something wrong?"

"No, there's nothing wrong," I blurted. "I'm fine."

Around the room, dozens of bewildered eyes watched.

"Do you think you can wait outside? School will be out in twenty-five minutes." She nodded at the wall clock to the side.

"I can come back another time, if you want."

"No, that's all right," she reassured me. "Just wait outside for me."

I turned, closed the door as quietly as I could, waited a moment, then walked back to Cathgate's entrance, unlocked my bike, and rode away. Miss O'Malley and I never saw each other again.

There was nothing in her voice or expression—or even in the classroom's laughter—that told me to leave. I understood, even anticipated, that I would interrupt her and probably be asked to wait. I expected her request that I wait outside. After being taken from Hope, Miss O'Malley was the first teacher—one of the first human beings—who had been genuinely kind to me. She taught me about old explorers like Vasco da Gama, who found the way from Europe to India, and Henry Hudson, who tried to do the same but got lost in the Canadian Arctic and died. She explained percents and probabilities. She listened to my accounts of the first books that I was assigned to read and convinced me that sentences worked best with verbs.

For the briefest moment, the fog of loneliness lifted when Miss O'Malley recognized me that afternoon at Cathgate and spoke my name. Still, one young woman—as much as I cared for her, as much as she may have cared for me—was never going to take the place of another. The loneliness would stay.

RUNNING LATE IN the morning had meant pedalling faster in junior high, but now in tenth grade, it meant missing the bus. I grabbed my jacket and backpack off my bed, then dashed out the front door and into the downpour. Past the front lawn and onto the sidewalk, I glanced ahead to the corner and saw the high school bus idling. The dank, cool air was already thick with diesel fumes. With my books pounding on my back and Rusty running alongside me in his yard, I hustled to the corner just as the folding door closed and the bus lurched into the street. The rain streamed down my face as I stared plaintively at the driver through the sealed door. The windshield wipers dragged across the windshield, squeaking over the glass. The driver's long, sallow face turned toward the soaked and skinny tenth-grader waiting at the curb.

Please! I mouthed at him through the glass.

He shook his head, looked at the intersection ahead, then reached reluctantly for the door lever. As the door opened, I ran into the street and leapt onto the stairwell. Slipping on the rain-slick tread, I seized the handrail just in time to save myself from tumbling backward onto the wet ground. The tyrant at the wheel ignored my struggle, and when I reached the aisle next to him, he yanked the door shut—his unspoken order to sit down and shut up. Caught in the stare of my high-school classmates, I scanned the rows for an empty seat. Predictably, the bus had filled from the back first, leaving only a front spot for me to take, in plain view of the large mirror and the driver's roving eyes. As the bus exhaled and sped into the intersection, jerking our heads against the tall seats, I dug out my novel for English class, though I had already done the reading the evening before.

We quickly cleared the neighborhood streets and entered the San Fernando Valley's larger grid of multilane avenues. Staring down at my book, I assumed that we were nearly at the high school when a chorus of moans rolled down the aisle. Looking up, I noticed several riders clearing the windows with their hands and sleeves. Breathing in the clammy air, I glanced at the street. The driver had taken a wrong turn. Amused and sure that he would find his way back, arming everyone with an excuse for tardiness, I kept reading.

Yet the driver confidently drove on. From a wide thoroughfare, he darted into an unfamiliar set of side streets. He rumbled past several blocks of older suburban homes before coming to a dead halt. As the bus trembled beneath us, its exhaust drifting through the windows that had been opened to break the stagnant air, the busload of eyes stared at a beige-painted dwelling that lay beyond. The structure was larger and set further back from the street than the surrounding homes and apartments that I could see, and though it resembled a single-story apartment building, its details betrayed something else. Down from an original front door, a set of newer, wider doors had been added, as if the fire marshal had insisted that everything be brought up to code. Unlike the other front lawns, this one was mowed and clipped to the point of being sterile. The cinderblock fence was not unusual—even the Leonards' property was bounded with one— but someone had taken the precaution of adding an additional layer of bricks, making this barrier taller than the fences around it. Two identical vans were parked side by side in the driveway.

Finally, the building's front door opened. A few seconds passed before a large man appeared. My stomach twisted. Umbrella in hand, the man sauntered across the walkway, then with a flick of his finger, he motioned toward the darkened threshold. Four boys trailed out the door, advancing in single file. Hardly dressed for school, they wore nearly identical sets of white T-shirts, blue jeans, and black sneakers. One of the boys was neater than the other three, but all four had shaggy haircuts and clearly none had washed up since tumbling out of bed. Without backpacks or books, the four waited obediently in the cold rain until the bus door jerked open.

"If you have a problem with these guys, you let me know," the boys' escort yelled as one of them ducked under his arm to get inside.

The driver looked down the stairwell and nodded, then watched the remaining three boys climb aboard before pulling shut the door. The seated crowd around me gaped at the unknowns. Unsure where to go, the bewildered boys stared back at us, searching for someone to make a space. No one volunteered. No one moved. The boys stepped forward, pausing between the first rows of smartly dressed students around me. An anonymous snicker challenged the intruders to halt. One of the boys glanced to the driver, who lifted himself slightly from his seat, glaring at the lines of his unyielding passengers. Reassured by the act of silent hostility, the boys quickly separated, wandered deeper into the aisle, and randomly forced themselves onto several seats.

With the strangers reasonably secure, the driver slumped back to his post, rested his arms on the steering wheel, and pulled into the street. Returning to the larger avenues, then staggering into the school's parking lot, we arrived only a few minutes late.

The boys were quickly ignored, if not forgotten. The rest of the day, I saw none of them in the halls. The next morning, the driver returned to his usual route, taking us straight to school without stopping at the boys' home. Nearly a week passed before I heard the whispers that there had been trouble.

On the day that the boys had arrived, a bully whom I vaguely knew shoved one of them against a locker between periods. Whether the bully had been told where the boys had come from or simply spotted a new target, no one was really sure. But when the new boy pushed back, a brawl erupted in the packed corridor.

Though the police were rarely called for other fights, they were for this one. The thug who started it all was suspended for three days. The boy from the group home was arrested and expelled.

Yet not even that was the end of it. As the bully later bragged, when his parents found out that the other teenager lived in a group home for boys in county care, they threatened to sue the school district for allowing "children like that" near their son. Faced with the prospect of a lawsuit, Mr. Phelpson, the high school principal, called the group home and refused to allow the remaining three to return. The group home offered no objection. Relieved, Mr. Phelpson telephoned the perpetrator's parents, informing them that the threat on campus had been removed. The suspension was revoked, and the cocky punk promptly returned to school the next day. The four boys were soon forgotten.

I told no one what I had in common with the boys who had arrived only for a day, then disappeared. Quietly, I felt ashamed that I had protected myself by saying nothing in their defense. Yet I saw how quickly they had left, leaving only a week's worth of rumors behind. No better than anyone else, I let the boys go.

TENTH GRADE WENT well. I joined the swim team, mostly to avoid the humiliation of basketball and baseball in physical education classes. After years of practice in the Leonards' pool, I was a middling to good swimmer. I joined several honors organizations, along with the school's debate team and the volunteer tutors. In the summer between my sophomore and junior years, I attended a four-week summer school program at UC Davis. Savings from my job as a box boy and a stipend from the sponsoring organization covered the tuition. The following summer, I attended Boys State in Sacramento, which the American Legion sponsored for free.

There were limits to what Miss O'Malley or any of the teachers that followed her could do. They could not change the family where the county had put me. They could not undo what had happened to Hope. They could never make me miss her less. They did what they said they would do and they were who they said they would be. Delighting in things like American history, geometry, and English grammar, they arrived and taught, day after day. Adults doing what they were supposed to do, doing what was expected, had become rare in my young life. Yet with the bit of attention that my teachers had given me, they had done the extraordinary. They had shown me that if the entire world was not safe, at least a region of it might be.

Every morning, the claxon was loud enough to taunt the boundaries of silence. Pricking thousands of eardrums, the blast walloped through the wide corridors lined with amber-colored lockers, then with nothing to stop it other than exhaustion, it spread over the large campus, across the lines of concrete and grass, dicing through the chain-link fences. Muted by it, students and teachers halted their progress for the slightest moment, then once it ceased, proceeded onward with their new day.

The hallways were always thickest in the morning. Dozens of ever-evolving cliques gathered outside bathroom doors. Boys shoved tongues into girls' mouths while knotted legs struggled for balance. Lockers rattled open, exposing interiors wallpapered with Care Bears or *Playboy* centerfolds, and shelves lined with notebooks or stuffed with trash. The younger and more timid students navigated the throng along its sides or wherever the safest clearing formed. The older and more confident ones cruised through with less care. I held mostly to the cautious edges.

Arriving at my classroom door on the third floor of the high school's most southern wing, I glanced at the neatly printed warning taped over the narrow window: ABANDON HOPE, ALL YE WHO ENTER HERE. The night before, someone had scrawled below it, "NO SHIT, SHERLOCK." I grinned at the lineup of possible culprits appearing in my head, then pushed open the heavy door, thinking of my twelfth-grade English teacher, who had posted the warning in the first place. *She'll never take it down now.*

Barely inside, a classmate shoved past me and I nearly tripped over the extended legs of another. I wandered to my desk, a spot that I had chosen off to the side of the thirty or so others arranged in the shape of a horseshoe. As I looked on, students streamed in through both classroom entrances, the doors slamming open and shut each time. The massing band of teenagers swung into their chairs, then dug out notebooks, pencils, and texts from overstuffed backpacks that barely fit beneath the small desks. They leaned, bent, and twisted to jabber about a new pair of sneakers, beg for notes on unfinished reading, or test out another clumsy romantic advance. At the head of the class, the large desk hunkered alone. Mrs. Ross's grade book lay unattended, taunting every set of passing eyes.

The tardy bell rang, silencing the room. The brasher among the boys slowly swaggered to their chairs. With the front desk still empty, though, the uproar quickly resumed. As she did every morning, Mrs. Ross arrived late, her heels clacking across the polished tile floor. Looking at no one, she swept around a cart stacked high with copies of a new novel and slapped a stack of marked essays over her grade book. She crossed to the front of her desk, leaned against its edge, and waited. The display quieted the class, except for one boy who continued yammering.

Mrs. Ross adjusted her hair with a sigh, locked her long legs at her ankles, and folded her arms. Her face assumed its familiar mild irritation as she looked down for a moment, before settling her eyes on the chatting boy, now draped across the desk behind him, his face nearly buried in a girl's chest.

"Mr. Sullivan," she called to the young man. I watched as the class giggled and shifted its attention to the prattling offender. "Tell us, are you talking to that young lady or breast-feeding?"

The boy finished a last tidbit of banter, then swung around and faced Mrs. Ross with a grin. "Well, I'm not sure." I could see the girl behind him already blushing. "Which would you recommend?"

Mrs. Ross ignored the question, twisted to glance at her desk. "Mr. Sullivan, while we're on the topic of little opuses"—she began limply picking through the stack of essays—"how long did yours take to develop?" She turned to the boy, mimicking his grin.

He furrowed his brow, stroking his chin and nonexistent beard. "As I'm certain you appreciated," he answered soberly, "I worked day after day, hour after hour, min—"

"Mr. Sullivan," she interrupted.

The boy straightened up in his chair.

"Mr. Sullivan," she repeated, rolling her eyes and sifting his paper from the pile. "I don't have time for this now. If you can pull yourself from your other activities, stop by at the end of the day."

The boy slouched back, dangling his arm to the side. "You know, I'm always happy to stop by whenever you need me." He clucked his tongue. "Whatever I can do to make you happy."

Mrs. Ross dropped the paper on her desk, then folded her arms and stared.

"You know," he continued, "since you and I'll be here workin' alone. Alone and hard . . ." A round of hoots tumbled through the class, encouraging him. "I can bring the candles, if you bring the wine."

Mrs. Ross pushed away from her desk, pulled a book from the cart, sauntered to the chalkboard, and wrote: *As I Lay Dying*. A few muted chuckles crawled through the rows of desks.

The boy gloated from across the room.

Mrs. Ross tossed the chalk on her desk and looked him straight in the face. "You know, *sweetheart,* I teach all day." She glanced at her feet then back at him. "The last thing I want to do is teach all night."

The class erupted. The boy's smooth cheeks turned pink. Mrs. Ross turned to the day's lesson, and from my inconspicuous spot, I smiled.

Mrs. Karen Ross was the incontestable commander of an English Department seething with rebels. Principal Phelpson hated her, and rumor had it that he had called her a name during a heated meeting that would have gotten any one of us expelled. She was in her mid-forties and commuted into the San Fernando Valley from Malibu every school day. We gossiped that she was married to a wealthy stockbroker and had a daughter who went to a private boarding school in Switzerland. Her teaching job was not something that she needed but rather an irritating hobby. She regularly threatened to quit, simply not show up at school the next day, though all of us knew that she never would do it.

She was the only high school teacher whom I ever approached for help. She was tough. She was not an angel or savior, parent or confidante. Had she offered to be one, I would have rejected it. Those promises had been made and broken, and now it was too late for more. She and I never discussed foster care, the Leonards, or my mother. When I did badly on a paper or answered a question poorly in class, she was deadly honest but kind. She was the first to teach me that I could disappoint someone without losing her.

Finally, there were the little reminders of Hope that I looked for in nearly everyone. The two of them looked nothing alike. Mrs. Ross was tall and blonde. Hope was petite and dark. Yet both women snapped out retorts that left their opponents sputtering. Both challenged the world. Both seemed braver than I could ever be.

When she strolled into class on our first day of twelfth grade, Mrs. Ross had promised that we would—as we had in earlier English classes—read books and poems, only this time a little better. Some of what she taught appealed to me by accident. When we read *As I Lay Dying,* she never knew that the story of a mother who had died and the son who could still hear crying in the night would mean so much to a shy boy sitting at the edge of her class. When we read *Catch-22,* she never knew that the same boy had already understood that heroes may not be as pure as we like, that they may not act or appear as we expect. She taught me poetry, especially her favorite poem about a pitiful and proper middle-aged man named J. Alfred Prufrock, who imagined himself lingering on the floor of the sea, listening to the distant songs of mermaids who sang to others but refused to sing to him. Mrs. Ross never told us what to do with our lives, in high school or beyond. Instead, she warned about old and frightened Prufrock, a man who had wasted his life in silence, too frightened to challenge the world, too timid to demand his place in it.

Mrs. Ross never denied that life could be horribly unfair. Occasionally she even implied that she thought it would be for some of us. She merely claimed that unfairness need not be the end of it. She believed that words mattered, that they could persuade, that now and again they could make us better than what our nature might have us be. Fair or not, life could still be something important, something meaningful. On the last day that I saw her, she handed me a note, quoting from the poem that she loved. Reminding me that the future could hold more than empty silence, she wrote that the mermaids who had never sung to Mr. Prufrock would someday sing to me.

I believed her.

CHAPTER FOURTEEN

∽

*Y*OU'VE NEVER BEEN *good at drawing the* S, I thought, staring at the poster board. *The letter always comes out looking like half of a swastika.* I surveyed the jumble of crooked letters, then grimaced. *That B isn't so hot either.*

From the desk in the bedroom, I looked down at the carpeted floor. Only two clean orange sheets remained, and I had already spoiled the back of one. The collection of cardboard and pens had been expensive, sapping most of my salary for the week. Besides that, the bike ride back to the Leonards' house from the craft store had not been easy, balancing seven poster boards across the handlebars and clutching a fistful of markers in each hand.

I glanced around the empty bedroom. Other than an occasional crack from the settling hallway, the house was quiet. Sometime between my rush to finish *Wuthering Heights* for Mrs. Ross and my first poster attempt, Mrs. Leonard had retrieved her husband from the garage. I had heard the two of them walk past my closed door, signaling that they were off to bed and leaving me to tiptoe around my room. I crept to the edge of my bed and stretched for the bag of marshmallows that I had stashed under it the evening before. Glancing up, I halted at the darkened window, smiled at my mirrored face under the ceiling light, my cheeks stuffed with pillows of sugary air, then reached for a thicker marker to fatten out my misshapen *S* and finish what remained of ANDY BRIDGE for Student Body President.

The next day, with my five posters and two rolled banners in hand, I waited outside the principal's office for him to review my campaign materials, sanctioning them as sufficiently bland. My two opponents stood in front of me—a quiet senior girl who had recently ended her term as student body parliamentarian and who posed the greatest threat to my candidacy, and a homely sophomore boy who had been elected sophomore class president unopposed. A semester earlier, I had concluded my own term as student body vice president. The three of us—a collection of little titles—had dawdled there in single file through most of lunch, shielding our materials from one another's nosy eyes and ignoring the contemptuous stares of fellow students passing by.

Finally Mr. Phelpson emerged from his office, stuffing the corner of a sandwich into his mouth. Beneath a block of silver hair, his expression normally defaulted into a tense, insincere smile. Prior to his career in education, he had been in the military, but speculation over his branch of service ran rampant. His friends on the faculty claimed it had been the Green Berets. Mrs. Ross insisted that it had been the weekend reserves. Whatever his credentials, the school district recognized his strengths, allowed him to skip the usual stint in the classroom, and placed him directly into high school administration.

He and I were already acquainted with each other. As student body vice president, I had presided over my high school's student assembly, a collection of bored homeroom representatives. Mr. Phelpson once addressed the assembly, urging the adoption of a Students for a Spotless Campus Campaign to assign homeroom classes responsibility for picking up trash from the school grounds once a week. Under the caption "RE: Gulag Plan—aka SS Campus Proposal," Mrs. Ross and her fellow English Department seditionists had promptly banged out a memorandum refusing to serve as "chain gang bosses." After I shared the memo with several homeroom representatives, the assembly had rejected Mr. Phelpson's idea. When he returned on appeal, one especially rebellious member pointed out that only students were allowed to offer resolutions for consideration. I refused to recognize Phelpson's claim as an "honorary homeroom representative" but promised to establish a committee of interested students. No one volunteered and the idea died.

After audiences with my opponents, Mr. Phelpson called me in from the corridor. Overlooking the campus's center quad, his office burst with sunlight. The smell of tuna fish and mayonnaise hung in the warm air. Standing behind his desk, his hands resting on his hips, he nodded at me to spread my posters and banner on the floor.

"Well, aren't these colorful?"

"I guess," I responded, exhausted from the late night and rolling my eyes.

He paused, then pointed at our feet. "Shouldn't the *for* in ANDY BRIDGE FOR STUDENT BODY PRESIDENT be a little bigger? I mean you are running *for* Student Body President, right? You don't have it, yet." He nudged me in the arm, chortling. "Gotta keep things honest, don't we?"

Idiot, I thought, mutely stepping away.

He circled the center of his office a few more times. Then, after I promised to add glitter to every *for,* he extracted his rubber stamp, slapped an inky "PRINCIPAL M. PHELPSON" on everything, and dismissed me. I never bothered with the glitter.

The following day, my opponents and I addressed the student body over the school's closed-circuit television system. I gave a nervous speech about election reform and presenting student proposals directly to the faculty assembly. Over the next four days, I walked the hallways, watching the little squads of my two opponents' supporters passing out flyers, carrying posters, and replacing the banners, which were inevitably covered with graffiti by the end of each day.

I had friends, or more accurately, classmates who knew me. After nine years in foster care, I had told no one that my mother had disappeared. Though I saw reminders of her in teachers at school and in strangers on the street, I said nothing. Like lying in the field and whispering to the crows, I protected my losses. There were some who tried to befriend me. But after I declined enough invitations to eat lunch together, to go to the movies, to hang out after school, to answer questions about my parents and me, most gave up. I learned early that people generally move on.

For the few who persisted, I endured their advances but held to my restrictions. If classmates insisted on stopping by the house, I did my best to meet them on the sidewalk or at the front door. For those who made it inside the house, I made introductions quickly, then did my best to shuttle them back outside. I avoided lunchtime pep rallies and nighttime open houses. During classroom breaks, I anxiously paced. Skipping lunch or eating along the way, I strode through the halls and the lawns, the lunch area, and the quad, never considering where I might be going. I knew that some classmates had noticed that I was always alone, and when I thought about it too much, my face flushed with embarrassment. Yet I kept moving, knowing that it felt better than keeping still.

Rarely, someone insisted on intruding and pushing across the line. David Sullivan, the boy who joked so easily in Mrs. Ross's class, made that effort. He had arrived in eleventh grade, after he and his mother had moved to the San Fernando Valley from Boston. Smart and good-natured, if a bit cocky, he transitioned well. He carried straight A's, until Mrs. Ross had the audacity to give him a B-plus. He bragged that he was going to go to Princeton University, and eventually he did. According to rumor, David's mother was also a single woman who had raised him on her own. I never told him that I had heard it and never confessed that I envied him for it. True or not, he gave the impression that things came easily for him. I admired him for that, too. Our friendship was little more than talking in the halls, maybe some before class. Still, I was proud of having mustered even that.

With a tap on my shoulder during a passing period, he offered more. As I glanced from my locker, he greeted me with a teasing tone. "Good morning, Mister Bridge."

"Morning," I answered before quickly turning away.

David took an awkward breath. "You know my sixteenth birthday is coming up later this month, and my mom promised to take me and some friends skiing. So, if you're not busy, you wanna come?"

I shook my head.

"Come on, it'll be fun. We'll just go up to Big Bear for the day." He grinned at me in the crowded corridor. "My mom's paying for everything." With an invisible ski pole clasped in each hand, he began swiveling his hips.

"I've never been skiing." I reached for my backpack, pretending to dig for a pen.

"We'll take lessons. It's not a problem. She'll pay for that, too."

I understood that he was being kind, felt the offer of friendship. But there was something in the threat of closeness that was more than I could sustain. In the moment that it arrived, even the offer itself was too much. "I can't do it. I'm sorry. I just can't," I answered, holding my back to him.

Yet the confident boy, so good at friendships, refused to give up. He ticked off the names of two other boys whom I barely knew, then rattled casually though the protocol: "You give me your phone number. She'll call your parents. They'll say yes, and we'll go."

I turned, ready to smile and decline firmly for the last time, when, less than a footstep away, he abandoned his ski poles, reached one hand to each ear as though he was talking on two telephones, then teasingly imitated the sound of his mother's voice with a nasal drawl.

"Hello? You don't know me, Mrs. Bridge, but my name is Joy Sullivan. Your son and mine are friends at Monta Vista High School." He tilted his head toward his other hand, then shifted his voice to reply for Mrs. Bridge. "Oh, of course, you know his father and I are always trying to get that boy out of the house."

He could not have known the intrusion I would have felt in his calling the house, or the taunt I did feel in his imitating my mother. Yet, like shoving someone's hand away from an uncovered wound, self-protection required no thought.

"At least I have two parents for her to call" shot from my mouth.

Stunned, David stared at me briefly, then walked away.

My hand shaking, I closed the locker door, then disappeared into the crowd. I regretted what I had said, understood that it was ugly. I also knew that I could not have thought of a more deeply wounding lie. But an apology would have required an explanation, and an explanation would have required too much. I had stopped hiding in restrooms and in bushes as I had done in elementary school, but I could not bear to surrender the lies that hid Hope and those who replaced her. David and I never spoke again. A year later, when we were seniors, when I watched him joking from across a classroom, I still longed for the chance at friendship that he had offered, but could do no more than that.

Walking through the school hallways with my election posters in hand, I knew not to rely on popularity or friends lobbying on my behalf. Instead, I chose the quality that childhood had taught me best: endurance. I carried the posters myself, replaced the banner when I needed to. Each day during lunch, I waited alone outside the heavy doors that channeled students to the hash lines, and one by one, I approached each, introduced myself, then personally escorted him or her to the polls about a hundred yards away. At school, as at the Leonards' house, I excelled in being known and unknown at the same time. At the end of the high school's weeklong student election, endurance proved to be what it had always been for me—the way that was safe, the way that prevailed. I carried close to seventy percent of the vote in a turnout that the faculty advisor noted was unusually large.

If asked why I wanted to be student body president, my honest answer would have been close to my opponents' responses. I wanted it for my school résumé. I wanted to impress admissions officers and get into a good college. Looking out at my bedroom window that first night, the Leonards already in bed, my mouth bursting with marshmallows, I would never have allowed myself to know, much less say, the other reason: I wanted a different title than foster child. I wanted a title that said I belonged where I was.

Two months after the election, the school district convened a meeting of all student body presidents. The gathering was at a different high school, which was close enough to ride my bike to. Still, I had to ask the Leonards' permission to go. That was the first time they knew I had run, let alone won.

"WHAT ABOUT APPLYING to school in Paris?" the plump, redheaded woman bubbled over the half-door. "I know a great school." She hustled to the back of her windowless office, which was not much bigger than a closet. I waited for her to finish sifting through the stacks of college flyers and SAT preparatory courses, as several transcripts fell to the floor. Her certificate in college counseling hung from the wall in an oversize frame. "See!" She glanced up from her desk, returning with a brightly colored brochure in hand. "I knew it was here."

I stared at the tattered piece of glossy junk mail, focusing on a picture of the Eiffel Tower teetering on a roll of French bread. "A boy like you couldn't have been to France, huh?" I looked up at the woman's hopeful, grinning face.

"I don't speak French. I don't even know anything about France, except that they like to eat."

"Think of it as a learning experience. My husband and I love Paris," the woman mused, pointing to a small picture frame nearly buried on her desk. "You know, we took our youngest daughter last summer. She's still talking about it."

I examined the pamphlet. "It says here that you don't get a college degree at the end. Don't you think I should get a college degree?"

The woman took the advertisement from me, pushed up her glasses, then began whispering through the text. "Ah . . . just like I thought." She looked at me. "It's right here." She tapped at a line. "See?"

I began slowly reading aloud, "Some students may be permitted to transfer earned credits to colleges in their countries of origin. . . ."

"Keep going." She pointed lower on the page.

I continued reading, ". . . toward obtaining a degree in the arts and sciences."

The woman smiled and waited.

I hesitated for a moment. "I really think I should look at some other schools. You know, the kind that give diplomas."

The woman's smile waned, then disappeared. "Well, have it your way. That's no problem for me," she said curtly. "Be sure to bring your recommendation forms at least three weeks before they're due. It's already November. You're getting late."

I glanced over her shoulder at a thick paperback book resting on a shelf above her desk. "Do you think I could look at your college guide? I promise to bring it back."

"I had two of them," she announced. "The last one I lent out was never returned." She paused to allow the full weight of adolescent larceny to sink in. "Students are no longer allowed to take it with them. You can review it in my office on Tuesdays and Thursdays." She added with an undertone, "Most students buy them."

Still looking at the book, I felt the woman's glare. "That's OK. I was going to buy one anyway." I reached for my backpack and scampered down the hall.

Later that afternoon, the manager at the grocery store let me clock out a few minutes early, and I biked to the largest mall in the neighborhood. The bookstore was about to close; still, the clerk was friendly enough. No guides were left on the shelf, but she retrieved one from the back room.

Returning to the house, I glanced at the open door to the garage and caught Mr. Leonard's eye as he looked up from a stereo that I assumed he had recovered from someone's garbage. He silently shook his head, then continued with his project. I sheepishly walked through the front door, unsure what I could have done to upset him. Lit only by the light above the stove, the kitchen was empty. Mr. Leonard and his wife had eaten, leaving me responsible for getting dinner on my own. Relieved that she was watching television in her bedroom, I glanced at a note on the counter, apparently intended for me: "Get the trash out, NOW!"

The college advisor had not been helpful, and the Leonards were likely to be even less so. All of the Leonards' children had moved out in succession. Living on their own, Becky and Christopher had already dropped out of junior college, while Jessica was still struggling to finish at UC Riverside. Though I was now a senior, no one had inquired about my future plans.

I crept to my room, laid my backpack and the bag from the store on the bed. Slipping through the rooms of the house but avoiding Mrs. Leonard's, I collected the trash from the wastebaskets, then stole back across the kitchen floor. I dumped what I had into the trashcans outside, before hauling the week's worth of garbage to the street. Finished, I returned to my room and gently shut the door.

I listened for Mrs. Leonard to pace down the hall. Several seconds passed. Nothing. Relieved, I slipped the college guide from its bag, turned on the small desk light, and slid into the chair.

The entries were short, mostly two or three paragraphs long. I flipped through the book's index, discovering that the schools had been ranked. I tiptoed to the bedroom door, back down the hall to Mrs. Leonard's desk in the kitchen. Counting out ten envelopes from the drawer, I stuffed them down my pants. In the dim light from the stove, I eyed a roll of stamps but left them untouched.

Back in my room, I wrote my SAT scores beside my best estimate of my most recent grade average, then compared each to the rankings in the guide's index. I chose a few schools that I had heard of. Thereafter, my first criterion was distance, preferably enough to require a plane trip. Envelope by envelope, I scrawled out the names and addresses. After the tenth envelope, I stopped.

Over the next three weeks, the applications dribbled through the mail, which I picked through before Mr. Leonard arrived home from work. By early December, I had sorted through the stack of materials, selecting four colleges, all in New England, all thousands of miles away, all unseen. I drafted two personal essays, unread by teachers or the Leonards, one on what I thought it would be like to have brunch with Sigmund Freud, and the other on Heathcliff, the vengeful orphan in *Wuthering Heights*. Both essays came from what I had read in Mrs. Ross's class. I gave the recommendation forms to my teachers. Then, over Christmas break, I finished up the applications, sent them in, and waited.

Yet, I never wrote and no college committee ever read what would have been my most honest essay:

Dear Admissions Officer:

My name is Andy Bridge. I am a senior at Monta Vista High School, and I have lived in foster care since I was seven years old. I don't think that you get many applications from foster children. I am not sure why I feel that way. No one told me not to do this, and no one said that I should. It's the quiet space in the middle where people say the most. The quiet is what tells you not to expect much and that not much is expected of you.

Before you have finished, and maybe already, I suppose that you will want to know what made this particular foster child apply. I suppose you will also want to know what made me different from the others who have never written to you.

From the grades and organizations that I have listed, you may want to believe that I am a popular boy, the kind of boy who takes easily to others and who even in a crowd of friends still stands apart. But I am not that kind of boy. I have stood apart, but have done it mostly alone. I am a boy who needed to keep everything separate: who needed to keep school separate from home and who he was separate from who was around him. I hope that you will not think less of me because I have found my way to honors and titles that did not require friends.

I also think that you may want to learn about someone who has always been there for me, someone who helped me along the way and, in the end, got me to you. I have to tell you that I would have liked that, too. But, if I could show you MacLaren Hall or the house where I have grown up, you would see that angels and saviors are rare. Then, like me, you would know to stop looking for them, too.

What I can tell you is that I learned my lessons quickly. I learned the importance of my County bed, and I have always known not to lose it. I learned never to be just another boy who came and went. I learned to please my teachers and to make them like me. I studied hard and managed tests especially well. If I am not close to my classmates, I learned from them what it means to believe that good things lay ahead.

My mother warned me that she would not be around forever, that I would have to fend for myself. I wish she had warned me that I would miss her and feel this alone. It's like when you're little in a crowded store with your mom, and holding your hand, she bends down and says, "If I lose you, just stay where you are. Don't wander off." Sometimes when you're lost, the most you can do is wait. More than anything else, that is what I have learned to do best: to wait, to outlast the fear, and to hold on just a bit longer.

Finally, when you read this, I hope that you will not feel sorry for me. Because even in years of quiet, a boy can still find his way.

"THEY WANT YOU there next Saturday, at eleven o'clock in the morning," the college advisor told me from her side of the half-door, retrieving the envelope from her desk. "Don't be late. No interviewer likes that." She glanced down at my shoes and pants. "And let's make ourselves presentable, all right?"

I nodded, tugging the letter from her fingers.

"It's in Sherman Oaks. Do you know where that is?"

"I can ride my bike," I said anxiously.

She stared incredulously.

"It's only a few miles. Don't worry. I can do it."

She shrugged and returned to her desk.

That Saturday, the rains were torrential. During the night, the downpour had flooded the Leonards' pool, flowing under the sliding glass doors and sopping the white living-room carpet with gallons of murky rainwater. Mrs. Leonard sounded the alarm just before five o'clock in the morning, running through the house, flipping on the lights, ordering me up. She called up her youngest daughter, Becky, who rushed to the house to help. By dawn, I was still in my pajamas, scraping plastic containers across the waterlogged carpet, filling buckets, then dashing outside and tossing the rainwater into the backyard swamp.

With the rain showing no sign of any clearing by eight o'clock, I approached Mrs. Leonard about driving me to my interview. "We'll see," she answered, and I continued nervously bucketing. At a quarter past ten, Mr. Leonard announced from the living-room entrance that he would take me. Soaked but unbathed, I ran to my room, peeled off my pajamas and pulled together a mismatched set of school clothes, then raced through the rain to the station wagon in the driveway.

I waited beside the locked car until, several minutes later, Mr. Leonard emerged with his car keys and an umbrella in one hand and a coffee mug in the other. He had donned his usual Saturday garb—threadbare jeans that he had had for as long as I could recall, a plaid shirt that his wife had salvaged from someone's trash, and a pair of flip-flops. Glancing at me from the driver's side, he rested the mug on the roof, fumbled to unlock the door, secured the mug on the dashboard, then swung inside and buckled up. He collected himself for a moment before reaching across the front seat and unlocking my door. I climbed in. My shirt clinging to my back, I handed him the soggy letter with the interviewer's address. He scanned the note, nodded, and placed it on the seat.

"So, where is this school?" he asked, his arm extended behind my neck as he pulled out of the driveway. The question was his first about my college plans.

From across the front seat, I smiled. "You mean Bowdoin College? It's in Maine. Brunswick, Maine."

"Oh," he answered, then wordlessly drove into the street.

Overhead, the rain hammered at the car, flooding over the windshield. As we plunged through the streets, water surged from the gutters, glutting the sidewalks and roadways, sloshing against the brakes and wheel wells beneath our feet. Mr. Leonard said nothing as we veered into the hills of an expensive suburb. The houses and yards around us grew larger, before finally disappearing behind walls of hedges and brick. We drove up and down the same stretch several times before spotting the small sign beneath the appropriate driveway's call box.

Mr. Leonard pulled up slowly, rolled down the window, and examined the metal cube. Several moments passed, and we were already ten minutes late. Finally, I leaned toward him and whispered, "I think you push the button."

"I know that you push the button," he snapped, but continued staring, gathering his courage.

"Do you want me to do it?"

He threw me a glare.

I retreated. "Just tell them who I am. They know I'm supposed to be here." Outside the car, the silver button waited. I reached for the passenger door, ready to get out.

Then slowly, Mr. Leonard began extending his forefinger into the rain.

"May I help you?" an impatient voice asked.

Mr. Leonard's finger flew back.

"May I help you?" the voice repeated.

"You need to answer them," I whispered anxiously.

Mr. Leonard straightened his back. "Uh, yes. This is Andy Bridge, for his appointment."

Without another word, the dark green gate in front of us opened leisurely, revealing no more than a private road canopied with oak trees. Mr. Leonard slowly accelerated, nearly pressing his forehead against the windshield as he canvassed the grounds. The leafy passage emptied into an egg-shaped driveway, which led to a white-columned house with pink-painted brick and French windows. In the center of the driveway, a crowd of life-size bronze statues of children circled what appeared to be an immense, dancing toad. Mr. Leonard stopped the car. Peering into the driving rain, the two of us quietly examined the scene, then looked at each other across the seat and shrugged.

"It shouldn't take much more than forty-five minutes." I reached for the door handle, then glanced back at him. "Thanks for taking me."

"No problem." He smiled shyly. "Do a good job in there."

I grinned at the encouragement, then darted into the downpour.

A woman answered the door and asked me to wait inside, then disappeared toward the back. Alone at the entrance, I peered through a wide archway into the living room, noticing not one but several sofas. A darkened fireplace occupied an expanse of the farthest wall. A pile of neatly stacked wood rested to the side. Vases filled with pink and white roses sat atop tables with baby-blue porcelain lamps. The house smelled empty, without the odor of stale cooking from the kitchen— wherever it was—or the whiff of Pine-Sol from the floors and walls. These rooms held only the empty scent of authority. *Rich people's houses smell different,* I thought, then jolted back to the purpose of my visit when I heard the woman approaching across the hardwood floor.

"Your talk with Mr. Bennett"—she lifted an umbrella from a gold stand beside me—"will be in the library." She reached for the front door, and I stepped awkwardly out of her way. As we walked around the driveway, she glanced at Mr. Leonard, who was staring from the driver's-side window, sipping at his coffee. Trailing behind, I focused on the woman's polished brown shoes. Opposite the main dwelling was a smaller, identically designed structure, which gave it the appearance of a matching playhouse. The woman entered, still leaving me to tag after her. She pointed to an overstuffed chair in a small waiting area, then rapped once at a closed door. Without waiting for a response, she entered the next room and shut the entrance behind her.

Moments later, the door swung open. "Mr. Bennett will see you now." She glanced to the side, cuing me to get up, then promptly walked out.

Leaning back in a leather chair, his legs crossed, a large gray-haired man sat behind a dark wood writing table. In front of him, a carefully stacked set of papers lay at one corner of the desk, balanced by a gold pen and a large picture frame at the other. He wore a deep blue suit and a crisp pink bow tie, and though he certainly knew that I had entered the room, he continued flipping through a file. Wall shelves held a few books but were mostly cluttered with other framed photographs of what I assumed were his family—two girls who had long blonde hair and were a bit older than I was, and the man's wife, who had a brittle smile. On the wall behind him, a collection of college banners hung, each name sewn in clean block letters onto backgrounds of yellow, blue, brown, green, and crimson.

The man continued reading as the rain beat at the roof, cascading down the paned windows. I glanced at my fingers, the nails soft from scooping the flood in the Leonards' living room. Eyeing a torn cuticle, I shot a look at the man, who remained occupied, then I nervously bit at the flap of skin.

"Would you like to sit down?" the man's deep voice called.

I quickly dropped my hand to my side. The man pointed to a wooden chair across from his desk. "Yes, thank you, sir."

He tossed the file on the desk. "So, your name is Andy? Andy Bridge, is that correct?"

"Yes, sir."

"Now, is that Andy or Andrew?"

"Andy, sir." I smiled at him. Two questions followed by two excellent answers.

"And you're a senior in public high school, just a few miles down the road at Monta Vista?" He glanced out the window, as if he was thinking of making the trip.

"Yes, sir."

"And why are you and I here today?" He turned and waited.

I fumbled for an answer. "Well . . . because Bowdoin College is a very good school, and I would like to go there very much?"

Grimacing, he leaned closer. "But what about the school do you like? What makes it a good fit for you?"

I felt my face warming. All that I really knew was what I had read in the guidebook and what I could remember from the application that had arrived over a month before.

Can I tell you that I just need to leave where I live? That I promise to do my best and not to disappoint you? I thought, looking back at him.

No, his impatient eyes seemed to answer.

"Well, of course, Bowdoin is one of the very best schools in the country. . . ." I crossed my legs but felt prissy and put my foot back on the floor. "Bowdoin is also known for its excellent English Department. As a matter of fact, Henry Wadsworth Longfellow went there," I added, remembering something from the school's brochure. *God, I think he might have gone to Amherst.* I stumbled for another fact. "Maine, and Bowdoin especially . . ."

The man suddenly glanced out the window again, then stood up and approached it. "*Who* is that man sitting in that car?"

I thought of Mr. Leonard, hunched over the wheel, ogling my interviewer through the driver's window in the rain. "What car?" I innocently asked.

The man looked at me and pointed toward the glass. "*That* car!"

"Oh, *that* car." I paused. "Umm . . . that's Mr. Leonard."

"Who is *Mr. Leonard?*"

I hated the words and could count on one hand the times that I had said them. "Mr. Leonard is my foster father."

The man turned to me, dropping his jaw incredulously. "Well, don't you think that we should invite Mr. Leonard in?" He returned to the window. "He looks cold out there in the rain." I watched as he settled back into his chair then smiled at me to retrieve the stranger from outside.

Judging from Mr. Leonard's expression, he had no more desire to be in that library than I now did. Dripping wet, we entered the room. The interviewer extended his hand, glanced at Mr. Leonard's flip-flops and splattered feet, then pulled another chair from the corner and motioned us to sit down. Posting his plastic coffee mug on his knee, Mr. Leonard stared across the man's desk. Side by side, he and I waited, awkwardly aware that we were now expected to act like father and son.

The man nodded for me to continue where I had left off. "Well, I'm very interested in English." Mr. Leonard glanced at me surprised. "My English teacher at school wrote one of my recommendations." I scanned the man's desk and the file that I assumed was mine. He raised an eyebrow, indicating that the desk was off-limits. I switched topics, still trying to gain some ground. "Bowdoin College—"

"Young man," the man suddenly interrupted, throwing his arms across his desk. "The name of the college to which you have chosen to apply"—he paused to press his mouth closer, lowering his voice to a whisper—"The name B-O-W-D-O-I-N is pronounced BOW-din, *not* bough-DOYN."

I stared back at the man's watery eyes, noticing a trace of satisfaction.

"It's really very simple," he continued. "Repeat after me. BOW, like an Indian's *bow* and arrow."

Native American, I thought to correct him, then weakly whispered back, "BOW."

"Good." He nodded approvingly. "Now, din, as in a jumble of senseless noise." His jacket hunched up around his shoulders, exposing his monogrammed cuffs.

"Din," I repeated.

The man raised his hands like an orchestra conductor, signaling me to combine my lesson.

"BOW-din." I pronounced the two syllables together.

"All right," he pushed back in his chair. As I waited for his next question, the man took a moment to think before an awkward smile crossed his face. "Forgive me, but I just have to ask. How *long* have you been a foster child?"

Outside, the rain had strengthened and was now sheeting against the roof. "A little over ten years," I said softly.

The man turned his ear toward me.

"Ten years," I repeated myself.

"And why did they take you from your parents?"

"I'm not sure." I looked ahead. Mr. Leonard cleared his throat but let the lie pass.

The man nodded, tapping his pen against his knee. "Are there other foster children at the home where you live?"

I held my stare on him and answered, "Not anymore."

"He's the only one, huh?" The man turned to Mr. Leonard. "Do you and your wife have children of your own?"

"We have three of our own children," Mr. Leonard replied stiffly.

"You must be very proud of them." The man paused. Mr. Leonard smiled nervously, anticipating another inquiry. "What are they doing? I mean with school."

Mr. Leonard straightened in his chair. "Our youngest has just started college. The two others are nearly done."

Returning Mr. Leonard's favor, I let him have his lie.

The man looked at me. "Well, how are they different?"

Confused, I hesitated.

"You know, this man and his wife. How are they different from the ones that you came from?"

I glanced down at my soaked black sneakers, noticed Mr. Leonard's veined feet. Raising my head and trying to avoid the man's stack of papers, my eye was caught by the large frame resting at the desk's other corner—a picture of his family sailing, with the ocean at their backs. The room waited for my response. I deepened my voice, stared at the man's jowls. "They're not my parents." My eyes lifted and sunk into his. "And, they never will be."

Mr. Leonard twisted next to me. Mr. Bennett appeared shaken for a moment but caught himself quickly, and cleared his throat to acknowledge what I had said. He stood, leaned across his desk, extended his hand to Mr. Leonard and then to me. "Thank you both so much for coming."

"Well, I know Andy appreciated this," Mr. Leonard blurted. I glanced at him, irritated by the parental tone, then looked down and noticed that a stream of coffee had dribbled from his mug, across his foot, and onto the man's carpet. "It sounds like a very good school," he blithered, unsure how to end the encounter.

The man smiled faintly, but kept to his side of the desk. "You won't mind if the two of you show yourselves out?"

"No, no. Not at all, we . . ." Mr. Leonard rushed to answer. Then, before he could finish, the man reached for a pad of paper and began to write.

Driving back through the rain, Mr. Leonard asked if I wanted to stop at the drugstore for an ice cream cone. I was already cold, so I declined, but he said that he wanted one for himself. He drove into the parking lot, leaped out of the car and into the store. About five minutes later, he appeared under the red and white awning, briefly hesitated, then ran back to the station wagon.

Chilled from the cold rain and the ice cream, he flipped on the dashboard heater. Fog spread over the windshield. I watched him struggle with the dripping cone for several moments, until he finally looked up.

"You know, Andy"—he licked a knuckle—"sometimes people just don't know what they're doing."

Briefly, I appreciated his vague effort to behave like a father. "I know," I answered. In front of me, a narrow gap in the window fog began to widen. "I know. Thank you for driving."

.   .   .

IN EARLY MARCH, a social worker that I had never met called to wish me good-bye. The woman was the last in a line of dozens of caseworkers, male and female, whom the county had assigned after removing me from my mother. I vaguely recall Mrs. Raspberry, Mrs. Hart, Donna, Mr. Harris, Ms. White, Conni. Throughout junior high, their changing pace only increased, and by my senior year in high school, I had forgotten most of their names and lost count entirely.

"I could come out, instead of doing this over the phone," the woman told me through the line.

"No, it's not a problem, really."

"You sure?" A bit of guilt hung in her voice.

"Completely," I replied.

"Well, you don't have to be at the hearing anyway." The woman paused, reassuring herself. "In six months, Los Angeles County will emancipate you. Do you know what emancipate means?"

I thought of President Lincoln freeing the slaves.

Clearly reading from a prepared text, she continued. "Emancipation is the judicial act releasing a child from the custody of the County of Los Angeles." Her voice warmed. "It really means that you've grown up, and that it's time for you to leave the Leonards. It's just a big formality." She waited to hear something from me.

"OK," I answered.

"Of course, you'll need to pack your clothes. And, it's always a good idea to start saving some money. Your foster mother mentioned that you have a job at a grocery store. Is that true?"

"Yes."

"Oh, that's wonderful, sweetheart."

I listened to her smile.

"But all of this brings me to what we really need to talk about and why I called." She stopped. "The Leonards have told me that you may want to go on to college."

May? I thought.

"And all of us think that that is an excellent opportunity to learn about setting priorities and moving forward." The woman's condescension squeezed through the line. "But, sweetheart, you never discussed this with any of us."

Suddenly, panic and anger stabbed at me. *You and I have never discussed anything,* my mind screamed back at her. She knew none of it: the A average, the test scores, the swim team, the state debating awards, student body vice president and president, all of it going on my careful résumé.

"Now, I understand that the schools that you have applied to are very expensive and very far away," she continued.

Suddenly, I felt like a prisoner, one who would never be allowed to leave.

"Your college advisor called me. I'm very concerned that these schools just aren't appropriate for you. Do you understand what I'm trying to say?"

"No." My head was pounding. "No, I don't understand."

"My goodness, sweetheart. Your advisor tells me that they're all in New England. You'd have to buy a plane ticket to get there."

I thought of my classmates' string of absences during the fall semester while they jetted to schools that they thought might interest them.

"I've been saving money from . . ." my voice faded away.

"Your advisor and I really think that you ought to try a closer school. You know, near the Leonards and where you grew up."

That advisor wanted me to go to Paris!

"Independence can be difficult. . . ."

I've always been independent.

"I think it's important to understand that a boy with your . . ." The line went quiet while the woman struggled for the right word. "A boy with your *history* needs a more *appropriate* school."

My hands trembled against the receiver.

"If you stayed in California and went to a state college, the county would pay for your tuition and help with almost everything else, too."

She paused, frustrated with me. "I don't know if the Leonards mentioned that to you."

No, the Leonards didn't mention it. I thought of the humiliation that had always come with the county paying for and helping me with everything—waiting in the school cafeteria lines hiding the yellow ticket that entitled me to a free lunch; watching the secretary at the doctor's office grimace at my Medi-Cal stickers; listening to the dentist explain to Mrs. Leonard that the county would not cover braces to straighten my teeth, though he was sure that it paid for cleanings; being given a summer job picking up after dogs in a park. About to graduate from high school, I wanted nothing paid for or helped with again.

The woman waited on the line for a response.

"What school did you want me to go to?" I asked weakly.

"Well, your college advisor and I talked about it." The woman's tone perked up. "We were thinking that Pierce College accepts applications through mid-August and *on a noncompetitive basis,*" she emphasized. "Your advisor tells me that many students transfer to a full college after a year or two."

Founded in 1947 as the Clarence W. Pierce School of Agriculture, Pierce was an unaccredited community college. The campus was close by. Pierce was the school that both Christopher and Becky had briefly attended before dropping out. No one in my high school classes was applying.

"Your counselor promised that she could get you an application form. Will you promise to pick it up?"

"Yes," I whispered.

"Oh, that's a good boy," she praised. "Wow. Hasn't this been a long talk? I'm so happy we got that settled." She laughed. "From the sounds of it, both of us have got some things to do." Promising to call me before my emancipation in August, she hung up.

The next day, I went to the college advisor for Pierce's admissions sheet, saying nothing as the woman handed it to me. When I reached the end of the corridor, just outside the school's library, I glanced at the pencil-bubbled questions, then crushed it into a ball and threw it in the trash.

Over the remainder of March, several college admissions letters arrived, and among them was one from Wesleyan University in Connecticut. I had never interviewed for its admissions office—perhaps fortunately. I had never seen the campus. I had never called to ask any questions. However, when Wesleyan's acceptance was followed with the offer of a generous scholarship and then a personal letter from its Dean of Admissions asking me to attend, I accepted.

My classmates bragged about their own results, about which schools they wanted to attend. Some gloated over their array of choices as if they had known all along that they had been bound to get in. Wesleyan was as good, even better than some of the schools that were bandied about. Yet when I read the acceptance letter, my eyes swelled more with relief than joy. I sent in the forms, told Mrs. Ross, who was pleased, then sometime in the next week mentioned my choice to the Leonards. Neither of them had heard of it. Four months later, in the middle of July, Mr. Leonard thought to ask me where it was.

∾

CHAPTER FIFTEEN

THAT FINAL SUMMER at the Leonards' house, the heat was blistering. In the far corner of the San Fernando Valley, the swelter descended relentlessly, settling on the yellowing front lawns, the tar streets, and the asphalt sidewalks, rising week after week, until by early August, the neighborhood lay heavy with it. Nearly six years had passed since the last of the other county children had come and gone. Only wife, husband, and I remained.

A light click caught my attention, and glancing at my desk, I noticed that the clock had flipped to 6:28 A.M., Monday, August 11. *They'll be up soon,* I thought.

Alone in the emptiness of a blue sky, as the sun streamed through the pale green curtains of the bedroom window, warming the back of my neck and shirt, I sat at the edge of my bed. That morning, like most others, I woke and dressed before the Leonards rose. Listening to the stillness, mindful of its safety, careful not to disturb it, I waited for the day around me to wake.

The Leonards' voices broke the quiet first. Their footsteps approached my closed door, shuffled past it and into the kitchen. Mrs. Leonard dropped a metal pot on the stove. The house pipes stirred as she measured out a cup of cold water. Still in his bathrobe, Mr. Leonard cracked open the front door, fetched the *Los Angeles Times* from the lawn, returned to the kitchen, then sat at the table and waited to be fed.

A brief pause. I strained to hear, noticing a bar of sunlight had broken through a gap in the curtains and lengthened across the floor.

The electric percolator expelled a congested snort. Mrs. Leonard scraped clean the simmering pot of instant oatmeal, then joined her husband. Sitting at the table, the two remained oblivious to the seventeen-year-old boy—more of a tenant than a child—who vigilantly listened from a bedroom down the hall.

A second pause. I lay down, resting my head on the pillow, leaving my shoes to dangle over the side.

Mr. Leonard ate quickly and, as was his habit, surely lifted his bowl to slurp down the last spoonfuls of milk. He pushed his chair across the linoleum floor, muttered to his wife, and left her reading at the table. His bare feet echoed through the kitchen, then down the hallway to their bedroom. A moment later, the shower sputtered to life. Eager to catch what remained of the morning cool, he hurried. He pulled on the slacks and buttoned the short-sleeved shirt that Mrs. Leonard had laid out the evening before; then he strode through the hall again and past my closed door.

He's leaving, I thought, lifting my head from the pillow.

The couple briefly kissed good-bye in the foyer, whispered something that I could not hear. The front door slammed. Mr. Leonard's heavy dress shoes clacked down the porch. I turned to the window, peered through the curtains, and watched as his backside waddled to the sidewalk, a calculator holstered to his hip and a briefcase hanging from his hand.

A third pause. *She and I are alone.* I eyed the bedroom door, listening.

Back in the kitchen, Mrs. Leonard slid the percolator across the counter tiles, poured another mug of coffee, thumped to the table, and returned to the morning paper.

She might ignore me, I reassured myself. *She might let me stay inside.* The bar of sunlight had finally reached the door.

I stretched, then perched myself on a corner of the bed, running through the rules for remaining in her house. Staying in the room would mean exactly that—staying there. For the ten hours until Mr. Leonard returned home and Mrs. Leonard set dinner on the table, I would not open the bedroom door or do anything that would remind her of my presence. I would not walk too heavily, play the clock radio, or slide the closet door. Lunch would be the chocolate bars, cookies, and sticky buns that I had brought home from the grocery store and stored under my bed. I had tried building models—balsa airplanes and plastic cars—but I had knocked the oil paint onto the carpet floor. With nothing to soak up the pool of paint, the enamel hardened into a deep red splotch at the foot of my bed, igniting Mrs. Leonard's fury at the end of the day. Thereafter, model-building had also been banned.

Even the bathroom would be off-limits, though I had not used it since the evening before. This problem had required considerable thought. I eventually learned to wedge open the bedroom window noiselessly, teeter on my bed while unzipping my pants and, in the absence of wind and with sufficient pressure, send a glistening arc of urine cascading directly into Mrs. Leonard's prized gardenias.

I glanced at the door. *What if I opened the door, walked through the hallway, then meandered through the house?* I smiled at the imagined intrusion.

"This is not *your* house, mister. This is *my* house," she had reminded me, most recently while I was getting ready for bed the night before. Indeed, she left no space for doubt. Everything was hers: the kitchen, the table, the countertops, the mug, and the cooking pot; the hallway and the foyer; the family room, the library of magazines, and the television; the living room, the carpet, the sofas, and the fireplace; the guest room and the queen-size bed; the other bedrooms and my own; the bathroom, the tub, and the toilet. It all belonged to her, and during the day, she would rebuff even my most piddling trespass.

I glanced at the clock again. *It's almost half past seven,* I thought, resting my eyes on the numbers. *It's getting late.*

Mrs. Leonard's chair moved in the kitchen. My head jolted and my eyes darted back to the bedroom door. Her empty coffee mug echoed as it landed in the sink.

"Andy," she hollered down the hall. "Are you still here?"

She knows I am. I slid off the bed.

She rapped at the door, then flung it open before I could answer. "Andy, are you up?" she asked, reviewing me from the door frame.

"I'm up," I whispered back.

A sleeveless housedress hung from her shoulders, halfway down her thighs. She insisted that summer was no time for shoes, stockings, bras, or panties, and this morning was no exception. Her body jostled under the faded fabric as she stepped into the bedroom.

"What are you still doing in the house?" she snapped. "It's a beautiful day out there." I turned toward the window. The day was sunny and might have been beautiful, had the hundred days before it not been identically hot and deathly still. "You need to be outside." Arms dangling at her sides, she held her stare on me, waiting briefly for a response before adding, "Why do you think we paid for that bike, anyway?"

It was stupid to have stayed, to have waited for her, I chided myself.

She glanced over my shoulder at the window, assessing the rising heat through the curtains' filtered light. "Time to close up," she whispered to herself, then returned her attention to me. "You know, it's never good for either of us when you're here, inside," she declared, locking her gaze on me a second longer before turning back for the hall.

I lingered behind, giving her time to leave, then slipped through the house, out the front door, and onto the porch. To my side, she suddenly appeared at the kitchen window, pulling shut the curtains that hung above the sink. She despised the summers, complained day and night about the uncompromising heat, and while remaining in her house, did all she could to hide herself from daylight's malevolent rays. In a morning ritual that put me, the sun, and the world out of sight, she advanced through the house, shuttering every window, closing every door behind her. I looked across the courtyard and, seconds later, saw her at the family room's sliding glass door. Ignoring me, she tussled with the tangled cords hanging to the side. Amused but trying not to grin, I looked down at my feet, then glanced up just as the drapes swung shut.

I walked to the front lawn. Around me, the neighborhood rested under the morning heat. The crows quietly watched me from overhead.

In third grade, my first full school year with the Leonards, my teacher had had a passion for ornithology. The young woman could not resist impressing her zeal on her clutch of eight-year-olds, instructing us to memorize the names of dozens of birds and what they were called as a group. *A bunch of chickens gives a peep. A congregation of owls holds a parliament. A gathering of crows marks a murder.* About to leave for college, I could still numbly recite the lesson.

The neighborhood barely resembled what it had been when I had first arrived at the Leonards' house. Across the street, a sprawling maze of fresh tract homes now covered the field that once faced the front yard. I had hidden in the knee-length grass until the owner plowed it, forcing me to tunnel into a mammoth pit of muck to escape from the Leonards. A row of swaying eucalyptus trees, planted to mark a forgotten property line, survived the grassland and watched over the broken earth for years. But after the workmen pounded the last nails into the new homes, they arrived in ladder trucks, armed with chain saws. Hoisted into the sky in waist-high baskets, the men leaned from tree to tree, slicing through the long row like a great hedge. Then, lashing chains around the stubborn stumps, the workmen spent days wrenching the deepest roots from the earth, until at last, their unrelenting hands had ripped away every last trace of the past.

The crows, it seemed, had been the only constant. Circling high above, they had no roots to lash. They descended from their exile in the surrounding hills, rested on the shingles of new homes, on the wires of utility poles. The trees, the grass, even the mud had been taken from them. Still they returned, refusing to forget the home that had once been theirs.

I ambled across the lawn, even considered staying there for the day. Yet if Mrs. Leonard spotted me through a finger-parted blind, the sight would only anger her. I mulled over my other options, then walked to the side of the house, crept under the Leonards' bedroom window, and retrieved my bicycle. The gate banged as I left, which I was sure Mrs. Leonard heard. I leaped on the ten-speed, sped down the driveway, maneuvering my way between the station wagon and camper, and blindly shot into the street. Pushing through the neighborhood, I rode past the elementary school that Jason and I had attended, then pressed up the fire lanes that wound through and over the hills. The roads ran deep, and briefly stopping at their base, I chose one that I knew would consume all of the morning and most of the afternoon.

The crossing's ascent was the hardest. At my feet, the bicycle's crank almost slowed to a halt as I struggled, panting in the hot, placid air. Each crest demanded a final shove, then a brief moment of wobbling balance, before throwing me down its backside, daring me to brake too quickly. Around me, the ravines and bluffs were sparse, but hardly barren. Clumps of sycamores appeared in the distance, though as I approached, they scattered into single trees that clung to the earth, their trunks blackened from the fires that roamed the hills in the dry autumns. Manzanitas and other thorn bushes whose names I could never remember gave themselves more freely to the flames, only to flourish in the aftermath.

My bike between my legs, I rested at a familiar peak. My calves were dark with dust, and the back of my neck was pink from the sun. Slick with sweat, I wiped my eyes with my forearm and squinted at the sprawl of the San Fernando Valley below. The basin stretched for miles, pushing back the range of mountains that eventually circled it beyond the horizon. Among the lines of homes, the Leonards' house was indistinguishable. The elementary school and its playground were easier to find. I spotted the supermarket where I had bagged groceries and, beyond that, my high school. Farther than I could hope to see, in the same valley, lay the remote markers of another past: the apartment where I had lived with my mother, the beauty school where she had tried to learn a trade, the motel where I had left to buy her a pack of cigarettes only to return in the back of a sheriff's deputy's car.

Eleven years had passed since I had lived with Hope and nearly nine since I had seen her last. From MacLaren, to the Leonards, to now, I had waited in a home that was never mine and watched for a mother who had never returned. I had no idea what became of her, and if those around me knew, they refused to tell. Still, I had done my best not to be greedy, not to need more certainty than I was allowed. The Leonards' constant address had been enough. The string of numbers stenciled on the curb had been my assurance that Hope had what she needed, that at any moment she could arrive to reclaim me. If I could only be still, when the time was right, when she knew that I needed her most, she would find me. She would remember the house, even chuckle at the sight of the dirty camper in the driveway, at the sound of Rusty barking in his yard. She would end her years of drifting through the streets that tangled in the distance. She would keep the oldest of her promises, the first that I could recall. She would come back for me.

But soon the marker in front of the Leonards' house would lead Hope to nothing. She would walk to the porch, knock at the door, and be told that her boy was gone, that he had been taken by a school in New England thousands of miles away. Then she would forget the address and the family in the valley. And the house would be no different from any other in the clutter that lay below.

I glanced above me. The crows slid through the unblemished sky, wary but tolerant of my intrusion. Alone on a roadside, I looked at what was theirs, at all they had claimed, all that they had lost, and all that they had refused to forget.

Dozens of children had left the Leonards before me, but someone had always come for them, someone had always led them away. I was the only child who made it to the end, the only one who remained to leave on his own, and to fend for himself completely. I would take

clothes, money, and every bit of life: high school papers covered with
a favorite teacher's notes; useless awards that I had accepted with false
smiles; notices from the court that had taken me from Hope, put me
in the house that I was leaving, and finally informed the world that,
after all of a childhood, I was free to go. But of all that I would pack
and ship, save and protect, the only stuff of consequence would be my
memory of Hope. I would remember all that she gave me, all that was
taken from her. I would remain the constant guardian of the piece of
eternity that belonged to her and me.

The crossing I had chosen that morning was a long one. It took me
hours to make my way over the hills and then back again. Yet when I
stepped onto the Leonards' porch late that afternoon, I warned myself. *You've come back too soon. She'll be angry.* Still, I reached for the
knob.

When I walked through the front door, the drapes remained
drawn and the house was dark. Only the muffled sound of a television from the Leonards' bedroom disturbed the quiet. My T-shirt
was soaked and in the chill of the air-conditioned house, a shiver
ran across my back and down my legs. Cotton-mouthed, I tiptoed
to the kitchen and bent my head under the tap for a slurp of water.
Then I saw it.

Dangling from the refrigerator by a magnet, Mrs. Leonard's note
was brief:

"Your Mother Called."

THE GIRL FROM the exhausted farmland of Colorado had telephoned the Leonards' house. After one judge deprived Hope of custody over her son, another robbed her of custody over herself. Yet,
after years apart, something—if just a whisper—told her that her boy
needed her, that the time had come to claim him.

Sometime after her final visit to the Leonards' house, Hope found
her way to downtown Los Angeles and to the bus station. With no

reason in mind, other than she had heard good things about it, she bought a one-way ticket for Phoenix, the city named for the bird whose song had summoned Apollo. Arriving in the sun-scarred desert— without friends to call, money to spend, or a son to protect— she was left with only her whispers. She caught the attention of the police and was soon picked up. Evaluated and judged unsuited for a normal life, she was confined indefinitely to the long-term unit at the Arizona State Hospital, formerly named the State Asylum for the Insane. Of the seven years that had passed since she had last seen her son, Hope had spent nearly six locked inside a public hospital's wards.

Then, late one evening, she vanished from the institution's grounds.

Hitchhiking her way back across the desert to Los Angeles, she did well for the first few days, until the pills from the hospital dwindled and the restless voices returned. Ahead of her, the highway sliced through the landscape in a clean line, but somehow the route began to tangle along the way. Roadside Samaritans promised ill-fated shortcuts that only added to her confusion. Repeatedly stranded, away from her intended path, she was left to stray back to the everlengthening road that led to her boy.

After nearly a week, Hope reached the boundaries of the vast sprawl of Los Angeles County where her son lived, somewhere. Years earlier, she had written down the address and telephone number, even known them by heart, but the paper and memory had long since slipped away. She wandered the labyrinth of sidewalks and alleys searching for something that she could remember but only descended deeper into delusion. Finally, as her doctors in Phoenix had predicted, she succumbed, overwhelmed by whispers. Screaming in agony on a street corner, she was arrested while a pedestrian audience drew closer to watch.

Late that night, she woke in the clouded calm of another institution. She pleaded with a succession of state-employed psychiatrists that she had a son. She begged that her boy needed her, that she had come to help him. Lost in the hospital's slurry of purposeless life, her days passed quickly. She grew desperate. She ranted, over and over, the same story of the little boy whom she had lost years before. Then, if only to quiet their new patient, the hospital staff gave in. A nurse called the county, tracked down the foster care department, and re-trieved the facts of what had become of Hope's boy.

Handing Hope the note with the Leonards' telephone number, the nurse must have thought it would lead to nothing. Area code 818 was a toll charge, and hospital rules were clear: Patients could make or re-ceive calls only from the pay phone, mounted at the end of the ward beside the nurses' station. Hope had arrived with nothing, and the isolation of asylum life inflated the value of even a few dimes. The required change was an almost impossible sum.

Hope's currency was limited to the useless hospital points that staff could award, withhold, or remove from her chart at will. With suffi-cient points, she could enjoy the reward of watching television in the patients' lounge. She could qualify for the free cigarettes that the hos-pital dispensed each week. Or, on a very good day, she could spend a hot afternoon in the patio's blinding sun.

Though money might have helped her, points and punishment were what really mattered in Hope's life. Losing points meant notch-ing down a scale of restrictions, summoning a host of penalties. Staff could confine her to the ward or even to her room. If circumstances required more, her keepers could strap her to her bed, choosing from an assortment of apparatuses, all painstakingly designed and approved by psychiatric professionals. Buckled leather straps, amply cushioned with cotton wadding to avoid marks or bruises, could moor her an-kles to a metal bed frame. Wristlets could likewise shackle her hands over her head, forcing her arms into a position of surrender. Longer, reinforced straps could lash across her shoulders, chest, or abdomen, though these required more care. If her torso were bound too loosely, Hope could slip to the side and strangle herself in the inches of air between the bed frame and the floor. If bound too tightly, she could suffocate without moving at all. But in the end, convenience might trump invention altogether, leaving Hope's keepers to the oldest, most reliable therapy of all: locking her in the seclusion room at the end of the hall.

Yet Hope knew the system better than any nurse, and the trip from the hospital in Phoenix to the one in Los Angeles had already taken too long. In the silent trade among patients, in the quiet of a bathroom or the warmth of a stairwell, Hope gave whatever was necessary. She acquired the needed coins, and before they went missing or stolen, she surrendered them to the telephone.

She had to have felt a moment of doubt, waiting for the connection, listening to the line pulse at the pace of her quickening heart. Even Mrs. Leonard's voice must have brought relief, though to call the exchange a conversation would have flattered the moment— perhaps a hello, followed by a few curt words that her son was out, then the drone of the terminated line and the wait for her boy to respond.

IN THE SHADOWED kitchen, my eyes still clearing from the afternoon sun, I stared at the note's thickly printed letters. Mrs. Leonard had left the message intentionally vague, forcing me to walk to the far end of the house and ask for more. The hallway was blackened entirely. Pausing outside Mrs. Leonard's closed bedroom door, I could hear the sharp chatter of an afternoon game show. I tapped lightly, waited a moment, but heard no response.

She knows I'm here, I thought. Hesitantly, I knocked again.

"What?" Her voice shot out over the television.

"May I come in?" The audience's applause rolled through the darkness, diverting her attention. I waited.

"Did you read the note?" she bellowed.

"Yes, may I come in?" I paused but heard nothing.

Reaching for the knob, I cracked the door to give her time to order me out. I walked past the master bathroom, toward the bedroom.

She lay belly down on the king-size bed, her midsection sloped up-right, like a staring walrus, her face glazed with the glow of the television. Over the edge of her bed, she clasped a diet cola can. A large plastic bowl, half-empty of popcorn from the kitchen microwave, rested at her side. She ignored me for several seconds before turning her face in my direction. Her blank, heavy stare told me to start.

"Do you know what she wanted?"

"Who?"

"Hope. Did she say what she wanted? Where she was?"

"How would anyone ever know what Hope wanted?" She grinned at her clever reply, returned to the television, and shifted her voice into a flat tone. "They found her on the street or something, how would I know?" Still distracted, she gulped at her soda can and swallowed.

"Is she all right?"

"As good as ever. She did something stupid. They locked her up in the Norwalk mental hospital. And now"—she dragged herself to the tale's complicated conclusion—"she apparently feels the need to see you."

Stunned, I waited for more.

She glanced back at me incredulously before grabbing a fistful of popcorn and garbling, "If you're going, you better call your social worker for a ride. Don't think I'm gonna do it."

She returned to the television.

That evening, I rode my bike to the bus stop and returned with a travel schedule. After digging out a map book from the front seat of the Leonards' camper, I sat at my bedroom desk and flipped through page after page until I reached the city of Norwalk. A splat of rose-colored ink designating the Metropolitan State Hospital was immense, consuming square centimeters of space. California's legislators had selected the site in 1914, choosing it over Beverly Hills because of its superior access to railroad lines and well-paved roads. Pulling the desk lamp closer, I did my best to measure the strands of freeways and surface streets that tied the Leonards' house in the San Fernando

Valley to the psychiatric ward in Norwalk. Round-trip, the distance was over ninety-five miles.

The next morning, I did as Mrs. Leonard had told me and called the social worker who had recommended the local community college over the schools back east.

"Oh, I heard Priscilla was back," the woman commented, interrupting her babble of job grievances. "Why don't we plan on seeing her in a few weeks? I don't think she's going anywhere, sweetheart."

I toadied to the woman's authority, trying to make the trip seem more like a chore than something I really wanted. "I don't know why she came now. I'm leaving for school. Don't you think we can get it over with sooner?"

The woman apologized, again blamed her packed schedule and burgeoning caseload, then unexpectedly paused before finishing up. "You know, sweetheart, everyone around here is so proud of you," she divulged effusively. "It's too bad the department doesn't have more kids that go to college, don't you think? How long have we had you in care now?"

"Eleven and a half years," I answered, taking on the easier of the woman's two questions.

"Well, I can tell you that everyone here is very proud of you." She lowered her voice. "You know, none of us really had any idea how much you'd accomplished. I'll call to see how things are going and arrange something for you and Priscilla next week. I'm so happy you called." She hung up.

I replaced the receiver on the telephone.

The woman meant well, wanted to bolster me with a compliment, offer a reassurance that an army of county social workers and bureaucrats stood behind me. Though she had never met me, she had a childhood's worth of court documents, case files, her colleagues' old notes, Medi-Cal and Denti-Cal applications, free-lunch requests, monthly payments to the Leonards, and more, all at her fingertips. She knew everything about me as a case, as a list of obstacles and childhood traumas, and as an improbable high school graduate, much less a college freshman. Yet there were the other facts that never made it into the county's files—ones that she and her predecessors might have easily guessed but had pointedly avoided.

Yes, nightmares bothered me, and I rarely slept through to morning.

No, the Leonards never treated me like one of their own.

Yes, I felt ashamed when people asked about my mother, and I had no idea how to answer their questions without lying.

Equally important were the details that make up any boy's life, whether or not a foster care department pays for his bed.

Yes, I had friends who disappointed me.

No, I tried not to back down from bullies, though I worried that I was too skinny.

Yes, I had crushes that I did my best to hide, and I fretted over acne.

What it meant to be a boy growing up was irrelevant to what social workers asked if they visited the Leonards, to what they wrote in their reports to the judge. After an hour chatting with Mrs. Leonard around the kitchen table, a caseworker might dash by my bedroom. "How are you, sweetheart?" he or she would ask, leaning into the room. "I'm fine," I would answer, then look up with a smile and wait for the door frame to empty again.

I stared at the telephone that squatted mutely on the kitchen table. The woman never called back. That morning's conversation was the last that I had as a boy with the Los Angeles County Department of Children's Services.

TWO DAYS AFTER Hope called, I left the house before the Leonards woke and walked to the bus stop. After several transfers, I arrived at the edge of the San Fernando Valley. By midmorning, I had only begun the long journey through Los Angeles County's immense inner core.

Adding and surrendering passengers, the bus ambled through the streets. Mounds of low-slung buildings, no more than one or two stories high, lined the route. The outcropping of a bolder enterprise occasionally broke the anonymous landscape, reaching a few feet higher but giving up in exhaustion well short of the sky. Stuccoed apartment buildings clumped around shoebox bungalows. Yet they were sufficient to sustain the people who walked and drove its streets, who worked in its convenience stores, laundries, fast-food joints, and garages, and who, when asked what they wanted—for themselves and for their children—inevitably answered with a self-conscious grin, "Something better."

In the bus's heat and sway, I gazed at the aisle floor and thought of the woman whom I had refused to forget. I recalled mostly fragments. Yet even they were enough to recount the story of her, me, and as much of the truth as I could withstand. Alone among the seated strangers, all waiting for their own destinations, I rehearsed for mine, whispering what I remembered:

When my mother walked down the street, men noticed.

She smoked Parliament cigarettes, which she had me retrieve from the corner drugstore with her handwritten notes. She played cards, mostly solitaire. Despite her modest height, she never wore high heels, preferring boots—especially the kind that zip up the back or the side and wrap around a woman's calf.

She had little patience for childishness. More than once, she snapped at me to stop acting my age.

Her hair was dark and matched her eyes. Her spoken voice was soft, even a little low for a woman. Yet when she wanted, her words could leave a man stammering as though his tongue, or something more, had just been skillfully excised. She was prankish with her girlfriends. Sometimes, a little vain.

She liked rock music, mostly the Doors and the Rolling Stones.

She was smart and said that I was, too.

Other than occasional lipstick, she wore little makeup.

She thought that Izod shirts looked best on me, and I liked the alligator.

She enjoyed my company, toted me everywhere with her, and refused to compromise, regardless of what others thought. She sat me on bar stools, took me to Disneyland, and taught me how to bet at racetracks.

She protected me when she knew that I needed it; left me to fend for my-self when she knew that I could.

When I was seven years old, they took her from me on a street in North Hol-lywood and called me a foster child. In all, she was mine for barely two years.

But even now, if I were to walk down one of these streets with her, though slightly aged, she would still catch the eyes of a passerby, who would assume that the young man at her side was the son that she had raised—the same son who was now assuming, for the first time, the role of her protector.

When the bus halted in front of the parking lot of the fenced and walled fortress, I was the only passenger to stand. Exposed to the sun, the terrace of cars and black tar expelled a swath of heat, a first warn-ing to intruders. I made my way to the gray granite stairs and arching portico that served as the facility's entrance. With a light pull, the heavy metal door flew open at me. Startled, I stumbled inside.

The reception area was quiet, empty but for a collection of plastic chairs that rested against one wall. Behind a shield of wire-mesh glass, a woman's perturbed expression immediately greeted me.

"Did you need something, young man?" the woman asked with bored eyes, after witnessing my struggle with the door.

I approached the glass cage. "I'm here to see Hope Bridge," I an-swered through the partition, assuming that she would know my mother and would be happy, or at least relieved, that someone had come for her at last. "I'm her son."

The woman was unimpressed. She slid a tattered clipboard from the corner of her desk. "Did you make an appointment?" She stared a moment longer, then without waiting for my answer, began leafing through the pages, descending through the lines of names and corre-sponding numbers.

"Are you sure she's here?" the woman asked, her finger still travel-ing halfway down a page. "I don't see the name." She looked up, feel-ing that she had done enough.

"Do you think she could have left?" I anxiously asked through the partition. "Do you think I could have missed her?"

The woman hunched her shoulders. A silent standoff developed between the two of us.

Desperately staring at the woman, I reached for the name that was farthest from the mother I had known. "Could you look for Reese, please? I mean Priscilla Reese?"

She laid her arms over the clipboard in front of her, removing any doubt that her search had ended. "Just when was *Ms. Reese* admitted?"

"A week or so ago, maybe two. I'm pretty sure."

The woman shook her head, grunted. At last, armed with the piece of information that she required, she reached for a second clipboard, rapped it with a pen, then shoved both under the glass divide. In my best high school scrawl, I printed my last and first name, glanced at my watch to note the time. Then beside it, I did my best to spell "Priscilla Reese."

Glowering through the glass at my handiwork, the woman snapped into the telephone. "I need a visitor's escort out here," she announced, pulling the clipboard from under my hand. "The client should be in adult intake." She paused, listening to the line. "It's a family visit. How would I possibly know?" she barked back, then covered the mouthpiece and glared up at me. "Excuse me, young man, but do *you* mind?"

I blushed and jolted backward, hurriedly surveying the lobby for someplace to land my attention. A smiling, though slightly askew, portrait of California governor Jerry Brown beckoned me from the far wall. I quickly strode over to return the governor's greeting. His face hung over a line of unfamiliar head shots, each apparently of a lesser sovereign. Feigning the discerning eye of a museum tourist, I lingered, reviewing each photograph, gleaning factoids from the plastic nameplates below, wondering if my aggrieved gatekeeper had ever crept over and done the same.

From behind me, the woman suddenly thumped her hand against the glass enclosure. An attendant dressed in a misfitting uniform opened, then lurched through, the door next to her. Glancing at me, he nodded in the direction of the hallway behind him, inviting me to follow. He waited while I walked past him. The entrance slammed behind us. Then he quickly took the lead, humming a light tune several feet ahead of me.

Around us, the interior passages were bright with fluorescent tubes that connected one to another and ran the length of the ceiling. The cinder-block walls were a glossy tan, and along each side, an occasional door punctured the wall. At our feet, a scent of fresh cleaning fluid rose from thousands of linoleum tiles. We made our way through the windowless maze, deeper into the hospital's interior. As the succession of locked doors lengthened behind us, my escort's confidence grew, his soft purr now clearing into a full-blown melody.

He glanced over his shoulder. "Hey kid, you like the Chairman?" I looked at him, confused. "Sinatra?" he persisted. "You like Frank Sinatra?" He hummed out a few more bars, swinging his arm to the beat, snapping out the tune. "Come fly with me, let's fly, let's fly away. . . ."

I smiled pathetically. He grimaced in disgust, dropped his performance, and turned back to the hallway, wordlessly shaking his head.

Halfway down another passage and still ahead of me, he called out dryly, "Well, this is it." While I watched over his shoulder, he punched in the security code. But the door denied him, catching both of us by surprise. He sucked in a frustrated breath, then reentered the cipher. Acknowledging the second effort, the lock sprang open. The man swung the door wide, then stepped aside, waiting at the entrance for me like an overly gracious host.

A few feet into the room, I glanced back to thank him, but he had already turned toward the hallway. "They'll send someone when you're finished," he yelled, his last words scrambling inside as the door slammed shut.

The new space felt more like a large closet than a waiting room. In front of me, behind more heavily fortified glass, another gatekeeper sat with her back to the door, this one wearing a nurse's uniform and a pink sweater. I approached the cage, then stared down at the top of her head while she flipped through a newspaper. Several moments passed before she sensed my presence and swiveled around in her chair. She looked up from her reading, then waited with a set of blank, expectant eyes.

"Excuse me, ma'am." My voice quavered. "But I'm looking for Priscilla Reese."

The woman's face immediately brightened.

I felt encouraged. "I'm her son. Do you know if she's here?"

"Goodness, so you're Priscilla's boy," she declared, like an effusive aunt surprised to see how much I had grown. She leaned toward the glass, bending slightly to whisper under the partition. "Did you know that she's getting to be one of our favorites?"

"No," I answered, then gave her a close-lipped smile.

"You take a seat, just over there." She strained to point at the single chair outside her enclosure. "I'll go find her." I glanced at the seat and looked back, wondering how long she would be. "It's all right. It'll only take a minute." She got up, then leaned back toward the glass. "You did say Priscilla, didn't you?" I nodded at her. She smiled, waiting while I sat down.

Only a few seconds could have passed before I stood again. With no area to pace, I fidgeted in the room's center, glancing back and forth between the woman's abandoned desk and the empty chair that she had assigned me. Over the sound of a television, a mournful yowl suddenly slammed against the glass and the adjacent door. Picking at a hangnail, I tore too deeply into the cuticle. The thumb quickly laced with blood. I thought of Jason, who had tried so desperately to please the Leonards, scalding his hands in the bathroom sink.

Be sure to get the blood out before it dries, he had lectured, poking under his fingertips with a nail clipper to prepare for Mr. Leonard's dinnertime inspection.

I glanced at the wound, sucked at it through my teeth, then examined it again. *No use,* I thought, grimacing while the blood reappeared. Stuffing my hands into my pants pockets, I returned to the chair. My eyes cast down, I stared at the linoleum tiles gleaming around my feet.

Why are you here? I thought. *You never really wanted to come, did you?* Suddenly, guilt seized its opportunity. *Didn't she claim you? Didn't you promise not to forget?*

The sharp clack from the door's lock startled me. My head jolted to the side. The receptionist had reassumed her post, and from behind the newly opened threshold, yet another uniformed man appeared. Whether for me at MacLaren Hall or for my mother here, the county was always well stocked with caretakers. At the Leonards' house, I never doubted that another social worker would be assigned to supervise my childhood, or that if Mrs. Leonard ever made good on her threat, another bed for me would be found. The county knew how to replace people, just not how to keep them. The attendant gave me a smile, which I returned. Then, suddenly she was there. Boxed in the door frame, the woman who had last clung to me in the middle of the night while Mrs. Leonard screamed at her to get out stared at me vacantly.

She was not what I had hoped, not what I had rehearsed. Her face and neck sagged, too early for her age. Her hair was still dark but cut randomly, as though the hospital barber had grabbed only as many clumps as he felt were required, before moving on to the next patient's head. The bright, flowered muumuu that she wore was really more of a bag than a dress. Beneath the threadbare sack, she was clearly naked. Her once slender form had swollen—the side effect of institutional food that fed more than nourished and drugs that restrained more than cured.

Of course, in our years apart, I had grown. Yet as she waited for the attendant's permission to leave the doorway, more than her height appeared blunted. The vanity that I remembered, even admired, had surrendered completely. Her mind must have been stubborn, and the endless protocols of tranquilizers and antipsychotics—chlorpromazine, fluphenazine, haloperidol, benztropine mesylate—that her doctors had prescribed had demanded their tribute. From the doorway, her eyes were impassive. Medical science had extracted the anger from her stare, then left her eyes empty.

She shambled across the threshold, and I jumped to attention like an anxious schoolboy. Barely a footstep now separated us. Below the shoulder straps of her dress, tremors ran down her arms, through her hands, and into her fingers. The precise, razor-thin scars that had lined the undersides of her wrists had thickened into a single mass extending from her palms to her biceps, resembling the jaundiced belly of a snake. A smile of faint recognition crossed her face as she lifted her arms to hug me.

Then, like that day when the county had rushed me into an idling car, I pulled from her reach. Her face flushed with pain. Briefly, the room was silent until, in her still familiar voice, she whispered, "Andy." I stepped forward to make right what I had twice done wrong. I gripped her, and once again, was wrapped in the only body that had ever possessed me entirely.

"Would you like to go outside?" she muttered, dropping her arms to her sides and avoiding my eyes. I looked at the attendant, who nodded permission. I glanced down at the stained, powder-blue house slippers she wore. Her feet were half-covered, her white, flaking heels exposed.

"Don't you want to change into your shoes?" I asked.

"I'll be fine, thank you," she answered formally.

"Won't you be cold?" I suggested, embarrassed by the sight of her scantily covered body.

She looked at me blankly, her modesty long discarded. "I'll be fine, Andy, thank you." Then, without another word, she turned back to the patients' wing, leaving the aide and me to follow.

Inside the unit, icy air blasted from the vents above our heads. Men and women absently wandered, all clad in flowered muumuus like my mother's. At the far end of the corridor, in what appeared to be a gathering room, a television screamed at its assembly of viewers. Closest to us, less than a quarter of the way down the hall, an older woman rested upright in a reclining chair. Balancing an ashtray on her bare knee, she smoked. A square of chocolate cake, laid on a slice of white bread for a plate, waited for her at the edge of the armrest. As my mother and I passed, the woman noticed us, then locked her head in my direction and smiled. Embarrassed, I turned away.

In front of the enclosed nurses' station, a man lingered several feet from the counter, his hands respectfully clasped together at his waist. "When's dinner coming?" he loudly asked a ward keeper. "When's dinner coming?"

The woman ignored him, continuing with her paperwork.

The man raised his voice. "Dinner always comes at five. When's dinner coming?"

I glanced at the station's clock. It was half past one in the afternoon.

"Soon," the nurse answered without looking up.

Satisfied, the man turned from the counter and saw my mother and me. "Priscilla," he shouted through the ward, "does your friend have a cigarette?" My mother proceeded ahead, ignoring the man's question, leaving him to yell it out repeatedly until the same nurse leaned over her counter and warned him to quiet down.

Barely down the hall, my mother suddenly turned to the side, then paused in front of a door. Her back to the attendant and me, she rocked from one foot to the other. The man squeezed past her, pressed a code into the lock. The exit popped ajar. My mother promptly pushed her way through the gap, and I rushed to follow.

The sunlight immediately punched at my eyes. I stumbled onto a glaring patch of concrete, trying to keep pace with my mother. A narrow patio separated her ward from the next, where dozens of men and women remained locked inside. Reaching for her shoulder, I kept by her side until just beyond the dormitories the concrete broke into a wide lawn, releasing us from the glare. I paused, then surveyed the closely cut green that spread for acres, interrupted only by clumps of slender palms and lines of sidewalks, each neatly bordered with patches of orange marigolds. Fenced and quiet, the heart of the asylum was empty.

My mother strayed farther onto the grass, her feet shifting in and out of her house slippers. A few steps ahead of me, she turned. "Would you like to go to the canteen? I haven't been to the canteen today. Would you like to go with me?"

"Of course, Mom. We can do whatever you want." I smiled.

She promptly turned and shuffled toward a covered rest area. The oasis blossomed from a plot of hard-packed sand. Though sheltered under an awning, the air was hardly cooler than it was on the concrete patio. Several faded green picnic tables, like the kind that I had seen at school or in public parks, occupied the center shade. Ash-pocked aluminum bowls rested everywhere, yet scores of dying cigarettes had marred the tables' thick plastic, leaving their edges bubbled and blackened. My mother halted at a block of vending machines that lined one side. Still no one was in sight.

"Andy, can you lend me some change?" she asked, facing a machine. "I'll get it back to you."

"That's all right, Mom." I dug into my pants, retrieved the small fistful of nickels and dimes from the bus, then panicked, thinking that I had forgotten the money to get back to the Leonards. While my mother patiently watched, I reached into my hip pocket, tugged out my wallet, and flipped through the bills. Reassured, I laid the coins on her outstretched palm. She picked through and counted them, studiously pumped them into a machine, and retrieved a paper cup of steaming black coffee.

"Did you want something to drink, Andy?" She turned to me.

"No, thank you."

She held out the remaining change, which I declined. Her dress pocketless, she clutched the coins in one hand and, trying not to spill the hot coffee in the other, inched her slipper-covered feet toward a table. We sat across from each other. Like our hour-long visits at the Leonards' house, this one was mostly quiet. I watched as her eyes grew absent, fixing on something in her mind. She moved her lips in an unspoken conversation, briefly giggled back at herself, and was still again.

"Do you remember Mrs. Leonard?" I asked, breaking the quiet.

"Yes, I remember *Mrs. Leonard,*" she answered stiffly.

Something in her tone made me smile. "You know, she's still fat," I added, trying to be funny.

Her eyes faded again. She moved her lips, wordlessly.

"I'm going away soon. I'm leaving them," I said, competing with the nothingness, thinking the news might make her happy.

Silence.

I looked out at the lawn. "Did I ever tell you that I still remember when you picked me up at the airport after Grandma put me on the plane from Chicago?" I added a detail to prove it. "You and Carol came together. She drove, didn't she?"

Silence.

I pointed at the great lawn around us. "Remember, I was looking out the window from the front seat and asked if we were in Hawaii, because of all the palm trees?" I smiled, glanced at her across the table. "The question made the two of you laugh." She carefully released the coins onto the tabletop, then sipped at the searing coffee.

"I'm leaving for college in a week and a half. I haven't seen it, but it's a fancy school, better than any of the ones that the Leonards' kids got into. It's back east," I bragged.

She gently squeezed at the paper cup, her fingers mustard-colored from the hospital's cigarettes, the black coffee rising and falling.

"Do you still play cards? Remember how you used to play soli-taire? I always tried getting your attention, hanging around you, mak-ing a pest of myself." I grinned at her and the memory. She sipped again, placed the cup back on the table, but continued clutching it. "Remember how you always gave in to me?" I lied.

Silence.

What seemed like minutes lapsed before she finally broke from whatever had called her attention. She looked me in the face, then asked, "When is your birthday, Andy?"

The question seared through me. I looked at the table and no-ticed that the undersides of my arms were covered with dust. The groundskeepers had missed a chore.

"February," I whispered back, filled with shame for both of us. "February the sixteenth."

"Oh, that's right," she nodded slightly. "Would you like to have a lighter? I have one in my room that I could give you."

The question came from nowhere, and I forced a smile. "Sure. A lighter would be great." I thought of the collection of gifts she had brought to the Leonards' house. I watched as she suddenly giggled again, whispering with a lifeless gaze. Her eyelids deepened, nearly eclipsing the blemish that my father had left behind.

Don't go, I thought. *It's too early to go.*

"Do you still hear them?" I asked her, impulsively reaching into the heart of her mind. "Do you still hear the voices?" A breeze blew through the covered plot.

She looked up, smiling bashfully. "Yes."

I waited while she lifted the cup to her mouth, slurped at the steam. "What do they say," I asked, surrendering wholly to voyeurism.

She turned away, ignored my clumsy question, briefly gave in to another distraction before volunteering, "Sometimes, I hear your voice."

Startled, I asked, "What do I say?"

She waited, then answered, "I can never understand it." Her blunt stare returned.

We sat a little longer, watching nothing happen. Then, remembering the return trip to the Leonards, I glanced at the time. Less than an hour had passed. Most of the afternoon remained for the bus ride back to the west corner of the San Fernando Valley. But without thinking, I pulled myself from her again. "Mom, it's time for me to go."

"All right," she answered compliantly, releasing me.

I watched her, regretting what I had said, hoping to linger a moment longer. But without warning, she slid the coins from the tabletop and stood. She glanced down at the coffee, quickly swallowed what remained, then began making her way across the lawn back to the ward where she slept. I lagged behind her. A few yards short of the door, she halted and turned to me. The light sound of the traffic beyond the hospital fence caught my attention. She lifted her hand to my face, ran her fingers across my temple, brushing into my hairline.

"It's still blond," she observed with a faint smile.

"And yours is still dark," I answered back.

She looked to the side, then muttered to the emptiness as much as to me, "You know, I tried."

"What?" I asked, having heard her perfectly well, but wanting her to say it again.

But as always, she saw through my ruse and said nothing.

I narrowed my eyes to seal them, concentrated on the space over her shoulder, and the closed door that waited beyond.

"I know you did," I answered weakly, feeling the burn of a first tear as it escaped and tickled the side of my nose. My throat tightened. "I know," I repeated, almost inaudibly. "I know."

My escort led me back through the maze of hallways and wards. I reached the hospital's front door, walked to the bus stop. I made good time and was back at the Leonards' house before Mr. Leonard returned from work. The next day, I bought an airplane ticket from Los

Angeles to New York City and a bus ticket for the trip to Connecticut. Over the next two weeks, I packed and sent ahead what I could.
Childhood had ended. I tucked three hundred dollars into my wallet,
my total savings from bagging groceries. Then I boarded the plane,
leaving Priscilla—my mother—to the care of the state.

CHAPTER SIXTEEN

⚭

MRS. LEONARD'S BOOK of foster children was off-limits, though she never hid it. The neighbors had long grown tired of her stories, and their visits had stopped. The book lay alone, deprived of the attention it had once so enjoyed. For years, I could have taken it whenever I wanted. Yet I waited until the very end to break her rule, until I was ready to leave her house for good.

Just before dinner, she said she was running an errand and left me to myself. I walked to the kitchen, opened the drawer, and pulled the cardboard-bound scrapbook from the clutter. I held it briefly before opening it. I expected to find my own page at the front or the back, making me the beginning or the end of something. But the hope was foolish. Children had come before me, and I had seen even more leave. My page was wedged somewhere in the middle.

As with the other children, yellowed transparent tape barely held my face at the corner of the page. The photograph had been taken shortly after I came to the Leonards' house from MacLaren Hall, already halfway through the school year. Dressing me for the day, Mrs. Leonard had buttoned the shirt collar tightly around my neck. With a head-on stare into the camera, my eyes were vacant, lost in thought; my smile was closed, faint, and compliant. The facility had fed me a nearly constant diet of pasta and cereal, and my bloated face was empty and resigned.

The book described me as a nervous boy whom Mrs. Leonard found watching her as she moved around the house. Sometimes she put me on a step stool that she used in the kitchen, and I sat there quietly for hours, staring at her while she made dinner. I must have made her uncomfortable. Yet the book offered no reason why the Leonards had taken me or what had made me different from all the other children who had come and gone.

Skipping over pages, I ran across Jason's entry. His picture was the one that Mrs. Leonard had taken of him wet and shivering by the pool on his tenth birthday. Under a chilly, overcast sky, his head was cocked to the sound of her voice. The picture cut Jason off at the waist. Called to attention, he smiled self-consciously as he balanced a pink balloon by its rubber knot between his fingertips. In the cool breeze of an early California spring, the balloon's string drifted through and below his hand. His wet hair was pasted to his skull like a rubber cap. Dark, rough clumps of a bad haircut stuck out over his ears. His skin was a smooth brown, yet just beneath his swimsuit, a white line would have wrapped around his waist.

Behind him, my blurred image was clearly an afterthought. Though our foster mother could have avoided me by taking only a few steps to the side, she locked me in with him, sitting in the distance at the pool's edge, wearing dark blue trunks that scratched when they were wet. Jason and I looked like visiting neighbors, not boys who were expected to act like brothers for as long as it lasted.

A few weeks before my high school graduation, the Leonards heard from Jason. They had forgotten to mention it, and when they told me, the news was already old. Sometime in his childhood, the county had returned Jason to his mother. But he ran away again. When the police found and arrested him, he told them he was looking for the Leonards.

What must he have thought, sitting alone in a police station, hoping that if only he named his rescuers, they would arrive. *Do they remember me? Will they take me? Can they still be angry?*

By the time he called, the Leonards had long stopped taking children. I was seventeen years old by then, the last child in the house. No room was left for Jason.

He must have argued with whoever told him, insisting that the Leonards had misunderstood. Even more likely, he suspected that they never had been called at all. Again, Jason had misjudged. He ran alone into the dark and disappeared with no one to chase after him.

In the years I had waited to open the forbidden book, I had wanted so much more. I hoped that someone had bothered to find it all out, write it down, protect it, not leave it to me alone. Yet, the book was in fact as it had appeared all along—just something Mrs. Leonard had picked up at the grocery store.

Standing beside the kitchen desk, I heard her car pull into the driveway. From our two pages, I peeled out Jason's picture and mine, slipped them into my shirt pocket, then hurriedly put the book away and rushed to my room. It was not the right thing to do. Yet with the neighbors gone, Mrs. Leonard never used the book anymore, and leaving my cold stare and Jason's stumped torso there in the drawer would have been worse.

AFTER LEAVING THE Leonards, my first years in college were anxious, difficult ones. I lacked the confident ease that so many of my classmates seemed to possess and, of course, the financial and emotional support that waited for them back home. Still more a boy than a man, I thought of Hope constantly. Still saying nothing of her, I quietly mourned her loss. I have difficulty explaining why I went back to them, but the Leonards remained in my life for several more years. I can only offer that, as my last county social worker had warned, leaving foster care behind was harder than I had thought it would be. They were a place to go for Christmas, a place to stay for a school break. That first college summer even, I went back. I was alone, and they were there.

After stumbling through my freshman year, I worked harder and improved my grades. Not every teacher was kind, but like in high school, enough were to fill the void. By my senior year, when I mentioned law school, my advisor suggested a surprising list of selective schools. I applied to a wider range, and with a promise to do public interest work, I wrote an essay about how easy it is to accept injustice as a part of life, rather than the result of choices that are made and changes that are avoided. Weeks later, I was stunned when the answer from Harvard Law School was yes.

When I graduated from law school, practicality briefly overrode idealism. With a pile of new educational debt, I joined a corporate law firm in Los Angeles. Then, less than a year later, desperately bored with mergers and acquisitions, I took a leave of absence for a Fulbright Fellowship in Germany. When I returned to the firm, I found myself continually tired. I chided myself for being lazy, not giving my all to a new corporate law practice. Then early one morning in the shower, I reached to the base of my neck and discovered a lump roughly the size of a tennis ball. Three weeks later, I was out when the doctor called. He left what he had to say on my answering machine. My blood had gone bad, he explained. I had Hodgkin's disease, possibly an advanced stage. The message arrived on the Friday before Christmas. The doctor promised to be back in his office the next week before New Year's Eve.

Outside my apartment, the afternoon had darkened to the sound of a chilly rain. The Leonards were not the first people that I called with the news. Still, I called. Mr. Leonard answered the phone in his silly, formal manner, "Leonard residence." My voice cracked; but with a deep breath, I recovered quickly and, in a low tone, I told him what had happened. I listened to the sound of a television in the background as he yelled for Mrs. Leonard to turn it down. In the space of the thought before he replied, I knew that I had made a mistake. I imagined dozens and dozens of doors, one after another, rapidly slamming shut as I realized that I had opened them in error. Mr. Leonard was clumsy and asked me what my chances were. He told me that he and his wife were about to start dinner, then asked if they could call back. Later that night, the answering machine clicked in the silence. The Leonards' voices spilled through the apartment, then ended with the dial tone. The rain hammered the roof. The apartment felt like a silent bubble of air in a deep sea. I never returned the Leonards' call. I never spoke with them again.

After a round of setbacks with the health insurance company, my law firm arranged for my treatment at the City of Hope National Medical Center, at no cost to me and under the care of one of the nation's leading and most decent oncologists, Dr. Stephen Forman. After seven months of chemotherapy, I was cured. Shortly thereafter, I kept the promise that I had made when I applied to law school in the first place, left the law firm that had twice taken me in, and began a career representing impoverished children, with a special interest in children left in the custody of the state. I began that career in Alabama and eventually returned to Los Angeles and the foster care system that raised me as a child.

While I was executive director of the Alliance for Children's Rights, we sued Los Angeles County over its practice of taking children from their parents, placing them in foster care, then failing to visit them to assure their safety and welfare. Having seen my own social workers rarely, I was familiar with the county's long-standing routine. After we prevailed at the trial court, the county's lawyers offered to withdraw their appeal if I agreed to a settlement allowing the county to obtain waivers from foster children surrendering their right to see their social workers on a monthly basis. The county's proposed settlement would have allowed children as young as ten years old to sign away that right. I refused. The County Board of Supervisors proceeded to the California State Court of Appeals, then to the California Supreme Court. They lost each time.

We did our best to work with the system, enlisting our own lawyers as well as volunteers from dozens of firms to complete thousands of foster children's adoptions in cities across the country, at no cost. In Los Angeles and beyond, thousands of children languished in foster care solely because child welfare agencies had failed to finalize the paperwork to allow them to join families who had volunteered—often years earlier—to care for them as their own. We argued that children in group homes—like the boys who had arrived at my high school for a day and then were asked to leave—ought to be allowed to attend public schools, instead of the on-site schools that reward group home operators with lucrative contracts but afford foster children only second-rate educations. We fought against the county's practice of confining foster children in psychiatric facilities, children whom the county acknowledged were not mentally ill. The county's psychiatric institution of choice was Metropolitan State Hospital, the same facility where I had seen my mother shortly before I was emancipated. After aging out of county care, many of the foster children at Metropolitan State Hospital were "rolled over" to an adult ward, though the best diagnosis of their condition would have been only desperate poverty.

Several years ago, I gave a luncheon speech at a weekend conference organized by the League of Women Voters. I talked about reforming foster care, made a few obligatory references to having grown up in the system myself, and finished in time to allow for a brief break before the afternoon program began. Ducking out through a hallway into a courtyard, I had nearly escaped when a woman called to me.

"Andy!"

Across the small lawn, the name caught me by surprise. Andy is the name my mother gave me, the name on my birth certificate. Yet sometime during law school, I had taken to using Andrew. I reserved my true name for my closest friends and the few people who had known me from childhood. I walked toward the stranger and met her in the middle of the empty space.

"Do you think your mother could have kept you?" she asked.

The inquiry was abrupt and more than a little intrusive. Answering, I masked my face with my brightest smile.

"Oh, that's a hard question."

I glanced at the exit, signaling that I wanted to end our exchange. But the woman persisted.

"I saw your name in the paper and called Phyllis."

Again, the woman surprised me. Phyllis had worked for the Department of Children's Services for more than twenty-five years, rising through the ranks from frontline social worker to deputy director. In various conference rooms across Los Angeles, she and I had tangled over any number of departmental policies. Phyllis was tough, nurtured a long memory, and, when provoked, was willing to offend. She had enemies, but I liked her. She made a point of smiling when I walked into a meeting late. On more than one occasion, she had pulled her punches in an argument with me. Others had noticed and commented on it.

"When I saw the picture, I thought it couldn't be you," the woman in the courtyard continued, "but I had to call Phyllis and ask what she thought. You know, if you could be Hope's son?"

My mother's name slammed into me. When I talked about her in public, I rarely revealed her name.

"Phyllis said she had no idea, but she couldn't imagine you belonged to Hope."

Something about the woman was becoming familiar.

"Do you remember me?" she asked.

I held onto my distant smile. "No. Sorry. I don't."

She paused for a moment, gave me a hard look in the face, then seemed relieved.

"It is you." She reached out her arms to hug me. But blocking her affection, I quickly extended my hand, which she accepted in a moment of awkwardness.

The woman had been a social worker and had carried me on her caseload for nearly two years, from third grade to fifth—overlapping with Jason's stay at the house, though he had not been assigned to her. She told me her name, which I vaguely remembered, and explained that Phyllis, at the time, had been her regional supervisor. Apparently, the woman thought I might have doubted her, and she launched into a description of the room where I slept in the Leonards' house, running through the names and ages of their children. For a moment, she confessed to having worried that the Leonards might have treated me differently than their own children.

I still had not said much of anything when she returned to my mother.

"You know, she just had a way of slipping up at the last minute. I can't tell you the number of times that she almost had you back. But then, she'd do something. Curse out Mrs. Leonard. Miss a court date. She'd be so close to getting it together, then mess it up."

I nodded blankly. *Did you ever think of helping her?* I thought but never asked. *Couldn't you have told her son that his mother was trying, that she wanted him back?*

The woman rubbed me affectionately. "Just look at you. Who would ever think that you were Hope's boy?"

I smiled back mutely, waited for her to finish, then accepted her telephone number and walked to my car. The woman never meant any harm, and the circumstances of my childhood went beyond any single person. Still, why was it so hard for her to believe that Hope's son could have succeeded? That Hope could have been a part of his success?

As when I was a child, foster care largely remains a world of young mothers and frightened children. Ask about their lives, and their grief fills the air. Mothers speak of wrenching loss, and children speak of unyielding loneliness. When those children age out of foster care, they return in overwhelming numbers to the families from which they were taken, and their families in overwhelming numbers take them back. In the rush of bureaucrats, social workers, lawyers, and judges to determine the best interests of the child, the uncomfortable subject of love quickly becomes irrelevant. Children say they want nothing more than to be returned to their mothers, and mothers say they want nothing more than to be given back their children, but courtroom professionals stare at their shoes, uncomfortable at the sight of love existing alongside failure.

Of course, some families cannot be saved and their children cannot be returned. Yet, even then, their love for each other must be worth something. Of the infinite number of virtues by which we judge a mother's value, if she only possesses one, then even that single bit of love must be worth saving for her child's sake and for hers. Love may not be enough to wake a child in the morning, dress him, and get him to school, then to feed him at night, bathe him, and put him to bed. Still, can any of us imagine a childhood without it?

Historically, Los Angeles County has operated one of the largest and most violent foster care systems in the world. Over the last decade, dozens of children have died in Los Angeles County foster care and hundreds more have simply disappeared. The exact figures are difficult to know. The county has generally refused to release the numbers, and when it has, few have believed that the counts have been accurate.

Nationally, the outcomes for our poorest and most vulnerable children are little better. Over a half million American children live in foster care. The majority of them never graduate from high school, and overwhelmingly, they enter adulthood only semiliterate. Fewer than ten percent of former foster children graduate college; many experts estimate the number is closer to three percent. Thirty to fifty percent of children aging out of foster care are homeless within two years. They crowd our shelters and our prisons. Perhaps their lives might have been better had the system that fed and clothed them as children also let them know that, in spite of everything, the families that they remembered, their real families, had not only failed them but loved them too.

Did Hope's visits to the Leonards' house have to be so hostile? Did she have to be limited to one visit a month for an hour? Could someone have asked her what she needed to assume more of motherhood's responsibilities, to assure her son that she was there for him, to ease her son's unyielding loneliness? Was it necessary to leave her boy to think that she had just disappeared?

My mother loved me more than she could care for me. Despite the failings that I knew and those that I was told of, I have never doubted that love. My mother's struggle on the street to hold me was the strongest moment of love in my life, though it came too early. Her arms challenge every subsequent embrace. No act can ever be as strong, as weak; so self-sacrificing, so defining. It was love as love should be. Love as we want it. Everything.

Time, sweet, redeeming time. Harsh truth can give way to gentler memory.

Though I know less of flawed, fragile, exquisite Hope than of the time she took to lose me, I will protect her and all of it, forever. She fought voices that refused to leave and struggled against a fear that refused to let her rest. Despite it all, she did what we ask of every mother. She taught her boy to survive without her. She told him to be careful, not to be too brave, and to stay safe. And I remembered her lessons.

Some people are born for battles. Their bravery endures, regardless of frailty or strength. They are the ones we look to, and our admiring hearts tell us, "They'll know what to do." They are the great winners and losers of history. We remember them less for their outcomes than for their glorious acts. And, with the gentle wash of time, they become our heroes. There would be nothing unusual in a boy, now a man, claiming his mother as a hero—unless he had been taken from her. That changes everything. It is easy to forget that a woman who lost her child may have done her best, done more than any one of us could do ourselves, and still have been defeated. Even Hope could be a hero to her boy.

Then there was Grandma Kate, Hope's mother, my earliest protector. I was the last of Grandma Kate's family to slip away, and even after Hope lost me, Grandma Kate refused to.

During my senior year in college, I flew to Chicago. We spent a week together, not in Lincoln Park—which had long been returned to those with wealth and means—but in a basement that she could afford on Chicago's South Side. We went to Marshall Field's and up to the restaurant where she bought me an ice cream dessert as she had done when I was small. This time, she indulged in one herself. We took a trip to the little zoo, not that far from the lake. I had the idea of going to the Chicago Museum of Contemporary Art. It was her first trip there, and she loved it so much that several guards had to ask her not to peer so close to the paintings and not to touch them. In the evenings, while I watched television, she prayed at the kitchen table for her salvation, Hope's, and mine.

Years after leaving the Leonards, I asked why she had not taken me, why she had left me to them. She admitted to having thought about it, but she was sure that a little boy had to be happy living in a big house with a pool. "I never had all that to give you, sweetheart." I let the matter go, never asked again.

Shortly after my graduation from Harvard Law School, the voices that had seized Hope arrived for her mother. Eventually, Katherine, too, trusted no one but me. Yet even then, there were weeks, sometimes months, of calm, when the whisperers held their tongues. During one reprieve, she called to tell me that she had withdrawn all that she had saved and bought two tickets—one for her and one for me—for a summer cruise to Alaska. She described the glaciers and the blue water that dripped from their exhausted edges. "I think they'll look just like the mountains in Colorado. You know, the ones Grandma saw when she was little," she confided, seeming to forget that I had long grown into a man. We quarreled badly about how she could pay for the trip or how I could. Yet she refused to change her mind, proving herself every bit as stubborn as her daughter. In the early spring of that same year—only a short season before her trip and before we had the chance to reconcile—a lump in Katherine's breast killed her. She was sixty-seven years old.

In the blackness of some nights, the Night Man still makes his way to me in my sleep, entering my room through a careless opening, circling

the bed, whispering my name and that he has come for me. With every
visit, I feel the urge to open my eyes, as he demands, to confront his
stare in my sleep. But I do not. I lie quiet and still. I hold it in, as Hope
taught me, outlasting my fear in a silent race to sunlight.

I visit Hope, though admittedly not as much as I should. I have offered to be her guardian, in place of the one the state has provided.
She has refused my offer but steadfastly volunteered to share the few
dollars of her federal disability check with me if I ever need it. I have
asked if she would like me to investigate another place for her to live,
some place better than a group home. Again, her answer is no. The
facility staff call her Priscilla and are usually confused when I refer to
her as Hope. Mostly, I have gone back to using Mom, at least when
the two of us are alone. Like the afternoon when I visited her at the
Metropolitan State Hospital, her caretakers tell me that she is "one of
their favorites." I appreciate their kindness, but wish that they had
known the real Hope—my real mother—not the docile, whispering
woman with gray hair.

Years ago, I lost the only picture that I had of my mother and me.
Mrs. Leonard had snapped it while we sat in my bedroom during one
of her visits. She wore a beige suede coat and had spiked her black
hair. She was defiant, as she wrapped her arms around me and waited
for Mrs. Leonard to finish messing with the camera. How could I
have been so careless as to lose the photograph?

The picture of Jason and me by the Leonards' backyard pool is
one of the few that remains from my childhood. Balancing that pink
balloon between his fingers, he appears slight, frail, nearly feminine.
Though the photograph shows otherwise, I remember him as the older
and stronger of us because he was the braver. I have no idea what became of him, and if I knew his last name or where he came from, I
have forgotten. Yet, he is still the boy who revealed his love, however
misplaced, and who challenged love to prove itself. And now he has
traveled with me for years, across countless miles. Beneath all the false-
hoods, despite my unwavering rejections, he was one of the few who

knew me. For his strength, he remains in my memory that smiling boy, shivering beside the pool, in a childhood that has lasted forever.

Jason, stay with me. Forgive me.

I wish you knew that, unlike everyone else, I kept you.

If I could, I would, with all my heart, unwrap the lies. I would tell you everything that happened to me. I would listen to what happened to you. I would hold your hand, walk with you the three blocks to school. I would call you my brother.

Like memory, you are the braver of us. With the rasp in your voice, you reassure me.

Andy, you can tell the truth now.

Epilogue

THE RAIN NEVER stopped that night in Alabama, but I made it back to Jeff.

Outside Eufaula's dark gate, I yelled for the guard through the call box. My soaked jacket hung at my shoulders while I listened to the man's voice complain that it was late. Hours earlier, Dr. Carlton had gone home to his family. It took a threat to call a federal magistrate before the guard relented and walked me across the grounds to the basement door.

Down the hall, inside the room, the lights were still bright. I found the boy as I had left him, clothed and balled up on a blotted mattress. Standing at the door frame, I whispered his name.

"Jeff? Jeff, I've come back. I didn't forget. I'm here, like I promised."

I startled him, and he jumped from his sleep. Yet the boy remembered me and smiled.

I walked across the room and sat on the mattress next to him. We talked about the weather, the bad food at Eufaula, the upcoming weekend, and his friends back home. He asked if being moved from Birmingham, so far from his family, meant that everyone had given up on him. I told him no, that I was there.

He countered. If they really wanted him to go back home, why did he have to use the pay phone upstairs to call his parents, and why did he always have to call them collect? I told him that we had asked the court to let children use a private phone.

He stared back at me, unimpressed, then continued. What good was family therapy when his dad had to take the day off work and drive five hours to get there? With that, the best I could do was to shrug in agreement.

Afraid that he had gone too far, that he had offended me, he smiled apologetically. Noticing my soaked suit and wet hair, he said that I must be cold. He offered me his blanket, which I accepted.

Happy to have done something, anything, for me, he asked if I liked being a lawyer. Had I always wanted to be one? Had my father been one, too?

I told him the truth, as best I could. I told him that I had grown up without a father. I told him that I had gone to college, then to law school, not really knowing what else I could do.

After a silence, he moved closer, then whispered to me, "If you don't like Washington so much, maybe you could get a job 'round here."

I didn't say anything. Just listened to the rain outside, until a tear escaped and I swallowed a gulp of air. "Maybe," I finally answered him, staring hard at the blank wall ahead of us. "Or maybe I could just stay here for now."

ON JULY 11, 1995, the Federal District Court for the Middle District of Alabama issued its ruling regarding the Eufaula Adolescent Center. Following his review of thousands of documents, dozens of staff depositions, numerous experts' opinions, and the testimony of two children, District Court Judge Myron Thompson concluded that Eufaula's "mission was, to speak kindly, confusing: in theory it was a treatment facility; but, in reality, it was essentially a penal institution."

Judge Thompson found that staff violence was widespread. One study indicated that during the three-year period preceding the trial, forty-two staff members at Eufaula had been the subject of two or more investigations for abuse and neglect involving children. Dangerous physical force to restrain children was found to be common. According to the court, staff practices included holding children in hammerlocks, bending the children's thumbs back to secure their submission, staff shoving forearms against their throats to hold them against walls, and forcing knees against their spines to pin them against the ground. One child testified that staff often "sat there and watched" when fights broke out between children rather than moving to break them up. Given that most police departments would regard the use of such techniques against adult prisoners as unprofessional, the decision to use them against children in a mental health treatment facility was reprehensible.

Gang activity was ongoing and widespread at Eufaula. Citing the testimony of a young girl who had been placed at the facility when she was fourteen years old, Judge Thompson wrote that gang members were sent on "missions" after which they received "higher ranks for beating other people up." Evidence indicated that gang missions also included males forcing females to perform sex acts.

Thompson described several individual incidents of staff misconduct that were especially disturbing. He noted that sufficient evidence existed to believe that a frontline mental health worker had "sexual relationships with a child at the Center." The frontline worker engaged in sexual intercourse with a fifteen-year-old girl in a bathroom stall but was never prosecuted. Evidence also documented Eufaula's use of dogs from a nearby adult prison to hunt down children who ran away, as well as a Eufaula psychologist who pulled a knife on and threatened to castrate a fellow staff member.

Considerable time was spent at trial on the seclusion of children. Judge Thompson expressed deep concern over the facility's practice of isolating children in a basement—the same basement where I had found Jeff—without "time limits or clinical oversight." However, Thompson determined that seclusion in Building 112's confinement cells was the staff's "most egregious exclusion practice." Staff had put David Dolihite in one of the cells shortly before his attempted suicide. His roommate, Eddie Weidinger, who later successfully hanged himself, had also been secluded in Building 112. The actual location of the cells on Eufaula's extensive campus remained a mystery until I discovered them by accident during a trip to Eufaula and videotaped them with a camera that we were using for children's interviews. The tape was later submitted into evidence. As Judge Thompson described: "Building 112 consisted of a long corridor with cells approximately nine-by-six. Each cell had a steel grate on the top with a light fixture hanging down through the grate. Other than the light, there were no fixtures or furniture, the building was unheated, and children had to sit on the concrete floor."

Most damning was the court's acknowledgment that "the vast majority of the 115 children residing at the Eufaula facility are not in need of the type of restrictive and isolated environment Eufaula currently provides, and . . . these children could be more appropriately served . . . closer to their homes and families." In other words, none of the abuse, pain, and loss that filled the daily lives of Eufaula's children had been necessary.

The court issued an injunction, appointed a monitor over Eufaula, then required Alabama's Commissioner of Mental Health, R. Emmett Poundstone, to send the court's opinion and findings to the parents and guardians of all children at the facility, "accompanied by a cover letter . . . [explaining] the need for parents and guardians to monitor the conditions at the Eufaula Adolescent Center by visiting it, personally and frequently . . . without fear of reprisal," either to themselves or to their children.

Presumably, Jeff's mother and father were among those who received Commissioner Poundstone's letter. They never responded. A year later, Eufaula was closed and Jeff was moved to another state placement.

Acknowledgments

I AM VERY lucky to say that this book was not written alone. These names arrive late on this last page, though every earlier page would have been impossible without them. Thank you to Jesseca Salky and Russell & Volkening for accepting a manuscript from a first-time author and then respecting the story that he wanted to tell. Thank you to everyone at Hyperion, a group of people who cared about that story and did so much for it. Most especially, thank you to my brilliant and delightful editor, Gretchen Young, who gave advice that was kind but always honest and who took a manuscript and made it into a book, which someone—quite unbelievably to me—may be reading now.

And before that, thank you to those who knowingly and unknowingly encouraged me to start, to keep going, and to finish. I needed all of you: Fred Ali, the Augustines, Juliana Coco, Paul Cummins, Sharon Daley, the Dolihites, Susan Estrich, John Farrell, Sue Fisher, Stephen Forman and everyone at the City of Hope National Medical Center, Adam Frisch, Michael Gordon, David Houston, Anne Jump, Mary O'Shea, Amy Pellman, Ben Polsky, Barbara Schlain Polsky, Megan Schulte, Patty Seyburn, Murray Shapiro, Michael Suscy, the Tuckers,

Peternelle Van Arsdale, Marci White, the men and women of the Alliance for Children's Rights and the Judge David L. Bazelon Center for Mental Health Law, and the thousands of foster children in this country, who wake each morning without their parents and each day are brave enough to do their best on their own.